ABOUT THE AUTHOR

Stevyn Colgan is an author, artist, public speaker and oddly-spelled Cornishman.

He has, among other things, been a chef, a brewer, a milkman, a comics publisher and the official artist for the 2006 UK National Children's Book Fair. He's written briefing notes for two prime ministers, TV scripts for Gerry Anderson, helped build dinosaur skeletons for the Natural History Museum and movie monsters for Bruce Willis to shoot at.

But for 30 years he was a police officer in London, during which time he was set on fire twice, was sworn at by a royal, met two US presidents and a pope, was kissed by Princess Diana and let Freddie Mercury wear his helmet. In between such events he was part of the Metropolitan Police's experimental Problem Solving Unit.

He is a consultant for change agency Left/Field London and was a judge for the 2014 Transmission Awards for the Communication of Ideas. He is a visiting lecturer at a number of UK universities and has given hundreds of talks across the UK and USA.

He is also one of the 'elves' that research and write the popular BBC TV series QI and its sister show, *The Museum of Curiosity*, for BBC Radio 4.

ALSO BY STEVYN COLGAN

Joined-Up Thinking
Henhwedhlow: The Clotted Cream of Cornish Folktales
Constable Colgan's Connectoscope
The Third Condiment
Colgeroons
Saving Bletchley Park (With Dr Sue Black OBE)

AS A CONTRIBUTOR

I Remember: Reflections on Fishing and Childhood
Ottakar's Local History: High Wycombe
The QI 'F' Annual
The QI 'G' Annual
The QI 'H' Annual
The 'EFG' Bumper Book of QI Annuals

Why Did
the Policeman
Cross the Road?

STEVYN COLGAN

unbound

This edition first published in 2016

Unbound

6th Floor Mutual House, 70 Conduit Street, London W1S 2GF

www.unbound.co.uk

Text Design by PDQ

A CIP record for this book is available from the British Library

ISBN 978-1-78352-233-0 (trade hbk)
ISBN 978-1-78352-234-7 (ebook)
ISBN 978-1-78352-286-6 (limited edition)

Printed in Great Britain by Clays Ltd, St Ives Plc

1 3 5 7 9 8 6 4 2

Dedicated to the unsung heroes who work in the public sector who never get the recognition they deserve ...

... but get all the stick they don't.

DEAR READER,

The book you are holding came about in a rather different way to most others. It was funded directly by readers through a new website: Unbound. Unbound is the creation of three writers. We started the company because we believed there had to be a better deal for both writers and readers. On the Unbound website, authors share the ideas for the books they want to write directly with readers. If enough of you support the book by pledging for it in advance, we produce a beautifully bound special subscribers' edition and distribute a regular edition and e-book wherever books are sold, in shops and online.

This new way of publishing is actually a very old idea (Samuel Johnson funded his dictionary this way). We're just using the internet to build each writer a network of patrons. Here, at the back of this book, you'll find the names of all the people who made it happen.

Publishing in this way means readers are no longer just passive consumers of the books they buy, and authors are free to write the books they really want. They get a much fairer return too – half the profits their books generate, rather than a tiny percentage of the cover price.

If you're not yet a subscriber, we hope that you'll want to join our publishing revolution and have your name listed in one of our books in the future. To get you started, here is a £5 discount on your first pledge. Just visit unbound.com, make your pledge and type **policeman** in the promo code box when you check out.

Thank you for your support,

Dan, Justin and John
Founders, Unbound

AUTHOR'S NOTE:

One curious fact about leaving the police service is that, as soon as you've handed in your warrant card and hung up your helmet and boots, it's like you were never a cop. All access to police buildings and IT systems is immediately rescinded, and you can't even read reports you wrote without applying for a copy via a Freedom of Information Act request. For this reason, much of this book is written from memory, supported by entries in my own personal diaries, press reports and by the recollections of ex-colleagues who were present with me when certain events took place.

I am also acutely aware that I signed lots of scary-looking pieces of paper – including the Official Secrets Act – when I was a naïve young recruit and I'm not stupid enough to write anything that might see me banged up in the Tower of London or living the life of a whistle-blower on the run. Therefore, some details have been changed and persons/places made anonymous to avoid corporate embarrassment, or breaches of security, and to protect individuals who may still be involved in sensitive or covert operations. Where I have not been able to clear permissions, I have used generalised or invented locations and have not named any of the individuals involved.

None of this will affect the validity of the stories you are about to read.

All views expressed are my own and do not necessarily reflect the views or policies of any of the organisations featured in this book.

CONTENTS

Prologue   xiii

1:   Slobby to Bobby   1

2:   The Tribe of Bin   21

3:   If the dragon says no...   46

4:   The Wizard of Waltham Forest   77

5:   The ape that moved a planet   103

6:   No one ever got sent on a linear thinking course   130

7:   Lobsternomics   155

8:   Rearranging the deckchairs on the *Titanic*   178

9:   The phantom bus stops of Düsseldorf   202

10:   The sensuous adventures of Kiki and Bouba   230

11:   The R Factor   258

Epilogue: To get to the other side   280

A bibliography and full list of sources used in this book can be accessed at:
https://colganology.wordpress.com/why-did-the-policeman-cross-the-road-references-and-sources/

Why Did the Policeman Cross the Road?

PROLOGUE

*For every complex problem there is a simple solution
– and it is always wrong.*

H L Mencken

*If you have always done it that way, it is
probably wrong.*

Charles Kettering

In 2002 a London council was getting complaints from the
public about drunks monopolising the benches in a particular
public park. So they decided to remove the benches and,
therefore, the source of the complaints. It was, they believed,
the simplest solution to their problem.

No benches = no drunks = no complaints.

However, the complaints increased tenfold and got
angrier. Most came from disabled people, pensioners and
young parents who now had nowhere to sit. But the strongest
complaints came from the families who had sponsored the
benches, all of which bore plaques memorialising a loved
one.

The drinkers, meanwhile, sat on the grass or, if it was wet,
on cardboard, creating an additional litter problem.

To their credit, the council responded quickly to rectify
the mistake. The Parks and Gardens Department varnished
the wood, polished the brass memorial plaques, and hastily
returned the benches to the park with a suitable white lie
about 'renovation and preservation' (which is why I've been

kind and kept them anonymous). Now everyone was happy again ... but the drinkers, and the complaints, remained.

So what should the council have done?

This is a book about effective problem solving. And problem solving is all about tackling the cause(s) of a problem rather than responding to the symptoms. Problem solving begins with defining what the problem actually is – which is surprisingly not as simple as it sounds. For example, did the council see the drinkers as the problem? Or was the number of complaints the problem?

This book also tells the story of my 30-year career with the Metropolitan Police Service and, in particular, my time with Scotland Yard's experimental Problem Solving Unit where we challenged many existing policing methods. However, I'm not setting out to slag off the police service. Far from it. While I can't deny that, like any large organisation or company, it can be rigid, inflexible and painfully slow to embrace change it is made up of thousands of professional, caring individuals doing the best they can with what they have. I also can't deny that policing doesn't have a few thugs, bullies and bigots. But they are a very tiny minority and it's been my honour and privilege to work with the splendid vast majority of good officers and police staff – some of the bravest, kindest, and most altruistic people I could ever hope to meet; people willing to put their lives on the line every day to keep you, me, and everyone safe.

This book is a celebration of good policing: of projects that made life better for individuals and for whole communities. The chapters bounce around a little in time and space[1] but each one focuses on a particular area of problem solving/crime prevention and there are some great stories between these covers. However, I haven't restricted myself to just talking about police work. Good problem solving can be applied to any work arena so you'll learn how fake bus stops can protect vulnerable pensioners, how bees can prevent elephant stampedes, and what tiger farms and sex workers may have in common. You'll come to appreciate the advantages of sticking gum on celebrities' faces, why the colour of your changing room might lose you the football match, and how eating lobsters helps to save lobsters.

You'll also find that this is a very optimistic book. I make no apologies for that. I absolutely believe that we could all be living, right now, in a safer, healthier and more crime-free society. Being a cop for three decades proved to me that almost any situation can be made better as long as you're prepared to invest some time, take a few risks, try new things, break with traditional and accepted ways of thinking, and constantly ask, 'Is there a better way to do this?'

Let me help you to cross the road.

---

1   How wonderfully appropriate that the world's most famous time and space travel machine is a police box.

1: SLOBBY TO BOBBY

I would rather have questions that can't be answered than answers that can't be questioned.
— Richard Feynman

The price to be paid for individuality is the abandoning of approval.
— Steve Aylett

1

There are many reasons why people choose to become police officers. For some it's a sense of duty or the desire to contribute to a better society. For others it's wanting to follow in a parent's footsteps. Or maybe it's simply the stability of a steady wage, or even the glamour and excitement.

I joined for a bet.

I don't actually recall making the bet because, at the time, I was celebrating my 18th birthday at the Devon and Cornwall Constabulary Social Club in Camborne. All I have are hazy, boozy fragments of memory: a desultory chat about my future career prospects with my homicide detective dad; a clacking typewriter; some congratulatory back-slapping and cheering; and beer, lots of beer. All I know for certain is that I woke up the next morning with one of the worst hangovers I've ever had and with the sinking feeling that I'd done something very silly. Searching through the pockets of my denim jacket, my worst fears were confirmed when I found a badly typewritten and ale-stained 'contract' stating that I'd accepted a £50 wager that I couldn't survive six months as a cop. I'd signed it. Dad had signed it. And, ridiculously, it was also notarised and signed on the back by two witnesses.

I bet my dad Myghal Colgan the sum of £50 that I can be recruited as a police officer and stay in the job for six (6) months.

If I fail, I will pay him.

Signed:

If I don't fail, he will pay me.

Signed:

Of course, I tried to wriggle out of it by pointing out that it (probably) wasn't legally binding and, even if it was, I (definitely) hadn't been of sound mind when I'd signed it. I didn't want to be a cop. I'd never wanted to be a cop. I'd spent my whole life surrounded by cops – my dad, his colleagues and our neighbours (we lived in police married quarters in those days). I was 18 and I wanted to be an artist. Or a writer. Or a rock star. A creative of some sort anyway. But Dad was unmoving. 'A bet is a bet,' he'd say, while adding the occasional taunt such as: 'Mind you, it does take a certain kind of person to wear the uniform. Not everyone is man enough.'

For a while, I quietly fumed. But, as the days passed, the idea started to put out roots. What else was I going to do for the next six months? I'd completely messed up my education – for reasons that will become clear in a moment – and had earned myself a set of grades so low that snakes could slither over them. And all of my friends were about to starburst to polytechnics and universities around the country leaving me alone in Cornwall, the poorest county in the UK, where almost all work was seasonal and woefully paid. Back in 1979, the advice doled out by the careers officer at my school was, genuinely, 'Get out of Cornwall.'

As it happened, my two best friends were doing just that. They were off to study graphic design at Middlesex Polytechnic. A thought suddenly struck me … what if I applied to join the Metropolitan Police and followed them to London? It would mean winning the bet with Dad, six months of partying with my best mates, I'd have wages in my pocket and I'd get to see gigs by all the bands I liked.[2] It seemed too good an opportunity to pass up. So I applied. And I presumably said nothing too outrageous or controversial at my interview because I soon received a letter requesting that I report to Hendon Police College on February 18th, 1980 to begin basic training.

Helston, 1979 and Hendon, 1980

2 'Live music' in 1970s Southwest Cornwall meant male voice choirs or beardy men in Fair Isle sweaters singing about pilchard fishing. If we wanted to see anyone more contemporary, we had to drive to the Cornwall Coliseum at St Austell or the 80+ miles to hedonistic Plymouth … as we had also done in the autumn of 1979 to see *Monty Python's Life of Brian*, because all of the repressed Cornish borough councils had banned it without ever having seen it.

I can't deny that my transition from slobby to bobby was tough. Many of my instructors seemed to be under the impression that we were in the army and I wasn't used to the discipline. There was lots of marching about on a drill square – a skill that I couldn't see being much use to me as a street cop if I'm honest – and barking of orders by a swagger stick-toting and pugnacious drill sergeant called Sid Butcher, who seemed to take great pleasure in making mincemeat of anyone who dared to be uncoordinated or casual.[3] He reserved a particularly baleful eye for me, it seemed, because I looked so rubbish in uniform. I have a long body, short legs and a large head; one chap in the uniform stores said that I had the same proportions as Sooty, the glove puppet. It took a fortnight for the stores to find a helmet that fitted me because, as another stores' officer helpfully explained, 'You have a head like a fucking watermelon.'

A typical day consisted of morning parade and inspection, marching about a bit, classroom sessions where we learned about law and police procedure, some PE or self-defence training, practical sessions where we pretended to arrest or stop and search each other, a bit more marching about, and then evenings spent in our tiny rooms attempting to learn large chunks of the *Metropolitan Police Instruction Book* by rote.[4] I wasn't a happy student, I'll admit. I was homesick and my Cornish accent made me the frequent target of yokel gags. And on my first day I made the unfortunate error of calling one particularly bullish sergeant, 'Sarge.' His reasoned response was to abbreviate 'Constable' every time he saw me for the next 16 weeks.

---

3   There are many great stories told about Sid who, after he retired, ran the student shop at Hendon. My favourite concerns an occasion when he prodded a scruffy Welsh recruit with his swagger stick and said, 'There's a piece of shit on the end of this stick', to which the recruit brilliantly replied, 'It's not at my end, Sarge.'

4   The 'IB', as it was known, was issued to every officer upon joining the Met and was the go-to place for advice or information. It covered everything from the history of policing, to powers of arrest, to how to dress and act appropriately. During the early years of your service you were tested on your knowledge of its contents.

Several times I got close to accepting that maybe Dad had been right; perhaps it did take a certain kind of person to wear the uniform and maybe I wasn't man enough. But then I'd remind myself that there was £50 riding on this – a substantial sum in 1980 – and I had my eye on a second-hand Fender Stratocaster. Besides, my curiosity was piqued: there were aspects of the syllabus that just didn't make any sense to me.

I should, at this point, explain that I am not a natural troublemaker, nor any kind of revolutionary. I've never protested at a march or rally, I've never stenciled political graffiti on a wall and I've never set fire to anything, or anyone, in order to make a statement. If anything, I'm a bit of a wet liberal and I don't look for confrontation. However, I do have an insatiable curiosity and I'm not afraid to ask difficult questions. And that hadn't always made me popular with my teachers at school.

I was that kid in the class who was always asking 'Why?' I wanted to know why the sky was blue, why things had to die (existence is very wasteful, isn't it?) and why, when we live on a ball spinning at 1,000mph, we aren't all flung off into space. The best teachers were the ones who knew the answers or who said 'I don't know, but let's find out, shall we?' The worst teachers were those who told me to shut up or to stop asking stupid questions. I became very resentful of the latter. And, although I'm not rebellious by nature, I do find it hard to stay silent if I believe that someone is fobbing me off, or something is being done the wrong way – especially if I think that there's a better way to do it. I realise how cocky and self-centred that probably sounds, but I'm a creative, thoughtful, analytical and, above all, ethical person and I can't be a 'team player' if I don't agree with the way the team plays. I'm even worse when I see dogma, orthodoxy, or bullying being used to support an inaccurate or unethical proposition. That was partly the reason why my school career was troublesome; if I didn't see the point of doing something I would challenge the

5

fact that I had to do it.[5] And, because I was a voracious reader and an obsessive collector of facts, I would argue with my teachers if I thought that they were bullshitting me or avoiding answering my questions. I couldn't help it – it's just the way I'm wired up.[6]

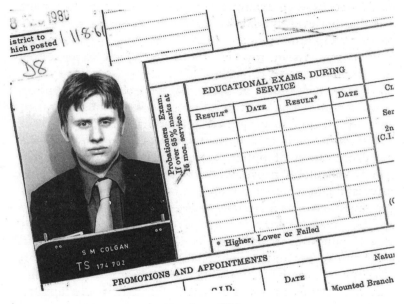

Hendon, 1980

5   Which is why I asked my teachers why I needed to learn things like logarithms, tangents, sines and cosines in what was supposed to be basic maths lessons. My O level exam result was 'ungraded'. But I have never needed them and my slide rule hasn't had a lot of use either. I feel vindicated.

6   Many of the tweedier old teachers at my school would have gone to university in the 1950s – some had even seen wartime service – so it's no surprise that their knowledge of rapidly-changing new areas of science and technology were often years out of date. Pointing out their shortcomings was never going to endear me to them, or help me to pass exams, but I was too cocky to see that at the time. I'm reminded of a story, often told within my family, about the time I questioned a primary school teacher's knowledge of dinosaurs. 'If you're such an expert, why don't you teach the class?' he said in exasperation. So I did just that. I was 10.

Which was why, almost from Day One, I found myself at loggerheads with my instructors at Hendon over the disparity between what I believed policing to be and what they told me it was.

Take Sir Richard Mayne's *Instructions to the New Police of the Metropolis* as an example. Written in 1829, this document was the first ever 'mission statement' for policing and it was considered so important and fundamental that, over 150 years after it was written, my classmates and I were expected to learn it off by heart.[7] It begins:

'The primary object of an efficient police is the prevention of crime: the next that of detection and punishment of offenders if crime is committed. To these ends all the efforts of police must be directed. The protection of life and property, the preservation of public tranquillity, and the absence of crime, will alone prove whether those efforts have been successful and whether the objects for which the police were appointed have been attained.'

That makes perfect sense, doesn't it? I'm confident that if you took a poll of the British public and asked them to express a preference between (a) being the victim of crime but the bad guy gets caught, or (b) not being the victim of crime, pretty much 100 per cent would opt for (b). People want to see justice being done but they would much rather that the bad guys didn't burgle their houses or steal their cars or mug them first. No one wants to be a victim and prevention is almost always better than cure. And if crimes can be prevented, there are other benefits too: people are spared the upset, hurt and loss; there's no cost in terms of victim support or medical services;

---

7   Mayne's instructions were based upon Sir Robert Peel's nine *Principles for Policing*. They included, for example, 'To prevent crime and disorder, as an alternative to their repression by military force and severity of legal punishment.' and 'To recognise always that the test of police efficiency is the absence of crime and disorder, and not the visible evidence of police action in dealing with them.' You can see that Mayne had Peel's vision very much in mind when he started writing, and his *Instructions* would go on to become the template for policing across the British Empire.

no increased insurance premiums or expensive repairs to, or replacement of, property; no lengthy judicial processes and bulging prison populations. With fewer crimes to report, there's less police paperwork and bureaucracy so officers get more time to focus on community issues and on investigating the crimes that have slipped through the net. It is almost always cheaper and ultimately less time-consuming to prevent crime than to deal with its consequences. Of course prevention should be the primary object of policing.[8]

So why then, I wondered, did my basic training not include any crime prevention? Not one minute of the whole 16 week training programme was allocated to the subject. Instead, the syllabus focused exclusively on catching the bad guys or, to be more precise, catching the bad guys *after* a crime had been committed. All of our classroom and practical sessions seemed to be based on the assumption that crimes were going to happen, regardless of any police activity, and that our role was to mop up afterwards.[9] There was no problem solving going on; everything we did was reactive rather than proactive. This was why I was confused. It seemed to me that the role we were being groomed for as shiny new police officers didn't sync with Mayne's 'Primary Object', Peel's 'Principles' or, more importantly, the desires of the public.

---

8   The message was spelled out even clearer in *Police Notices* – a forerunner of the *Instruction Book* – to the first police officers: 'It should be understood, at the outset, that the principal object to be attained is the prevention of crime,' it explained. 'To this great end every effort of the Police is to be directed. The security of person and property, the preservation of the public tranquillity, and all other objects of a Police Establishment will thus be better effected than by the detection and punishment of the offender, after he has succeeded in committing the crime.' As far as I could tell, nothing had changed in the intervening century and a half.

9   We also had some very scary Cold War 'Protect and Survive' lessons in which we learned how to use radioactive fallout meters, how to make chemical toilets, and what cops would be doing in the aftermath of a nuclear strike on London. Melting and screaming, mostly.

Hendon, 1980 (me, top centre)

My four months at Hendon passed remarkably quickly and soon it was time for me to to put on (literally, in my case) the big hat and learn 'The Job', as cops call it. I was subsequently posted to Uxbridge Police Station in the London Borough of Hillingdon and placed under the tutelage of a succession of experienced police officers who would 'puppy walk' me through my first few months of real police work.

I'd assumed that the lack of crime prevention training at Hendon had been due to time constraints, that what I'd been through was a compressed syllabus intended to front-load us with just enough knowledge to be able to hit the ground running. It followed, therefore, that, out in the real world, I'd be taught the other stuff. But that wasn't the case. I was smartly told that prevention was the domain of the dedicated Crime Prevention Officer and nothing to do with me. And yet there was just the one CPO for the whole borough, an older officer with 30 years under his expansive belt who was presumably expected to single-handedly service some 250,000 residents

9

and goodness knows how many shops, businesses, hospitals, schools and other premises.[10] Uxbridge nick fielded something like a hundred cops at that time. Imagine the impact on crime we'd have had if every single one of them had been given the same training and knowledge that the CPO had been given; a hundred officers equipped with the skills and expertise to advise people how to best protect themselves, their homes and their property. It was a point I was keen to make but I was told: 'That's not your job. Your job is to concentrate on bringing in as many bodies[11] as you can. That's what you get judged on.'

And that, I realised, was the problem.

Prevention is notoriously difficult to measure; not impossible, but challenging and time-consuming. By comparison, many other police activities, such as making arrests, stopping and searching people, appearing at court, etc., were easily countable. Therefore, back in the early 1980s, they had become the primary measure of police performance and my colleagues and I were judged on our 'figures'. But, of course, you couldn't arrest someone unless they'd committed a crime. Therefore, the irony wasn't lost on me that we police officers were reliant on criminals being good at what they did in order to prove that we were good at what we did.

So I followed my instincts and I learned all about crime prevention in my spare time. Then I got stuck into trying to solve local problems that impacted on people's lives even if, sometimes, they were quality-of-life issues rather than policing issues. I wanted the public to trust the police and I was convinced that getting the community and the police working together to solve local problems was the right way

---

10 By the time I retired in 2010, there were still no more than one or two dedicated Crime Prevention Officers – rebadged by the Home Office as Crime Reduction Officers, almost as an admission that prevention wasn't happening anywhere near often enough, for each London borough. They were the only officers who would be sent for specialist training in crime science and the use of crime preventative techniques and technology.

11 Police slang for arrested persons.

to go. After all, if the people of London are working with you, you have a huge resource to draw on, and several million pairs of eyes to help you to make the city safer. But problem solving, crime prevention and community involvement didn't generate enough arrests to keep my bosses happy. It seemed that my idea of policing was wholly at odds with that of my supervisors and my relationship with them became steadily more sour.[12]

Uxbridge, 1984

Six months passed and Dad paid out, but he didn't mind. For just £50 he'd got me out of his pretty little Cornish cottage and into a steady job.[13] I reckon he'd always known

---

12 I was frequently admonished for 'spending too much time chatting to the public', and in one of my old notebooks there is a written warning from one of my inspectors for having been seen 'drinking tea in a café in view of the public'. I was actually chatting with the owner about an issue he had with people urinating in the alley behind the premises. These days police officers are encouraged to make this kind of contact but, back in the early 1980s, it was a very different story.

13 I now realise what a shrewd piece of problem solving that was on Dad's part.

that, once I got to London and started getting a regular wage, I wouldn't be coming home. And he was right. I loved my job and the feedback I was getting from the public seemed to suggest that what I was doing was right. Hearing someone tell you that you've made them feel the safest they've felt in years is hugely satisfying in a way that collecting a shoplifter from a store detective will never be. Letters started arriving at my station, thanking me for my advice and for the time I was devoting to trying to solve local problems of crime and disorder.[14] I was also enjoying my social life and there was a lot more of London that I wanted to experience before I left. So I reset my target to two years as that was the length of my probationary period. By then you'd either made the grade or you got sent home. I was sure they'd be letting me go so I determined to make the most of the time I had left.

My reading habit was leading me to discover all kinds of interesting books and magazines about criminology and crime science. Hendon Police College had a brilliant library, and a brilliant librarian called Sue Clisby, and whenever I revisited the campus to attend a training course she'd point me in the direction of anything she thought that I'd find interesting. On one such visit I found myself reading an article by an American academic called Professor Herman Goldstein in a US journal called *Crime & Delinquency*. The article was called 'Improving Policing: A Problem-Oriented Approach' and I quickly realised that here was something special. Goldstein had been studying the way that police forces work for over 20 years and had come to the conclusion that there needed to be a shift away from the 'reactive, incident-driven standard model of policing', towards a new, proactive model that identified the causes of crime and disorder and tackled them

---

14 It says something about the state of affairs back then that there was no official book at my station in which to record the receipt of letters of gratitude. But there was a book to record complaints about police, so my inspector partitioned off a section of that book and recorded the letters there.

at source. In other words, everything that I believed in.[15] It's not an exaggeration to say that it became one of the most influential things I've ever read.

CRIME & DELINQUENCY, April 1979

Improving Policing: A Problem-Oriented Approach

Herman Goldstein

The police have been particularly susceptible to the "means over-ends" syndrome, placing more emphasis in their improvement efforts on organization and operating methods than on the substantive outcome of their work. This condition has been fed by the professional movement within the police field, with its concentration on the staffing, management, and organization of police agencies. More and more persons are questioning the widely held assumption that improvements in the internal management of police departments will enable the police to deal more effectively with the problems they are called upon to handle. If the police are to realize a greater return on the investment made in improving their operations, and if they are to mature as a profession, they must concern themselves more directly with the end product of their efforts.

Meeting this need requires that the police develop a more systematic process for examining and addressing the problems that the public expects them to handle. It requires identifying these problems in more precise terms, researching each problem, documenting the nature of the current police response, assessing its adequacy and the adequacy of existing authority and resources, engaging in a broad exploration of alternatives to present responses, weighing the merits of these alternatives, and choosing from among them.

I already knew that I wasn't alone in the way I thought; I'd met plenty of other officers who felt the same as I did. But now, here was a noted academic agreeing with us and, what's more, some of his ideas for improving policing had been trialled by a number of US police departments and *they had worked*. Crime rates had fallen. Satisfaction in policing had risen. People felt safer. The case studies were a revelation.

15 He also had much to say about the way that US law enforcement agencies were, in his opinion, wrongly focused on the 'means' of policing rather than the 'ends'. In other words, there was more effort going into deciding how policing was delivered and measured than into understanding what results it was achieving. It's a subject we'll examine in greater detail in Chapter 11.

On that day I crossed the road from reactive police officer to proactive police officer and I realised that, come what may, I could never go back. For what remained of my police career I would carry on policing with my gut, even if it meant that the Met would fire me at the end of my two-year probationary period.

Monday, February 18th, 1982 came along and I packed my suitcase as I expected to be back in Cornwall by the weekend. But, when the summons to Divisional HQ came, I was genuinely surprised to discover that, somehow, I'd passed my probation. My Chief Superintendent seemed quite begrudging about it, but he told me that the weight of appreciation letters had been a contributory factor, especially as some were from notable people, including the local MP.

I now had a big decision to make. Should I quit and return to Cornwall? Or should I try to make a career of being a cop even though I seemed to spend all of my time disappointing my bosses? In the end, I decided to stay. Goldstein's article had really resonated with me and, as arrogant as I know this will sound, I'd developed the ridiculous notion that I was somehow ahead of the curve and that, eventually, the rest of the Met would 'catch up'. Besides, Cornwall, as much as I loved it (and still do), had nothing for me now whereas London was brilliant. I was able to hang out with my best friends, I'd seen a host of top bands and, during one recent memorable St Patrick's night in Soho, I'd been hauled up on stage by a ceilidh band to sing 'The Wild Rover' with a very drunk punk rocker with nightmarish dental problems.[16] The die had been cast. I was in for 30 years and I resigned myself to a long and bumpy ride ahead.

---

16 It was, of course, Shane MacGowan. The Pogues (or Pogue Mahone as they were originally called) formed a few months later in 1982. MacGowan wasn't performing that night; I suspect he'd been hauled on stage just as I had been. But even back then his brilliantly shambolic drunken performance was an utter joy to behold. When he started to turn up on TV some time later I recognised him immediately.

2

I recently unearthed my annual report from 1986, which shows that, even a full fifth of the way through my service, I was still getting comments like:

This officer appeared for interview with some considerable trepidation, as well he might, for his annual appraisal rates are among the worst I have seen. Looking back over his first six years, one might be excused for asking why he remains in the service. His return of work is very disappointing and I have advised him of the necessity to improve.

Tourist Polaroid taken outside Downing Street, 1986

My appraisals were generally this scathing because of my 'very disappointing' performance or, more specifically, my failing to meet the criteria by which my performance was assessed. I was achieving some fantastic results in terms of crime prevention. But time spent on making people feel safer, reducing crime and nuisance, and building confidence in the police didn't get counted. On paper, I looked like the laziest cop at my station.

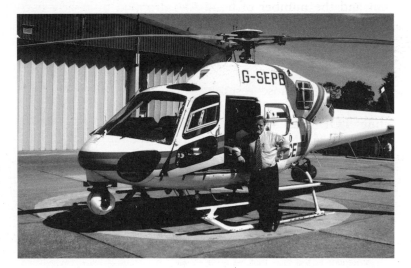

Me in 2000

But then, as the 1980s ended, there was a sudden sea change. I strongly suspect that the tipping point was the work that Mayor Rudy Giuliani and Police Chief Bill Bratton (and later Howard Safir) were doing in New York. In 1990, Herman Goldstein published his seminal book *Problem-Oriented Policing* and 'POP', as it became known, spread across the USA, scoring success after success. As the name suggests, POP means focusing police resources on solving problems – prevention in other words. It urges officers to understand the causes of crime and to remove them rather than to keep responding to crimes after they've happened. In partnership with other agencies, the NYPD performed detailed analyses of crime hotspots to discover why crimes were happening, and then designed tailored preventative solutions to fit. They used innovative predictive software to work out where best to assign their officers. Policing got scientific. Policing got smart. And the results were extraordinary. Major crime in New York City fell by 39 per cent, violent crime by 56 per cent, robbery by 67 per cent, aggravated assault (with a weapon) by 28 per cent and the number of homicides dropped by nearly two-thirds. New Yorkers said that they felt safer than they had in decades and staff at the NYPD reported that their workloads were more manageable and that they were enjoying greater job satisfaction.

Admittedly, those results were not due solely to POP. Violent crime was already on a downward trajectory[17] and, while POP was working to prevent new crimes from happening, the NYPD were simultaneously taking a hard line on those who continued to offend.[18] But no one can dismiss the effect that POP had on people's perception of crime, attitudes towards the police, and best use of police resources.

---

17 There are some interesting theories about why this was the case. One strong contender is the idea that we were seeing the effects of lead removal from petrol, paint and plumbing systems in the decades before. Lead is a very potent neurotoxin and alters the formation of the brain. It can lead to behavioural problems, reduced IQ, hyperactivity, and poor decision-making. Research by economist Jessica Wolpaw Reyes of Amherst College, Massachusetts, has found a US state-by-state correlation between the timing of anti-lead legislation being brought in and a subsequent drop in violent crime 20 years later. Correlation doesn't always mean causation of course, and more research is needed. But it's a fascinating idea.

18 This was known as 'zero tolerance policing', a term first coined by US politicians. As the name suggests, it meant that no crime, no matter how small or seemingly insignificant, went unpunished. The belief was that if you caught and punished people for committing lesser crimes they wouldn't then go on to commit more serious offences. However, its use was controversial because, by definition, zero tolerance means that police discretion is removed – all offenders receive some kind of penalty for their actions – and critics argued that this 'inflexible repression' of minor offences meant that police/community relations were damaged and that the poorest and most desperate people in society ended up receiving punishment instead of help.

More crimes were being prevented, fewer people were being victimised and everyone was happier.

It took a few more years for POP to drift across the Atlantic. Police chiefs on this side of the pond were naturally cautious about such a radical shift in the way that policing was done. But, soon enough, successes started popping up (if you'll pardon the pun) in California, Massachusetts, North Carolina, Michigan, Wisconsin, Kentucky, Pennsylvania ... and, all of a sudden, POP was hard to ignore. Which is why I suddenly found myself being approached in 1998 to contribute to the work of a specialist team being put together at New Scotland Yard to explore some of these 'new' ideas in problem solving policing. I jumped at the opportunity.

And so, for the final decade of my police service, I did exactly what I'd been doing during the previous two, only now with the sanction and support of my senior management, rather than their disappointment. There were six of us in what became known as the 'Problem Solving Unit' – five police officers and an analyst – and we were given almost no budget, laughable resources and a nomadic office that moved around central London like a travelling circus. Our curious brief went something like this: all over the capital there were problems of crime and disorder that hadn't responded to traditional enforcement methods. Despite a great deal of time, effort, money and resources being thrown at them, as soon as the police walked away, the problems popped straight back up again. We were asked to design ways to stop these problems from continuing, preferably with some degree of permanency, and to prevent them from happening elsewhere. We could pretty much try anything as long as (a) it wasn't illegal, (b) wasn't immoral, (c) wouldn't bring the police into disrepute, and (d) didn't cost very much (i.e. as close to 'nothing at all' as we could manage). We were also asked to develop ways of reducing people's fear of crime, which, for a number of reasons, was disproportionately high: certainly much higher than the likelihood of them actually becoming victims.

The Tilley Awards, 2009 (The UK Home Office POP Awards)

So that's what we did. And I can't deny that we raised a few eyebrows along the way with some of our more creative solutions, like using lollipops to reduce antisocial behaviour, wizards to prevent street gambling, and dog shows to stop young men killing each other. However, we had more hits than misses and, even though the unit only existed for 12 years, it made an impact upon the way that London is policed and, to some extent, the UK. We trained thousands of police officers and people from other agencies in crime prevention and problem solving skills. We had an input into national police training and sat on Home Office working parties. We lectured extensively throughout the UK and the USA. We helped create the Safer London Awards and we even won an award or two ourselves.

3

I retired from the police service in 2010 having stayed for 29 years and 6 months longer than I'd originally intended. I'd had a career of ups and downs but it had never been boring and I had enjoyed the challenges. However, a global economic recession was in full squeeze and budgets were being slashed and belts tightened. As each member of the Problem Solving Unit retired or moved on to new roles, they weren't replaced because, it was argued, we'd trained enough staff to ensure that POP continued without us. And as the cuts became ever more savage, the Problem Solving Unit was pretty much wound up. I briefly considered staying on for a few more years but, to be honest, it seemed like a good time to go. I'd achieved what I wanted to achieve and 30 years is a long time to spend in public service.

Charlotte, North Carolina, 2004

I assumed that as soon as I'd handed in my warrant card, my involvement with policing was over. What happened instead is that I found myself being asked to talk about problem solving by people and agencies from many different walks of life. And I was asked to write a book about my experiences while also passing on much of what I'd learned about solving problems. This is that book.

But now, let's return to 1980 and my first few faltering steps as a new constable.

2: THE TRIBE OF BIN

The police are the public and the public are the police; the police being only members of the public who are paid to give full-time attention to duties which are incumbent on every citizen in the interests of community welfare and existence.

Sir Robert Peel

Coming together is a beginning; keeping together is progress; working together is success.

Henry Ford

1

Uxbridge Police Station was not what I'd expected.

I'd expected my first station in the 'big city' to be something concrete and Brutalist with bustling open-plan offices full of haggard-looking, chain-smoking detectives. But Uxbridge was actually rather charming; blonde-bricked and arch-windowed with decorative keystones, cast-iron railings, hanging baskets and window boxes. Sandwiched between an old-fashioned book shop and a new-fangled video shop in Windsor Street, it was hard to imagine that this friendly-looking Victorian building was the seat of local law enforcement. It looked more like a location from a Boulting Brothers comedy and I chuckled at the thought that an ostentatiously moustachioed Jimmy Edwards wouldn't have looked out of place coming out of the front door in uniform and mounting his black bicycle.[19] Which is why, when an officer with a handlebar moustache like two freeze-dried ferrets, emerged from the station tapping out his pipe on the railings and clutching a copy of *The Racing Post*, I was somewhat taken aback. That he was immediately followed out by another older officer with huge white mutton chops, loudly tum-ti-tumming the theme tune to *The Archers*, just added to the surreality of it all.[20]

Uxbridge Police Station, 1964
Photo: Kenneth Pearce

19 Curiously enough, I recently found out that Uxbridge's front steps were used to film a scene for the 1965 MGM Agatha Christie whodunnit *The Alphabet Murders* starring a horribly miscast Tony Randall as Hercule Poirot. The scene features a delicious uncredited cameo by Margaret Rutherford and husband Stringer Davis reprising their popular Miss Marple and Mr Stringer film roles.

20 These, it turned out, were Home Beat Officers, a kind of community police officer that was being phased out. Mostly, they were officers at the end of their careers who had joined in the late 1950s/early 1960s.

Thankfully, inside the station, the officers were a little less Ealing Comedy in appearance and the Reserve Officer – the person who manned the telephones and radio (no computers back in 1980, of course) – was definitely under 30. This suggested that maybe I hadn't been accidentally seconded to a police retirement home or some sort of Bobby *Brigadoon* after all.

'You've been posted walking with 545,' said the Reserve – an officer called Chris Hale who would become a lifelong friend. His use of a number to identify a colleague was strangely impersonal, but I was soon to learn that an officer's shoulder number was a kind of business shortcut and that almost everyone was referred to by number, rather than by name. From that day forward I wasn't so much Steve Colgan as I was 227.

'I'll check where he is,' said Chris, reaching for a radio handset. '545 from Uxbridge. Are you receiving? Over.'

'Shhhhhh.'

'545 ... your signal is breaking up,' said Chris. 'Are you receiving? Over.'

'Shhhh!' hissed the radio. 'I'm on obbo!'

Chris's voice dropped to a whisper. 'I have 227 here. New guy. The guv'nor has said you have to puppy walk him. What's your location? Over.'[21]

'Odeon car park,' said the breathy disembodied voice.

'His name is Mick Butcher,' said Chris. 'He's on obbo.'

I thanked him, put on my helmet and prepared to step outside the station for the very first time. But what if someone asked me to do something? Was I ready for that? Would I forget all my training? And what on Earth was 'obbo'? I steeled myself, took several deep breaths ... and then realised that I had absolutely no idea where the Odeon Cinema was. The officer manning the station front counter,

---

21 In the Met, officers above the rank of inspector were referred to as 'Sir' or 'Ma'am' (and were saluted up until the mid-1980s) but many were happy to be addressed by the more familiar 'Guv' or 'Guv'nor', regardless of gender.

an elderly Scot everyone simply called 'Jock'[22] kindly gave me directions punctuated liberally with curse words – but it was such an embedded part of his natural speech pattern that, strangely, you hardly noticed. It was as if he used swearing as punctuation. In the five years I was at Uxbridge I never heard of him receiving a single complaint despite dropping the F-bomb almost continuously when talking to the public. I even heard him once split a word in half to accommodate a profanity. The word was 'disin-fucking-fectant'.

It turned out to be a short but nerve-wracking walk along the High Street to the Odeon Cinema,[23] most of which I spent hunched over like Frankenstein's Igor, hoping no one would notice me. The car park, at the rear of the cinema, had five or six cars parked there, but there was no sign of a police officer. My radio crackled into life.

'227. Up here.'

I looked around and up. And there, gesturing furiously at me from high up in a nearby sycamore tree, was a skinny, bald policeman. He beckoned me over.

'Up here! Make it snappy!'

With a conspicuous lack of grace, I climbed up to join him and found a safe perch in the crotch of two fat branches. I noted with some dismay that my brand new uniform had green and brown stains on it where I'd rubbed against the bark.

'I'm Steve,' I said. '227.'

---

22 Nicknames were very popular back in those pre-nicknames-are-a-form-of-bullying days. And they were very inventive. Among my favourites at Uxbridge were Bongo ('Books On, Never Goes Out'), Treasure (sunken chest), Opium (slow-acting dope) and Silas ('Sorry I'm Late Again Sarge'). One particularly disliked inspector was known as Kipper (two-faced, yellow, no guts) and one boss-eyed officer was called Uzi ('Uzi looking at?'). There was also a chap called Womble and, as I could see no resemblance between him and Great Uncle Bulgaria, I felt obliged to ask him why. 'Because I've got one ball,' he replied pragmatically. Apparently, he'd had a testicle removed following a grisly injury playing rugby at school.

23 Which, bizarrely, I instantly recognised as a location used in the film *Carry on at Your Convenience*. I soon came to recognise lots of other locations; Uxbridge isn't very far from Pinewood Studios and was often the first port of call when filming off set.

'Shhh,' he hissed. 'I'm waiting for a tea leaf.'

I'd yet to fully master the intricacies of Cockney rhyming slang but I knew enough to know that here was a police officer, up a tree, waiting to catch a thief.[24] I also learned that an 'obbo' was an observation – a 'stake-out' in TV detective show parlance – but it didn't get much further from *The Sweeney* than this. Mick Butcher was 30-something and painfully thin; a colleague once described him to me as a 'skeleton with a condom pulled over it'. He was a bag of nervous energy and every ounce of body fat had been rendered off his wiry, vascular frame.[25] His helmet, filled with sandwiches and Tunnock's caramel wafers, dangled from a nearby branch by its chinstrap like a hanging basket.

We sat silently in that tree for well over an hour, the only sounds the gentle rustle of the leaves and Mick's jaw muscles bunching under his skin as he obsessively nibbled around the edges of his sandwiches like a very hungry caterpillar. My bum soon went to sleep and there were several times when the rest of me threatened to join it, but Mick's laser-beam attention never once wavered. I later learned that he'd been up in that tree for over an hour before I'd turned up.

Eventually a short, stocky, dark-haired guy walked into the car park, looked nervously around and began trying car door handles. With a silent catlike leap, Mick launched himself from his perch and grabbed the man by the arm. Rather more clumsily, I fell out of the tree and ran across to join them just as Mick told the man he was being arrested

---

24 It took me ages to figure out why my colleagues kept saying that it was 'taters' when it was chilly. Potatoes in the mould = cold. Apparently.

25 Mick Butcher's nickname had been 'The Screaming Skull' but, in recent months, colleagues had taken to calling him Chi Chi. The reason he'd been on foot patrol when I first met him was that he'd been suspended from driving police vehicles because he 'fucked pandas'. (For foreign readers, I'll explain that British police cars used to be nicknamed 'panda cars' because of their black and white or blue and white liveries.) Having an accident in a police vehicle invariably meant a driving suspension while a fearsome Traffic Division Sergeant determined whether you should be trusted to drive police vehicles again.

for 'Sus' and cautioned him.[26] The words that I'd learned during endless mock arrests at Hendon suddenly took on a new reality:

You are not obliged to say anything unless you wish to do so, but what you do say will be taken down in writing and may be used in evidence.[27]

This was my first involvement in a real arrest, a landmark moment in my police career, which is probably why I can still remember the suspect's name, though don't ask me to spell it. All I recall was an extravagant number of rarely-used consonants. The next day I hit another landmark – my first arrest as the arresting officer (two young women for shoplifting) – and in the years to come I would be involved in many more.[28] Most of them I've forgotten, but I'll never forget that first one: that chap with all the Zs and Ks in unlikely combinations. Nor will I quickly forget the sight of

---

26 'Sus' was the slang term for Section. 4 of the Vagrancy Act, 1824, a controversial piece of legislation that gave the police powers to stop and search anyone suspected (hence 'Sus') of attempting to commit an arrestable offence. Mick was using it correctly in this instance but there's plenty of evidence to suggest that some officers did misuse it. Certainly, an allegedly disproportionate misuse of 'Sus' is considered to have been one of the factors that kicked off the race riots of 1981. It was consequently repealed and replaced by the Criminal Attempts Act.

27 The caution has changed over the years and is currently: 'You do not have to say anything. But it may harm your defence if you do not mention when questioned something which you later rely on in court. Anything you do say may be given in evidence. Do you understand?'

28 I've always found it strange that Americans choose to call their equivalent of our caution the 'Miranda Rights', because Ernesto Arturo Miranda was a very nasty piece of work indeed and the name almost memorialises him. Miranda was convicted of kidnap, rape and armed robbery in 1963. However, the prosecution case had rested solely upon his confession and he had not received legal advice. Miranda appealed and won the right to be retried without the now inadmissible confession. He was still found guilty, but a judicial review led to the introduction of new police procedures, whereby anyone arrested must be informed of their right to remain silent and to have legal representation before anything they say becomes admissible in law. As for Miranda himself, he was released from prison on parole in 1975 and supplemented his income by selling autographed Miranda cards until he was fatally stabbed in a barroom brawl in 1976. The killer was never caught.

Mick Butcher, like some predatory raptor, up a tree, eating sandwiches from a helmet.

It was the first time that I witnessed the lengths to which some police officers will go just to get 'a body'. While TV cop shows can hardly be called realistic, they do reflect the fact that, for many cops, their *raison d'être* is catching the bad guys.[29] And arresting people was seen by many as crime prevention; catch the bad guys and they can't commit further crimes. Sure enough, Mick had prevented a crime from happening in the Odeon car park that day. But it had been an expensive use of police resources just to prevent one criminal from committing one crime. Real crime prevention requires a degree of sustainability; there's always another opportunistic 'tea leaf' waiting around the corner. Didn't it make more sense to invest in ways to prevent *anyone* committing crime in the Odeon car park 24 hours a day, 365 days a year? But how do you do that? Even if police numbers were suddenly increased a hundredfold overnight and we filled the trees with cops, it still wouldn't be sufficient to keep watch on every car in every London car park. Or to watch every street for burglars. Or every town centre for street robbers. There can never, ever be enough police to cover every eventuality.

Or could there?

It all depends on your definition of policing.

2

These days it's common practice to group people together who have nothing more connecting them than a shared attribute and to call them a community: e.g. the gay community, the farming community, the Chinese

---

29   They may not be realistic but recent research shows that TV cop shows and movies have a major influence on people's perception of police procedure and available resources. It means that many people believe that a cop's primary job is to catch bad guys.

community, etc. But it's quite possible for members of these 'communities' to be geographically separated; to have no contact with each other; to have conflicting aims, mores or philosophies; or even to be in competition with each other. In extreme cases, there is infighting and violence between factions. Supporters of different football teams verbally abuse and sometimes even fight each other even though they are all fans of the same 'beautiful game'. Members of religious communities can clash violently over interpretations of their holy books. And if it's simply a matter of shared attributes, is there an equally valid paedophile community or dog fighting community or Hepatitis B community? I suspect not. If we have to use group labels, isn't it more accurate to simply say 'gay people', or 'farmers', or 'Chinese people'?

I believe that 'community' is something more intimate than a bunch of strangers all wearing the same team shirt or owning the same make of car.[30] It's something much more powerful than that.

For me, a community is a group of people who have shared concerns about the space in which they all live: their street, their block of flats, their village, etc. To some degree they care about each other too, especially about the most vulnerable members. There's usually a kind of 'bush telegraph' in place by which information is quickly disseminated, person to person, household to household. It helps to keep the community close. And it helps to prevent crime because potential criminals or troublemakers are quickly identified. The bad guys are up against everyone, not just a few individuals. A functional community is something intimate; it has social networks that are genuinely social and once it gets too large and impersonal it doesn't function

---

30 *Volkszone* describes itself as 'Europe's largest VW community'. It's just one example of the many so-called 'brand communities' out there. There are Lego and Barbie communities too, apparently.

any more.[31] And, it goes without saying, that police officers should be active within those networks. This is policing with a small *p* and I firmly believe that it's the way that we should all be living.

In his groundbreaking and influential 1972 book, *Defensible Space*, the late architect and city planner Oscar Newman argued that the presence of some form of police is not enough to create a safe and crime-free environment – the community has just as important a role to play. And Sir Robert Peel agreed, as you'll see from the quote headlining this chapter. There has never been a time in human history when we have been able to abrogate all responsibility for our own safety and welfare, and I suspect there never will be. There aren't enough police officers to assign one to every street (and would you want that anyway?). Therefore we, as citizens, have to do our part; the 'duty incumbent' upon us, as Peel put it. We all have to be involved in policing if we want to live in a safe and crime-free society. But that doesn't mean having to form community warden patrols or anything quite so organised or confrontational.

It can simply mean being a good neighbour.

3

A community police officer is running one of his regular clinics in a church hall where, over tea and biscuits, local people can come and have a chat and share their woes. In the past hour he's learned that kids are loitering in the alleyway

---

31 Research by British anthropologist Professor Robin Dunbar has shown that human beings, regardless of race or geography, are only capable of maintaining a finite number of stable relationships with other people. Although an exact figure is not specified, 'Dunbar's Number' is a cognitive limit somewhere between 120 and 170. Taking 150 as a round figure, it means that we could all know around 150 people well enough to know who they know. Research has shown that tribal groups larger than 150 tend to fragment into smaller tribes that each subsequently grow back to around 150 in number. Also, the number of academics in a discipline's sub-specialisation rarely exceeds 150. And many modern army battalions are divided into companies of around 150.

that links Laurel Road to Hardy Street, that the man at 29 Keaton Road is fed up with people putting rubbish in the skip that he's hired, and that inconsiderate people aren't always clearing up after their dogs.[32] But the flavour of the week is quite definitely burglary. Word has got around that there has recently been a 25 per cent increase in incidents. Even though that figure actually equates to one more burglary per week than the average for the area, it's still one too many. Being the victim of burglary is a distressing and painful experience for the victim and people are quite rightly worried. 'It's not safe to live around here anymore,' says one lady. 'I'm afraid to leave the house unattended.'[33]

Clinic over, the officer takes a leisurely stroll around the area, chatting to local people and asking the dog walkers he meets to keep an eye out for people who aren't clearing up after their animals. He promises himself that, towards the end of his shift, he'll have a look at the burglary records to see if anything jumps out. The Chaplin Estate isn't a burglary 'hotspot' – there are many places on the division that have far more burglaries per week and therefore warrant the most police attention – but perhaps there's something he can do, at local community level, to make things better.

A perusal of reported burglary records reveals to the officer that the offences have mostly happened on a Thursday between 9am and 6pm and he wonders why that is the case. Perhaps the burglar has a drug problem and needs money on a Thursday to replenish their stock? Is there maybe something that happens on a Thursday that brings certain undesirables into the area? Or is it perhaps something that the residents of the Chaplin Estate do on a Thursday that makes it the best day of the week for burglary? Over the next few days he speaks to homeowners, the regular postwoman, the

32 Over the years, I must have heard every possible euphemism for dog mess: dog toffee, dog eggs, doggy sausage. Urp.

33 Incidentally, whenever I ran such clinics, I always used raw numbers rather than percentages. A '25 per cent' increase sounds far worse than 'one extra burglary'.

shopkeepers on Arbuckle Parade, the dog walkers, the local vicar and others.[34] And what he discovers is a possible reason for the Thursday pattern.

Every week the inhabitants of the estate put out their wheelie bins for emptying, either on Thursday morning or the night before. Then, after the dustcart has gone by, all of the residents who are at home pull their bins back on to their properties. By 11am, the only bins still on the street belong to houses where the occupiers are at work or otherwise not at home. And, very handily, they all have the numbers of the houses they belong to stencilled on them. At 4pm, the same bins are still advertising that no one has been at home for at least five hours. If the same thing happens every Thursday, what message are those bins sending to a burglar?

The community officer knows that he doesn't have enough evidence – at this stage it's just a notion – to convince either his inspector or the local Burglary Squad to assign resources. No one would sanction a police operation based on such a flimsy premise. But, he realises, he doesn't need police resources to test his theory; he just needs the community to act like a community and to help police itself.

Over the next few days, he organises a series of house calls, clinics and meetings with residents' groups, landlords and the local Neighbourhood Watch. He explains the issue and asks the people of the Chaplin Estate if, in the spirit of good neighbourliness, they will do one small act of kindness: If they are at home on a Thursday after the bin men have been, would they be good enough to pull their immediate neighbours' bins off the street? It will take them, at worst, a minute of their time. As always, there are a few curmudgeonly old so-and-sos who say that it's nothing to do with them, but mostly the response he gets is very positive. And, he realises that, even if it transpires that the wheelie bins aren't contributing to the burglaries, the initiative will at least get people talking to each other. There's no downside to running the experiment.[35]

The following Thursday there are no burglaries. The week after, there are none. The week after that, none again. After a six-month review, the average number of burglaries per week has dropped to one. Most weeks there are no burglaries at all.

This may sound fanciful but it's based on a true story from Lancashire in 2006. And it's not an isolated incident; in 2007, people pulling their neighbours' bins off the street in one area of the London Borough of Harrow appeared to result in burglaries dropping by 22 per cent after just two weeks. And numbers continued to drop. No one was able to identify any other factor – seasonality, weather, improved home security, etc. – that could account for the

---

35 Focusing people's attention on wheelie bins is a good thing: if they are stored in a poor position, they can aid access to flat roofs and upstairs windows. I've even known burglars use them to cart away the spoils of their break-in.

reduction.[36] PC Stuart Hutchinson, the officer behind this 'good neighbour wheelie bin initiative' (I'm sure there must be a catchier name) told me that, 'Even if the wheelie bins weren't the culprits – and I have to accept that it's quite possible that they weren't – it got neighbours talking and looking out for each other. Maybe it was the very fact that neighbours were now cooperating that put the burglars off the area?' Whatever the reason, potential new victims were spared the upset of being burgled and those that had been previously burgled didn't get a repeat visit.[37] Stuart also cleverly had shiny high-visibility stickers made up to advertise the fact that the scheme was in place. Putting them on the bins had a triple effect: it told potential burglars that the residents were aware of them, it allowed occupiers to announce their participation, and it shamed some of the bellyachers into joining the scheme (or scared them as their non-stickered bins would possibly say to a burglar 'I'm not being looked after by my neighbours'). No one wants to be the person with no shiny stickers, do they? Most importantly Stuart and the community working together had created a sustainable crime prevention solution.

With ever more thinly-stretched resources it's impossible to guarantee a police presence in every residential street. But if residents work together, and work with their local police,

36 I say 'appeared to result' as more detailed research and analysis would have been needed to ensure that the wheelie bin initiative was definitely the cause of the reduction. Evaluation is a subject we will discuss in depth in Chapter 11. Don't worry, I'll make it interesting.

37 It's not uncommon for burglars to revisit a property that they have burgled before. There are good reasons for this: firstly, there's knowledge of what the property contains; they can steal the goods that they couldn't transport the first time, or goods for which they now have a buyer. Plus, if a decent period of time has elapsed, many goods may have been replaced after an insurance payout. Secondly, they understand the hazards they might face – dogs, alarms, neighbours, etc. – and they know the layout of the house. Therefore, if you've been burgled, the best thing to do is to add a new layer of security or a few obstacles that the burglar(s) won't be anticipating. Like a pair of permanently angry attack dogs.

there will always be plenty of people looking out for the burglars, and for each other.[38]

That's the power of community.

4

Moving to London was something of a culture shock. Quite apart from the much faster pace of life, I couldn't quite understand why everyone seemed to be so insular. People didn't say good morning to each other like they did in Cornwall; the commute to work was a solemn affair conducted in stony silence. I would frequently meet people who had never spoken to their neighbours, even to those who lived next door. It was all very puzzling; surely people are people, with the same needs, desires and fears wherever they

38 I remember a similar incident in which the empty flats in a block were identified by the empty spaces in the shared car park. Each parking space bore the number of the flat it belonged to. That problem was solved by giving the parking spaces a random letter for identification that didn't correspond to the associated flat number.

live? I'd transplanted myself from Cornwall to London but I hadn't been changed by the experience. I still said 'Good morning' to passers-by and engaged people in conversation on public transport. I did get the occasional horrified stare in return but, mostly, people seemed to enjoy the contact as if I'd somehow unlocked something for them. Why were things so different from Cornwall?

I was, at this time, living in a small cul-de-sac of around 30 properties just outside Uxbridge. I shared a rented, three-bedroom house with a Cumbrian helicopter engineer and a Scottish accountant, and we were all a long way from home. Every morning, they would get up, have their breakfasts and brave the rush hour. Then, in the evening, between six and seven, they came home, ate their dinners and then toddled off to the pub for a couple of beers, before settling down to watch some terrible, and possibly illegal, video nasty on our rented VCR.[39] The next morning they did the same thing all over again, as did nearly all of the good folk of the cul-de-sac (but probably without the dodgy films). My housemates were lucky because their work was fairly local. Many of our neighbours had a much longer working day with a commute in and out of central London to endure. Uxbridge is right on the western periphery of London and properties are more affordable in the 'commuter belt' than they are closer to the centre.

Things were different for me. Being a shift worker, I wasn't part of that whole 9-to-5 routine. It meant that I often got to chat with neighbours who were at home during the day; mostly mums and housewives but the work-at-home and retired people too. What I found out from them was

---

39 I'd join them when I could. Shift work is terribly antisocial. My shifts in those days consisted of a mix of 'Early Turns' (6am–2pm), 'Late Turns' (2pm–10pm) and Night Duty. If you were on Lates or Nights, your evenings were buggered. And if you were on Earlies your evening fun was always overshadowed by the fact you had to be at work at 6am the next day. I got one weekend off in four.

why Londoners acted the way they did.[40] It was all to do with tribes.

Had I stayed in Helston, or returned after my six-month adventure was over, I'd probably have found a job in the town and stayed friends with some of the people I went to school with. I might have married a local girl and our kids would have gone to the same school we'd gone to. I'd have rented or bought a house and, in time, I'd have died and been buried in the town cemetery. For the whole of my life, I'd have had several generations of my family nearby, along with many of my school friends and several generations of their families too. I would have belonged to the 'Tribe' of Helston.

However, I didn't belong to the tribe of London. Or even to the tribe of Uxbridge. I didn't even belong to the tribe of my cul-de-sac. But nor did my neighbours because there was no tribe to belong to. The majority of them, like me, had moved to London to find work. Some were hundreds of miles away from their childhood homes and nearest family. Consequently they didn't know anyone locally and – because they spent more hours at work, or travelling to and from work (sat in silence on the trains and buses, of course), than they did at home – they didn't really socialise outside of work hours. Most of them didn't even know anyone else in the cul-de-sac except maybe by sight. *That* was the difference.

Many years ago, I read Desmond Morris's book, *The Human Zoo*. There are a couple of paragraphs that always stuck with me:

Imagine a piece of land twenty miles long and twenty miles wide. Picture it wild, inhabited by animals small and large. Now visualise a compact group of sixty human beings camping in the middle of this territory. Try to see yourself sitting there, as a member of this tiny tribe, with the

---

40 Of course, I am generalising to simplify the narrative. There were lots of small, but strong and cohesive communities in London. But they were not the norm.

landscape, your landscape, spreading out around you farther than you can see.

Now imagine a piece of land twenty miles long and twenty miles wide. Picture it civilised, inhabited by machines and buildings. Now visualise a compact group of six million human beings camping in the middle of this territory. See yourself sitting there, with the complexity of the huge city spreading out all around you, farther than you can see.

Photos: Angella Rodgers

As he points out, all that separates these two hugely different pictures is a few thousand years: a mere blip in the story of life and a very small portion of the 200,000 years that *Homo Sapiens Sapiens* have been kicking around. We haven't changed much in that time. By the start of the Upper Palaeolithic Era (50,000 years ago) we had developed language, music and other cultural universals such as personal names, taboos and rituals, cooking, etc. If we found a man or woman from the Neolithic Era (the New Stone Age – about 12,000 years ago) frozen in the ice and were somehow able to defrost them and bring them back to life, they'd be quite capable of doing everything that we can do. They could drive a car, use word-processing software and assemble flat-packed furniture. In evolutionary terms, we are no different to our Stone Age ancestors. We may have smartphones, ergonomic office chairs and breadmakers but we still have the same needs, drives and desires as they had.[41] One of those needs is to feel that we are part of a tribe: whether it's the Women's Institute, being a regular at a particular pub, following a local rugby team, or dressing up as a favourite character from *Star Wars*. That's why there are so many fan clubs, appreciation societies and 'brand communities'; we are naturally communal creatures and, if we can't be part of a physical community, we will try to make do with a virtual one. And a community is a tribe – you either have to be born into it, or be adopted by it, or make an effort to belong to it. The alternative is social isolation.

Many aspects of our lives – such as happiness, motivation, health and our sense of worth – are affected by whether or not we 'belong'. 'There is evidence of a correlation between strong social networks and wellbeing,' says Nicola Bacon, co-founder of Social Life, an organisation dedicated to building communities. 'Those who know more people in their local neighbourhood tend to be happier than those who don't.' And research by psychologists, such as Gregory Walton of Yale University, has shown clearly that isolation can do enormous harm. There is even some evidence to suggest that *any* instance of exclusion can undermine IQ test performance. The need to feel like we're 'in the gang' – whatever that gang is – is something deeply coded into our genome; it explains why disenfranchised kids with no sense of belonging to a community and poor (or absent) adult role models, will gravitate towards forming their own tribes. That's how gangs are formed. It also explains why someone who doesn't feel like they belong, can feel desperately lonely and isolated even though they live in a hugely populous

---

41 In a 2008 report for the UK Commons Transport Committee, psychology professor Geoffrey Beattie of Manchester University explained why men drive cars differently to women: 'Our twenty-first century skulls contain essentially 'stone-age' brains and this can help to explain the differences between the sexes in terms of their risk-proneness while driving,' he says. 'Stone-age man did not drive. But the legacy of his hunting, aggressive and risk-taking past – qualities that enabled him to survive and mate, thereby passing on his genes to future generations – are still evident in the way in which he typically drives his car.'

city. It's probably no surprise to learn that loneliness is a leading factor in many cases of suicide.[42]

There are many reasons why people in London and other large metropolitan areas are either unwilling, unable, too busy or too uncomfortable to lift themselves out of their isolation. Just the fact that making eye contact with strangers is generally uncomfortable in Western society is one reason why commuters, travelling in cramped metal tubes, hide behind their newspapers and smartphones. Keeping ourselves to ourselves is learned behaviour and, paradoxically, even though we do it as a form of self-protection, it adds to our feelings of discomfort and disengagement from society.[43]

There wasn't a Tribe of the Cul-de-Sac for me or my neighbours to belong to. Despite our geographical proximity, we were all separated from each other by the walls of our houses and British reserve. It therefore seemed obvious to me that the first step towards creating a functioning community would be to get my neighbours talking to each other.

5

I have a friend called Dr David Bramwell. A few years ago, he

42 Every 40 seconds, somewhere in the world, someone commits suicide. That's a staggering statistic, isn't it? In the United States, it is the tenth most common cause of death among people over 10 years of age and, in the UK, it is the leading cause of death of men under 50 years of age. Loneliness and a sense of isolation is a common factor in many of these tragic instances; a 2014 survey by the Office for National Statistics found Brits are 'less likely to have strong friendships or know our neighbours than inhabitants of any other country in the EU'. We are, officially, the loneliest people in Europe.

43 People who talk to strangers on their commute to work almost always feel happier for having done so. Connecting with others is an important determinant of happiness and, according to Dr David Halpern, Director of the Behavioural Insight Team at the UK Cabinet Office: 'Loneliness is a more powerful predictor of whether you will be alive in 10 years time, more than almost any other factor.' The message is simple – be social, be happy. Perhaps this lack of communication is why a 2012 *Trip Advisor* survey listed London as the second least friendly city in the world.

went in search of Utopia – the perfect community in which to live.[44]

He travelled to anarchist communes in Denmark, to Californian free-love retreats and to an underground temple in the Italian Alps the size of St Paul's Cathedral. He didn't find what he was looking for but, upon returning to his home in Brighton, he discovered that a man called David Burke had done something quite extraordinary in his own backyard. Burke had created a thing called Zocalo[45] and the idea was simplicity itself; you pick a date and then, on that day, you take a chair and sit outside your house and meet your neighbours.

Photo: David Bramwell

44 The story of which is told in his excellent book, *The No.9 Bus to Utopia*, Unbound (2014)

45 A zócalo is a plaza in Mexican towns and cities where people congregate and spend time together. It's like the Italian piazza. Other countries seem to find this sort of thing so natural.

As David Bramwell describes it, 'At 5pm, like magic, people began to appear on the streets, in ones and twos at first, but pretty soon clusters were gathering. People brought their dinners out to eat, some played games of chess. One family dragged out the entire living room, complete with oriental rug and bean bags. Kids brought out table football and Jenga to play with passers-by. Elderly residents, wrapped in headscarves and woollens, came out with tea and cakes. All it needs is one person in every street to kick-start a Zocalo. No need for fundraising, sponsorship, bureaucracy or political interference.'

David now runs Zocalo and tells me that the best thing about it is that he and his neighbours now have keys to each other's houses. They take turns to cat-sit and water each other's plants when they go away. They borrow DIY tools from each other: why does everyone in the street need to own a belt sander that they only need once in a blue moon? Just the one will suffice because they all share each other's toolboxes. As David says, 'I do fantasise about a time in the future when, through overwhelming public demand, our government would be forced to establish a new national holiday – Zocalo Day – when we'd all have a day off work to plonk a chair outside our house and spend a little time with our neighbours.'[46] Crime in David's street is virtually non-existent because, as Sir Robert Peel wisely once said, 'the police are the public and the public are the police.'

But if you don't fancy a Zocalo, you could always organise a Big Lunch. I recently had the pleasure of hanging out with Sir Tim Smit, the palindromic co-creator of the Eden Project in Cornwall. For several years Tim has been encouraging us all to take part in something very similar to Zocalo. Although The Big Lunch is an initiative created by the Eden Project, it's not badged as such.[47] They deliberately don't advertise it because Tim doesn't want it to be seen as *their* Big Lunch but,

46   www.brightonzocalo.com
47   www.thebiglunch.com

rather, as *everybody's* Big Lunch. He believes that if the public takes ownership it is more likely to grow as a cultural event and he has hopes that it will one day become a nationwide 'Neighbours' Day' – just like David Bramwell's 'Zocalo Day' – when people get together to eat, drink and laugh, to find out about who they live next door to, who is lonely and needs help, and all the other benefits that come from belonging to, or strengthening, an existing community. When The Big Lunch began in 2009, 750,000 people nationwide took part. In 2015 the number had risen to 6.5 million. It is growing and growing fast because it's what people want.

Photo: David Bramwell

I now realise that, back in our cul-de-sac in Uxbridge in the early 1980s, my housemates and I hit upon something very similar. But rather than getting everyone to sit outside their houses, we invited everyone to ours for an all-day open house called 'Sociable Saturday'. We started with Elevenses, where anyone could drop in for tea, coffee, biscuits and cakes. Then we did a lunchtime buffet. Then we had afternoon 'Tiffin' at 3pm.[48] Finally, in the evening, we laid on a barbecue. To help lubricate the event, a friend's uncle had loaned us the complete kit for setting up our own small pub – some firkins with racks and taps – and, for nearly 24 hours, we partied, ate and drank and made friends. It was a great experience and even the people we'd thought unapproachable or antisocial were persuaded to come along: we called at their houses armed with chocolate cake and issued personal invitations. It turned out that they were more fearful than fearsome, more 'hard to reach' than 'don't want to be reached'.

The results were amazing. People felt less isolated. Neighbours watched out for each other's homes from that day on. We got invited to barbecues and parties. We'd helped to create a community, a real physical community, our very own tribe. More importantly, in the three years that I lived there, the cul-de-sac was crime-free.

In a nationwide survey organised by Neighbourhood Watch in 2014, it was revealed that one in ten UK residents couldn't name any of their neighbours and less than a fifth knew the names of even their immediate neighbours. Overall, fewer than 20 in 100 people said that they had a sense of 'belonging'. And yet 65 per cent of those polled said that they believed their neighbourhood would be a stronger and safer place if people were encouraged to get to know each other. At the same time, Neighbourhood Watch conducted a month-long experiment in a randomly chosen street – Lingard Road in Manchester – asking people to keep diaries of contact with their neighbours. The residents were also asked to make a conscious effort to smile at people and say hello, to offer help if it looked like help was needed and to try to strike up conversations. After just a month, *all* of the residents who

---

48   When I joined the social network Twitter, I did the same thing: at 11am and 3pm every day I would announce that it was time for Elevenses and Tiffin. By doing so I encouraged people to engage with me and others by providing a common point of interest – virtual beverages and biscuits.

had taken part stated that it had made a difference. 'People I've never met before have been a bit more sociable and said hello on several occasions,' said local man Jay Crawford when interviewed by *The Observer*, 'The study has been useful and really proven that we are a nice little street with a small community.' Despite living in the area for 24 years, he had never plucked up the courage to talk to anyone before taking part in the study. He also reported being delighted that he now runs a wheelie bin rota with his new 'tribe' – just to annoy the burglars.

I absolutely believe that helping communities to become stronger and more cohesive is a primary function of policing. A 2014 study produced by the N8 Policing Research Partnership reports that: 'This programme [community policing] has been associated with a range of beneficial outcomes including: stronger communities; more effective, motivated officers; reduced crime and disorder; and increased perceptions of neighbourhood safety.' It confirms the results of many previous studies that all made the same conclusion, that the 'bobby on the beat' isn't a luxury – it's a necessity. In places where communities are fractured or dysfunctional – like you find in some larger suburban areas where family links are few and where people are separated from where they grew up – a little nudge from the local police officer is sometimes all that's needed to make things better. People who are part of a community don't feel isolated. They don't feel so fearful. They feel empowered. And, if the community police officer is an integral part of that community, it adds to people's feelings of security.

Of course, this doesn't just apply to policing. If you treat the staff at your workplace as part of your 'tribe' and build a sense of community with your customers and other people you do business with, you'll excel. The late David Ogilvy CBE, called by many the Father of Advertising, had these words of advice for managers: 'You can never spend too much time thinking about, worrying about, caring about your people, because at the end of the day it's only the people who matter. Nothing else.'

In my first few years as a police officer I came to realise that preventing crime, disorder and other concerns negatively affecting quality of life is a community issue. Policing is something we all have to take a stake in. If we are all involved – simply by getting to know our neighbours and by looking out for each other – we'll all be better off.

We'll never live in a crime-free society unless we're willing to surrender a great many civil liberties. However, we can live in a society that is as near as dammit to crime-free if we all get stuck in. The alternative is that we abrogate all responsibility and leave the decision-making to others – the police, local authority, central government, etc.

But then we can hardly moan if what we get isn't what we wanted.

3: IF THE DRAGON SAYS NO ...

Some people become cops because they want to make the world a better place. Some people become vandals because they want to make the world a better looking place.

Banksy

The primary cause of unhappiness is never the situation but your thoughts about it.

Eckhart Tolle

1

'All units, all units from 227. Aged broken Conservative bonked in vicar's house. I repeat, aged broken Conservative bonked in vicar's house. Over.'

'227 ... can you repeat? Over.'

'All units, aged broken Conservative bonked in vicar's house. Over.'

It was February 1983 and I was on night duty. Elsewhere in the capital the streets would be awash with hordes of happy hedonists, with theatres, restaurants and pubs, strip joints, nightclubs and casinos, all brimming with pissed-up, pleasure-seeking, party people. But not where I was. The London Borough of Hillingdon had a cup of Horlicks and an early night. It was as if someone in authority threw a huge switch at midnight and turned the borough off. The result was a moderately brisk start to the shift followed by a rapid descent into five to six hours of desperately trying to stay awake until booking-off time. The temptation to find a nice dark wood in which to park your panda and snatch 40 winks was always there. But, as you couldn't do that, you had to find a way to stay conscious while driving around the dark and empty streets. And, as it turned out, a game of radio cryptic clue hide-and-seek was just the ticket.

An officer would find a location and give out a clue as to where they were, e.g. 'trick rope flying nearby' on their radio. The first colleague to guess the location (in this case 'Concorde Close') would drive there and announce the answer over the radio. Everyone would then meet at that location while the winner drove smugly off to find a location from which to broadcast a new clue. It was fun. And, more importantly, figuring out the clues helped keep our brains active and alert as we patrolled. I have no idea who initiated the first game but I immediately spotted its potential as a problem solving tool. More than 30 years have passed since I transmitted 'aged broken Conservative bonked in vicar's house' as a cryptic clue for Old Rectory Lane (*Old wrecked Tory lain*. You see?) but I could drive you there right now if you asked me to. Its location is ingrained on my memory. And that's the point.

There are many different ways to make memorising information easier but, generally, if you can employ the linguistic and visual parts of the brain simultaneously, the knowledge becomes more deeply embedded and more easily retrievable. Cryptic hide-and-seek ticked all the boxes and proved to be a really good way of learning your way around the area. Similar techniques are used by professional stage magicians and mentalists, and there are echoes of it in the 'memory palace' or *Loci* technique popularised by Thomas Harris in his Hannibal Lecter books and Benedict Cumberbatch's take on Sherlock Holmes – creating a mental map to which you can link things you need to remember, like objects, dates and people.[49]

Now that I had a little service under my belt I'd been given the task of 'puppy walking' a brace of new probationary constables. I suspect that it was an effort to make me toe the line by giving me some responsibility. But I didn't mind. In fact, I rather enjoyed the challenge. And cryptic clue hide-and-seek proved to be a far more effective way for them to learn their way around 'the manor' than the traditional method of 'learning beats' from a small book and a map.

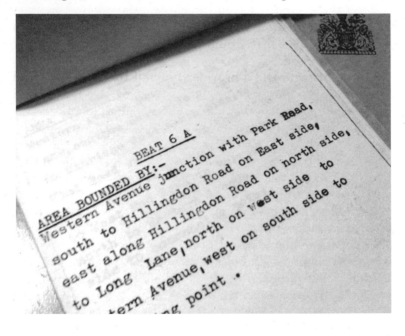

BEAT 6 A

AREA BOUNDED BY:—
Western Avenue junction with Park Road, south to Hillingdon Road on East side, east along Hillingdon Road on north side, to Long Lane, north on west side to ern Avenue, west on south side to g point .

That's not to say that there's anything wrong with the traditional way of doing things; after all, that's how London

---

49 The Aborigine peoples of Australia have navigated across their continent for centuries by chanting 'songlines' that describe the location of landmarks as you travel. It's an oral map that allows those who know 'the secret law' to navigate distances of over 300 miles. Most songlines relate to hidden waterholes and springs.

black cab drivers do The Knowledge.[50] And it actually improves the brain as you do it; studies of cabbies have shown that the learning process creates a greater volume of nerve cells in their brain's hippocampus region. However, cabbies have the luxury of time to learn The Knowledge because they can't start work until they've passed their exams. By contrast, cops have to learn on the job because when you arrive at a new station you're expected to hit the ground running and be operational immediately. So any system that helped the new cops find their way around more quickly was a good thing. And if I could make learning enjoyable, even fun, the information was more likely to stick; that was a lesson I'd learned that would prove to be very useful as my career progressed.[51]

In the meantime, I'd proven to myself that building small communities – person by person, street by street – helped to prevent crime. The next step was to think about ways to cement the relationship between the police and the public: to reinforce the idea that we were all on the same side. Little wins proved to be invaluable for this. I found that the policing priorities set by the Home Secretary and police chiefs were generally of little interest to the public; what they wanted was to feel safe where they lived. So I learned to identify the local issues that disproportionally impacted on people's lives and then set out to eliminate or, more realistically, reduce them to a more tolerable level. By doing so I could improve people's quality of life and build trust.

The first step towards tackling a problem – crime or

---

50 The Knowledge consists of learning 320 different 'runs' that take in over 25,000 streets and thousands of landmarks. These are contained within the infamous 'Blue Book' that all cabbies have to memorise. You will often see 'knowledge boys' (and increasingly 'girls') riding around London on scooters with a clipboard and maps attached to their handlebars as they explore the various runs.

51 In 2013 I told the story of my night duty hide-and-seek shenanigans at a live event for the Ig Nobel Prizes UK tour and, in 2014, on Josie Long's excellent Radio 4 series *Short Cuts*. On both occasions, people contacted me afterwards to say that they would try using the technique at their workplace. Those that got back to me were delighted to report that it had been a great success.

otherwise – is to identify exactly what the problem is. But, surprisingly, that isn't always as clear-cut as you might imagine.

2

In April 2008, British street artist Banksy unveiled an audacious new public artwork in the heart of London's West End. Having cunningly badgered a Royal Mail depot just off Oxford Street that work needed doing on the wall of an adjacent building, Banksy and crew were allowed to erect scaffolding in the depot's yard. A few days later, the scaffolding and safety covers came down overnight revealing a three-storey-high mural on the side of the building. The words 'One nation under CCTV' had been blocked out in large white letters. Below this was a red hoodie-wearing youth atop a ladder and supposedly writing the words with a large brush. At floor level, a security guard, accompanied by a dog, could be seen taking a photo of the youth.

Photo: Tom Eversley

Reactions to the work were mixed.[52] Some called the piece witty, well-executed, and a poignant comment on our increasingly scary surveillance society. Ironically, but no doubt intentionally, the secretive artist had created the work while under the watchful eyes of several CCTV cameras – some even mounted on the same wall.

However, Westminster City Council saw it as graffiti, nothing more. Robert Davis, chair of Westminster's planning committee, told *The Times*, 'If we condone this then we might as well say that any kid with a spray can is producing art. To go and deface other people's property is graffiti. Just because he's famous doesn't give him that right.' The mural was painted over in April 2009 and the site is currently being redeveloped.

52 It's hard to say how much the piece was worth but, in 2008, Banksy's *Keep It Spotless* sold for $1.87 million and a new work on a wall in Cheltenham in 2014 trebled the value of the house it was painted on. In 2014 Banksy came in at number 93 in Artnet's Rich List of the 100 top-earning living artists with a total sales figure of $18,244,497 (around £11,673,863 at time of the list's publication).

In 2009 Hackney Council removed a Banksy mural of the Royal Family that had been on the outside of a building for eight years, to the annoyance of the people who live there and fans of the band Blur whose 2003 single *Crazy Beat* featured the painting on its sleeve. The owner of the building, Sophie Attrill, told the *Hackney Gazette* that she was devastated when she saw the wall being painted: 'I looked out the window and saw what they were doing, so I ran downstairs and I told them to stop.' But Alan Laing, spokesman for Hackney Council, told the *London Evening Standard* newspaper, 'We can't make a decision on whether something is art or graffiti. The government judges us on the number of clean walls we have.' But perhaps the most famous Banksy to be removed in London was the one depicting John Travolta and Samuel L Jackson as their *Pulp Fiction* hitmen characters pointing bananas instead of guns. Originally painted in 2002 on a wall at Old Street tube station in Islington, it was removed by Transport for London (TfL) in April 2007, even though it had been valued at more than £300,000 and despite protests from locals. Asked to comment on the mural's destruction, a TfL spokesman told the BBC, 'Our graffiti removal teams are staffed by professional cleaners not professional art critics.'

Other London councils including Hammersmith and Fulham, Haringey, and Tower Hamlets have also removed or painted over Banksy's work in the recent past, but not every council takes such a hard line. Camden, Southwark and Sutton councils have all offered local people the chance to vote on whether they are removed or not. And in the London Borough of Islington, they regularly restore Banksy's artwork if it is 'vandalised' by other graffitists and taggers. Deputy leader and executive member for the environment, Lucy Watt, told the *Evening Standard* that: 'We generally remove graffiti within 24 hours when it is reported to us. However, residents have been telling us Banksy is in a class of his own, his art sells for thousands, and they don't want us to remove the work. Because of the quality and renown of his work in Islington, many people want to see it preserved.'

So, here's the question ... is Banksy a problem?

Westminster and Hackney Councils have entirely polarised views – one sees his work as vandalism, the other as art. You could argue, I suppose, that if his art is acceptable to some, then maybe the problem is not Banksy's behaviour but the intolerance of the other councils. Or, conversely, that the laxity of some councils makes the anti-Banksy councils appear to be overly zealous when they are just doing their job.

Whether something is a problem or not depends entirely on whose eyes you're looking through.[53] Perspective is everything.

One of my first assignments as a fully fledged member of the Problem Solving Unit involved an underpass in west London that ran underneath a busy dual carriageway. The problem, as it was explained to me by a local police officer, was that it had been 'claimed' by local youths as their place to hang out and, as a consequence, other people tended to avoid it. Most affected were the elderly residents of a sheltered accommodation block because the underpass provided the safest route between their homes and the local shops. The alternative was to risk crossing the dual-carriageway at a nearby junction but some of the residents were too infirm or slow-moving to get across before the lights changed. The pensioners were nervous of using the tunnel because the youths played loud music, smoked, drank and swore, and rode their skateboards aggressively. The police were called most days by at least one irate person demanding that the kids be removed or even arrested.

So I visited the site with a local officer and could immediately see why people didn't like to use the tunnel. It was poorly lit, covered in graffiti and it smelled nasty. The kids were challenging, disrespectful, borderline aggressive, and very defensive. They said that everybody hated them so they stayed hidden away down in the subway. They said that there was nowhere else for them to hang out.

---

53 Tracey Emin's controversial *My Bed* sold for £2,546,500 ($4.4 million) at Christie's of London's contemporary art sale. Taste in art is also a very personal thing.

I then went and spoke to the pensioners. They told me that they felt threatened and were scared of being robbed for their pension money. They demanded that the youths be removed. The police response up until that day had been to do exactly that but, as soon as they left the scene, the kids came back. The local officer told me that she and her colleagues were fed up with it. Police action could go no further because there were no actual crimes being committed. Therefore, there was now talk of ASBOs[54] or of closing the tunnel and inconveniencing everyone.

As an objective outsider, the first thing to strike me was that the two sides, despite having very strong views, had never actually had any contact. Everything they believed to be true about each other was anecdotal. But the kids weren't the murderous knife-carrying thugs that the pensioners thought they were; a few had minor convictions but none had ever been found to be carrying weapons and there had been no reported robberies in the underpass. The pensioners,

---

54 Antisocial Behaviour Order. A court can issue someone with an ASBO if they can be shown to have 'acted in a manner that caused or was likely to cause harassment, alarm or distress to one or more persons'. An ASBO can have conditions attached such as curfews between certain times and exclusions, meaning that a person may not visit certain locations. Breach of the ASBO can result in arrest.

meanwhile, weren't the moaning old youth-hating killjoys that the kids assumed they were. They were simply elderly and vulnerable and they wanted to feel safe.

The obvious thing to do was to get both sides together to dispel the myths and rumours but no one was having any of it. So the local officer and I engaged in a spot of subterfuge. We offered to run a 'walking bus' to chaperone the elderly people through the tunnel to and from the shops. The offer was gladly accepted by the pensioners who saw this as a form of police protection and visible support for their side of the argument. It was, therefore, something of a surprise to them when we made a point of stopping to talk to the kids. But that had been my plan all along and, bolstered by the security of being with two cops, the pensioners explained to the kids how their behaviour made them feel. Then the kids explained how they felt. The tension between the groups started to ease as the reality of the situation began to separate itself from the lurid stories and misinformation. Then one of the older people said something like, 'Here, I know you. You're Edna's grandson aren't you?' Consequently, we discovered that some of the kids had a connection to the elderly residents, which shouldn't have been a surprise really as they all lived locally. A kind of uneasy truce was born that day; the kids were still wary of the pensioners and the pensioners still didn't like the kids, but the fear had evaporated.

Over the next few days I organised several more 'walking buses'. On every occasion I insisted that the 'bus' always stop upon reaching the kids to have a brief chat. After just a week, enough trust had been built that the pensioners were no longer scared to use the tunnel without police attendance. Meanwhile, footfall increased dramatically; other local people had cottoned on to what was happening and had started to use the tunnel again. In time the local police officer got to know the youths a little better and subsequently helped them apply to the council for permission to decorate it with a mural. Giving them a sense of part-ownership made the kids look after the place a little better. Remarkably, a couple of the pensioners, who had contacts at the council, successfully lobbied to have the underpass steam-cleaned and to have better lighting installed. The police no longer needed to attend and calls dropped to a negligible level.

The problem that I'd been alerted to was kids gathering in the subway and what people had asked for was that the kids were moved on. But if I'd done as people had asked, we'd have returned to the cat-and-mouse game that had existed for over three years (based on the earliest recorded complaint I could find). We'd have continued to respond to the symptoms of the problem, rather than the cause.

Whether it's Banksy painting on walls or kids gathering in an underpass, a problem isn't simply an event or behaviour: it's how different people perceive an event or behaviour. Samuel Butler once wrote that 'cannibalism is moral in a cannibal country'. As I said earlier, perspective is everything.

3

Occam's Razor is the principle that states: 'All other things being equal, the simplest solution is the best.' Or, as Dr Theodore Woodward once put it, 'When you hear hoof beats, think horses not zebras.'[55] And it is true that, for many problems, the obvious answer is the right answer. However, life isn't always as simple as Mr Occam and Dr Woodward suggest, especially when people are involved.

For example, domestic burglaries mostly happen during the day when people are at work and the house is empty. Conversely, commercial premises tend to be burgled at night when the staff has gone home. People complicate things and the burglar doesn't want to meet anyone who could challenge

---

55 Also known as Ockham's Razor. The principle was named after Franciscan logician William of Ockham (c. 1285–1349). It is sometimes described as the 'KISS Principle' (Keep it Simple, Stupid!). Dr Woodward worked for the University of Maryland, Baltimore, School of Medicine and the term Zebra has since become a slang medical term for an obscure and unlikely diagnosis from ordinary symptoms.

them or act as a witness. For this reason they will also naturally look for a point of entry where they can't be seen. Side alleyways and service roads at the rear of buildings are favourites, which is why 'AlleyGater' type schemes have been so successful at preventing crime. A sturdy lockable gate keeps the burglars at the front of the premises where they stand a far better chance of being seen by neighbours or anyone passing by. This kind of passive security measure works very well; the more potential witnesses there are, the less inclined the criminal is.

However, the AlleyGater scheme misfired spectacularly when it was first suggested as a solution for burglaries in London's Chinatown. A number of older traders completely rejected the idea of gates and, despite many attempts to explain their crime preventative value, the traders stated categorically that they did not want them. No one could figure out what their opposition was until someone thought to ask the traders whether it was something specifically to do with Chinese culture. 'We do not want the gates because the dragon will not be able to lie down,' was their surprising reply.

Feng shui is an ancient method for creating aesthetic harmony. In the modern age, the concept has become somewhat diluted and bastardised by interior decorators, but older Chinese people take it very seriously and a true *feng shui* master takes 6–10 years to learn their art. The idea is that, by arranging structures and objects in certain harmonious positions, it increases the flow of *qi*, believed to be a potent life energy. An important aspect of traditional *feng shui* is that 'dragon veins' of energy should only ever be broken by another dragon vein. Therefore, buildings and their contents should be arranged to maximise the flow along the dragon's body. Try to visualise a long, sinuous Chinese dragon that wants to lie down with its face pointing in one specific direction and tail in another. Anything that stops the dragon lying down is bad for the flow of *qi*. In the case of Chinatown, a particular *qi* line associated with wealth and good fortune would have been interrupted by the gates.

Just to show that this is not a unique issue to London, in 2010 the proposed expansion of the light rail transit system in Edmonton, Canada was opposed by the Chinese community for the very same reason. 'The energy of the earth is along the neighbourhood of that meridian,' explained *feng shui* master Stephen Chan. 'The proposed new route will throw Edmonton's 'dragon vein' into turmoil, and could throw the entire city's positive energy into a negative cycle.' Director of facility planning in the city's transportation department, Adam Laughlin said: 'That is something that I haven't experienced before personally. But we've committed to consult with them and understand what their concerns are and try to address them through the planning process.' And in Hong Kong, there are a number of buildings – most famously the Repulse Bay Hotel, or 'The hotel with the hole' – where the architects had to amend their designs to accommodate the dragon's path from the mountains to the sea. Even the giant Disney Corporation was affected; a consultation with Feng Shui experts resulted in the main entrance to Hong Kong Disneyland being shifted by twelve degrees to ensure maximum prosperity.

Back in Soho, there was no simple answer to the alley gates in Chinatown so we took a different route, advocating barred windows, heavier doors and locks and anti-climb paint on drainpipes and window sills. It did the trick and the dragon, for the moment, was happy. However, time has moved on and the younger generation, especially those British born, simply don't believe in *feng shui* as strongly as their grandparents did. Consequently, the fear of burglary, theft and damage is now surpassing the fear of upsetting dragons and gates are starting to appear.

Simple, obvious solutions aren't always possible because people aren't simple. And, more often than not, the problem isn't simple either despite appearing to be.

Imagine that you live in a small farming community in Africa and one of your friends suffers a fatal snakebite while working in the maize fields. What would you do to stop this from happening again? Put a bounty on snakes? Are things as simple as they seem?

The majority of our thinking falls into one of two categories that the Nobel Prize-winning psychologist Daniel Kahneman has labelled 'System One' and 'System Two'.[56] System One thinking is emotional, intuitive and instinctive; it allows us to make snap judgements and offers a quick fix that answers our immediate needs. However, System One doesn't always result in solutions with any degree of permanence (e.g. chasing the kids out of the underpass, removing park benches). If you want a more long-term solution, you need System Two thinking, which relies on head rather than heart. System Two is about research and analysis. It works slowly but it finds solutions that are inevitably much more effective in the long run. By 'looking before you leap', you also get time to consider what the possible outcomes of your actions could be.

Putting a bounty on the snakes is a bad idea. Killing all of the snakes in the vicinity might solve our immediate problem, but what if those snakes had been controlling the rat population? Rats carry potentially fatal communicable diseases such as leptospirosis, typhus, salmonella, meningitis and bubonic plague.[57] And, as a rat's gestation period is just 22 days and a youngster can breed at just five weeks old, that's a whole new generation every month. Without any natural checks from predators, the numbers are going to explode. And, on top of all that, they're going to eat your crops. You now have a much bigger problem than you had before and, chances are,

---

56 Kahneman's hugely influential book *Thinking, Fast And Slow* is a must for any serious problem-solver.

57 We tend to think of bubonic plague as something that happened in the 'olden days'. In Europe, certainly, cases are now extremely rare. But it is still an issue elsewhere. As recently as 1994, an outbreak in five Indian states caused an estimated 700 infections (including 52 deaths). And between 2000 and 2009 more than 20,000 people became infected, mostly in Africa – but 56 (including seven fatalities) were in the USA.

more people will now die than would have done by rare instances of snakebite.

Thea Litschka-Koen and her husband Clifton run a charity in Swaziland, Africa, to provide antivenoms for snakebite victims. But they also protect deadly snakes, such as the black mamba, because they do more good than harm. 'Almost every day I fight the same fight, try and explain the same thing … that 20,000 families could not survive without snakes,' explains Thea, who is known by locals as 'The White Witch'. 'I work with snakebite victims and families who have lost children, husbands, mothers, etc. and it breaks my heart. But I also understand that without snakes in the sugarcane and maize fields, the rodents would destroy the crops and people would starve.'

The System Two thinker wouldn't have killed all the snakes. They would, as the Litschka-Koens have done, educate people. And they'd have stockpiled antivenoms, used snake repellents, set traps or, at worst, only killed the venomous non-rat-eating snakes.

Tackling problems effectively means not jumping at the simplest solution, or the most complicated, or the most outlandish, intriguing, or sexy solution. It means understanding the problem, and why it affects people the way it does, in order to pick the solution that is *just right*.

Goldilocks, it seems, had wisdom beyond her years.

So, let me ask you this: What's the simplest solution to the problem of tigers being killed in the wild? This is a question I've posed during talks and lectures many times as an example of how System One and System Two thinking can clash. But before we look at options, I want to digress slightly and talk about beef.

Photo: Ruth Bourne

I once saw the late Douglas Adams give a talk about the future of our relationship with the planet. This was around the time he wrote *Last Chance to See*, his book about the plight of some of the world's most endangered species. During the lecture he made a comment that went something like: 'Paradoxically, the best way to save an animal from extinction is to eat it.' I may not be quoting him verbatim here, but what he said stuck with me: if an animal acquires commercial value, people will invest in ways to increase its numbers.[58] Because beef has value, we make more cows. Or, rather, we use cows to make more cows and then we make more space for cows to make more cows in, and to hell with the bugs and plants that lived there first. The global demand for beef means that we are tearing down 35 million acres of rainforest a year to create grazing land for cattle[59] and some top-end estimates – backed by the UN Environment Program – suggest that as many as 150–200 plant and animal species are being made extinct *every day* due to deforestation. That's around 55,000–75,000 species per year being sacrificed to human progress and, in many instances, for nothing more than to service the burger cravings of fast foodies.[60]

I mention this because the tiger has commercial value too: almost every part of a tiger has worth, especially for use in Eastern traditional medicine. Demand for tiger products is

58 That said, we do some extraordinary things to help threatened species even if they have no commercial value. With only 126 kakapos – a large, flightless green parrot – left in the world (2014 figures), New Zealand scientists have been looking for ways to increase their numbers. Female kakapos are notoriously fussy, so when researchers observed that some kakapo males had better pulling power than others, they wondered whether they simply smelled better. Feather clippings were taken from the parrot gigolos and analysed using a gas chromatograph mass spectrometer, a machine that can identify and measure every chemical in the bird's scent. The result? A synthetic kakapo perfume that, hopefully, will encourage more breeding. The news is good: six hatchlings appeared in 2014, the first since 2011.

59 In 1950 rainforests covered around 15 per cent of earth's surface. Today it's around 6 per cent. More than 200,000 acres of rainforest are burned every day. That's over 150 acres lost every minute of every day, and 78 million acres lost every year.

60 Any serious environmentalist will tell you that one of the best ways to do your bit to save the planet is to only eat beef products once a week and to reduce your daily consumption of cow-based dairy. Fewer cows means less habitat destruction and, just as importantly, less methane production. Their massive herds are burping us closer and closer to a climate change catastrophe. We'd be much better off eating kangaroos, for example, as their meat is tasty, low in fat and cholesterol, and has a very high concentration of conjugated linoleic acid (CLA) which has anti-carcinogenic and anti-diabetes properties. And, crucially, kangaroos don't burp and fart the same amounts of dangerous greenhouse gases as cows do.

high but the species is facing extinction in the wild because supplies are dwindling and there simply aren't enough tigers to go around.

So what would Occam's Razor tell us to do? What would we do if we were running out of beef? We'd farm it, of course. So perhaps one simple solution to the plight of the wild tiger would be to farm them commercially in the same way that we farm cattle.

Of course, there are alternatives to farming such as reducing or voiding the tiger's commercial value.[61] But to do this we'd need to persuade people that tiger products have no efficacy, and that's going to take a very long time because entire cultures would have to change their view of traditional medicine. In the meantime, wild tiger numbers would continue to fall.[62] But what if we could provide the market with a cheaper alternative source for tiger parts that doesn't threaten wild populations? What if we flooded the market with cheap produce so that people can't earn money from killing wild tigers? It's a suggestion that has been considered by several organisations, including conservationists.

'Governments have repeatedly failed to save endangered animals by banning their sale. By contrast, does America have a shortage of chickens? No, because people own chickens and eat them,' says Terry L Anderson of PERC[63], a non-profit organisation that advises on improving environmental quality

---

61 In some parts of Africa and India, that's what conservationists have done to preserve wild rhinos. As it's only the horn that poachers are after (they are paid by the kilo), removing the horns has proven to be an effective deterrent, although it still has to be supported by anti-poaching patrols; even a stump of horn has some value.

62 Marine biologist Dr Helen Scales once appeared on an episode of *The Museum of Curiosity* alongside advertising supremo and behavioural economics guru Rory Sutherland. She asked him: 'What can we do to stop Chinese people killing millions of seahorses for medicine that, as test after test shows, doesn't actually work?' Rory stroked his chin and said, 'Well, if they're happy with medicine that doesn't actually work, convert them all to homeopathy. That way one seahorse would do them all.' Genius problem solving.

63 Property and Environmental Resource Centre.

through markets and property rights. 'Allowing private owners to sell animals for food or tourism saved the bison in America. It could save the tiger too if environmental groups would drop their resistance.'[64] And in a paper published in 1998, Michael 't Sas-Rolfes, a conservation economist from Johannesburg, South Africa, voiced some uncomfortable truths: 'Most of the interest in tiger conservation occurs in the developed countries but little of that interest translates to actual protection of wild tigers in their natural habitat. Few local people benefit directly from the presence of wild tigers, but they bear considerable costs. Meanwhile, rapid economic growth in countries such as China is leading people to pay increasingly high prices to obtain tiger products, making poaching more attractive.' He suggests that controlled hunting and/or tiger farming might be genuine responses to the problem. 'It is almost impossible for purchasers to be sure that they are buying genuine tiger bone', he explains. 'Farming would create a quality control and make poached wild tigers less attractive. Tiger farms would also create local employment opportunities and a legal fur trade.'

As unpalatable an idea as that may be, here in the West the majority of us do little to help the wild tiger's plight beyond making sympathetic noises and maybe a small donation to an animal charity now and again. Meanwhile, most of us are quite happy to accept the farming of other mammals, such as sheep or pigs or cows, but our Western sensibilities won't let us extend the idea to species like tigers. The way things are going, the wild tiger will most likely become extinct; I stress 'wild' tigers – there are already more pet tigers in the USA than there are left in

64   Via the John Stossell Show, *ABC 20/20* May 8th, 2009.

the wild so the species isn't going to disappear entirely.[65] However, if tigers could be legally and humanely farmed we could assure their wild cousins' continued existence. And there may be other benefits: with allegations already being made about cruelty on existing state-approved tiger farms in China, new international welfare standards might improve the animals' lot worldwide. Conservationists and tiger lovers would be 'sleeping with the enemy' – farmers and consumers of tiger-based goods – but the wild tiger would be saved.

This is the point where I take a step back and assure you that this is no more than a thought experiment and I'm not advocating or supporting the idea of farming tigers (I bet I'll still get hate mail, though). Personally, I'd much prefer it if people left the poor animals alone and used medicines with clinically-proven results rather than unscientific faith-based mumbo-jumbo. However, I am using the subject of tiger farming to make a serious point here. In many instances, our emotionally-charged System One thinking outweighs our logic-dependent System Two thinking and, as the result, we cannot bring ourselves to follow a course of action that 'feels' wrong or doesn't align with our moral compass, even though it might be the simplest solution and may even be the most effective. As Anaïs Nin once wrote: 'We don't see things as they are, we see them as we are.' Strong emotions can cloud the issue and logic isn't always the winner.

There is no simple solution to most problems because, once you add the human element, there are all kinds of human things to factor into the equation, such as funding,

---

65 It's difficult to know how many pet or captive tigers there are in the USA as the requirement to report it varies from state to state. Eight states have no rules on ownership whatsoever. In 2004, the WWF estimated that there were about 5,000 tigers in captivity in the US and only five per cent were in accredited zoos. That's significantly more than the estimated wild population of 3,200. China's government-regulated tiger farms, meanwhile, hold at least 7,000 tigers at any one time.

demographics, resources, beliefs, social acceptability, personal taste, compassion, politics, morality, legality, sexuality, practicality, and any number of other factors that end in '-ity'. Sometimes the simplest solution to a problem is simply unpalatable.

Which is why, curiously, there is a similarity between sex workers and tiger farms.

4

If you've ever visited a major UK city then you might have seen a vice card or two. Also more insultingly known as 'Tart Cards', they're those postcards you find inside public telephone boxes inviting you to contact a sex worker for fun and frolics.

It has been estimated that, at the height of their popularity, over 13 million cards were being deposited in central London phone boxes every year; a staggering 250,000 per week, or around 35,600 cards per day.[66] To remove them was no small task; in 2001 British Telecom (BT) were removing 150,000 cards per week from central London boxes alone. But there were hundreds of paid carders – often unemployed or homeless people or students – and so, however many you removed, there would always be more the next day.[67] Sometimes the carders worked in gangs and jealously guarded their pitches. Some even cheekily followed the cleaners around and re-stocked every phone box as soon as the coast, and the box, was clear. After all, that's how you get your cards displayed in the prime eye-level spots.

---

66 In his book *London, The Wicked City*, Fergus Linnane claims that in one eight-week period during the 1990s, more than a million cards were removed. Printing that many cards would have cost sex workers over £150,000.

67 A university student once told me that, during the summer holidays, she'd earned three times more from carding than she'd previously earned working in a supermarket.

The legal aspect of this problem used to be complex because prostitution is not a crime in the UK. A prostitute, or what we more kindly call a sex worker these days, is defined as someone who has 'offered or provided sexual services to another person in return for any financial arrangement on at least one occasion'. If this is done in private, the person commits no offence. However, while it may not be illegal to be a sex worker, it is illegal to 'solicit' or tout for business. Therefore the question often debated was this: was carding a form of touting? The prostitutes claimed that they were simply advertising a legal business and drew a comparison with minicab firms; their drivers weren't allowed by law to tout for business either but no one objected to their cards being placed in phone boxes and other public places. When does advertising become touting?

But, putting the legality of carding aside for a moment, why had carding become the sex workers' preferred method? Mostly it was to keep them safe.

There was a time when you couldn't walk down certain streets in London without being asked if you were looking for a good time, or words to that effect. But, for the sex workers, being on the street was fraught with danger. Quite apart from the threat of arrest, they risked assault, robbery and targeted violence against them solely because of their profession – which was why many turned to carding as a safer alternative to streetwalking.[68] Early cards were typewritten, handwritten or used rub-down lettering. After a while, images started to appear, sometimes hand-drawn, traced or photocopied but, with the advent of home computers and affordable printing, the cards began to include photographs. By the mid 1990s, full-colour cards could be produced in large numbers at reasonably low prices.

My colleagues and I were asked to look at the problem of carding in phone boxes because trying to remove the cards was simply not working; there were just too many. So we asked the question, 'What is the problem with the cards?' And we got some rather surprising answers. The main complainants were the people who'd asked us to look at the problem – the owners of the phone boxes and Westminster Council. But apart from them, and in a city that, at any one time, boasts a population of over 10 million people, we found that complaints about vice cards were surprisingly few. And those complainants that I got to speak to personally didn't actually have anything against sex work.[69] Their issue was with the photographs being used on the cards. Until recently, the cards had displayed quite modest images but the number of sex workers advertising in central London had significantly

---

68 Many sex workers don't approach the police to report crimes committed against them for fear that they themselves will be charged or that the police will be unsympathetic. However, a brilliantly effective campaign run on Merseyside since 2006 has seen crimes against sex workers dealt with as hate crimes. In 2010, their conviction rate for rapes of sex workers was 67 per cent. The national average is around 6.5 per cent. In 2011, the Association of Chief Police Officers recommended that all forces adopt the Merseyside hate crime approach. Sadly, none have (at time of writing) and none are obliged to.

69 In the UK, polls suggest that a majority of people are tolerant of sex work. Aggregating results from large polls conducted in the past 20 years, I've found a fairly constant percentage of around 51–53 per cent of people who agree that paying for sex shouldn't be a criminal offence compared to 30–35 per cent of people who think it should.

increased in recent years and competition had become very fierce.[70] As the result, the ante had been noticeably upped on the explicitness of the images. Interestingly, after talking to a number of sex workers, I discovered that most of them were also uncomfortable with the newer, more blatant cards too. One lady called Amanda told me, 'Pictures don't bring punters in, it's the services offered.' Another called Debra told me, 'I don't see the point. They know it's not going to be the girl who's on the card anyway. If they think that, they're idiots.'[71] And May, a 25-year-old mother, told *The Guardian*: 'I have children myself and I agree with the people who don't want children to see the pictures. But they should let us do cards with no pictures. You have to think about how many people use these services.' Some women I spoke to said that the reason they put the cards inside the boxes instead of on the outside was so that the majority of the public wouldn't see them.

What was generating the complaints wasn't prostitution itself – it was the images used on the cards. It followed, therefore, that if the images on the cards were toned down, or used appropriately worded text only, there would be a reduction in complaints – at least from the general public.

Sadly, we will never know if this was true. While we'd been doing our research, the anti-carding lobby had been pushing for a legal solution and, in 2001, all ambiguity about touting/ advertising was removed with the arrival of Section 46(1) of the Criminal Justice and Police Act, which made it an offence to 'place advertisements relating to prostitution on, or in the immediate vicinity of, a public telephone'. This resulted in a huge increase in prosecutions because the offenders could be traced by way of the phone numbers on their cards. Raids

---

70 One of the main reasons for the increase was the collapse of the economies in a number of former Warsaw Pact countries. It saw a large influx of sex workers moving from Eastern Europe to Western Europe.

71 More than one wag has suggested to me that the police would see more successful prosecutions if the card owners were dealt with under Trades Descriptions Act or Advertising Standards legislation.

were conducted on the workers' addresses and landlords were informed that sex workers operated on their premises, putting pressure on them to evict their tenants. Jenn Clamen of the International Union of Sex Workers publicly denounced the raids telling *The Guardian* that: 'The effect of the carding operation is very drastic. No one should be evicted from their home, lose their livelihood and risk deportation for placing cards advertising a legal service in a phone box.' And a spokeswoman for the English Collective of Prostitutes stated: 'Women have found a way of working without pimps and without being on the street. Some women will go back to that rather than go out of business. It is 10 times more dangerous to work on the street and it is more of a public nuisance than the cards.'

At the same time, BT had been cutting off any numbers that appeared on the cards. But all this did was drive the trade to use mobile phones, which made them significantly harder to block, especially when the phones were cheap, pay-as-you-go 'burners'. Meanwhile, the carding persisted. In August 2004, in a somewhat surprising move, an angry and frustrated Westminster Council distributed 20,000 mock vice cards to passers-by in Oxford Street bearing the names and business numbers of the heads of mobile phone companies who, they claimed, were not doing enough to prevent carding. At the time, they stated publicly that if this did not spur the mobile phone companies to do something, they would re-issue the cards with the CEOs' home telephone numbers on them.

The introduction of the new law took away any room we might have had for manoeuvre and concession. Carding in phone boxes was now illegal but there were always going to be sex workers wanting to advertise their services, 'Johns' wanting to buy those services, and people willing to be paid carders. It was therefore obvious to us that, despite the new legislation – a classic System One Thinking response – the problem was going to continue unless some method was found that either physically prevented carding in phone boxes or the sex workers found a different but equally effective way to reach customers.

We did briefly look into the latter option and we discovered that, back in the eighteenth century before the days of phone boxes, a gentleman in 'pursuit of sport' in central London might well have purchased a copy of *Harris's List Of Covent-Garden Ladies*.[72] Published annually between 1757 and 1795 this was, to all intents and purposes, a Yellow Pages for vice. The language used was somewhat more loquacious and florid than it is today and occasionally comical as a result. They have a copy of the 1787 edition at the Wellcome Library in London and, inside, I found descriptions like:

She is best pleased when her opponent is well armed, and would despise any warrior, who had not two stout balls to block up her covered way, and did not carry metal enough to leave two pounds behind him.[73]

Harris's List was by no means the first such publication; back in the 1660s there was a directory called *The Wandering Whore*, and in 1691, *A Catalogue of Jilts, Cracks & Prostitutes, Nightwalkers, Whores, She-friends, Kind Women and other of the Linen-lifting Tribe* was available in and around Smithfield Market. But Harris's was by far the most popular and the longest in print.

I wondered whether the re-introduction of such a directory might be the answer that everyone was looking for. Firstly, it would be more discreet than public carding. Secondly, it would keep sex workers off the street. Thirdly, it would surely be cheaper for them to place an ad in such a directory than

---

72 Actually, the publication's full name was *Harris's List Of Covent-Garden Ladies: Or, Man Of Pleasure's Kalender – Containing The Histories And Some Curious Anecdotes Of The Most Celebrated Ladies Now On The Town, Or In Keeping, And Also Many Of Their Keepers*. No one is entirely sure who 'Harris' was. The strongest contender is an Irish hack called Samuel Derrick who may have written the guide in cahoots with the self-declared 'Pimp General of All England', one John Harrison who traded under the name of Jack Harris. Derrick died intestate but, on his deathbed, he bequeathed the 1769 edition of *Harris's List* to Charlotte Hayes, his former friend and mistress, and a madam to boot.

73 The Wellcome also has a large collection of vice cards – 20-plus boxes of them – all collected by employee Stephen Lowther from 1992 to the present day. They provide a fascinating year-on-year view of changing design, printing techniques and sexual services offered.

to continually have cards printed and to pay carders. Fourthly, you could only be offended by the images and language if you obtained a copy and read it, in which case *caveat emptor*. Fifthly, as far as I could see, sex workers had been advertising their services using small ads placed in newspapers and magazines for decades; a bespoke directory might remove such ads from these publications and bring them all together under one unambiguous title.[74]

Inevitably, we were asked to submit our findings. Everyone already knew that eliminating carding was likely to be impossible without a massive increase in resources and almost constant attention to phone boxes. But what else, they asked, could we suggest?

Unfortunately, what our research tended to suggest was that unless someone was miraculously able to persuade all sex workers to stop being sex workers, the best option for everyone was to leave things as they were.

Even if we did find a way to successfully prevent phone box carding – by developing, for example, something like a non-stick surface – what would be the likely outcome of that? Either the workers would come back onto the street or the cards would move elsewhere, maybe to somewhere more publicly visible and, of course, not illegal under the new legislation. In either case we would face a worse scenario than we currently had. The cards caused no physical damage to the boxes and, with so few people using phone boxes anymore, there was a strong argument – supported by the sex workers themselves – that carding had less impact on society than the alternatives.

Then there was the issue of public complaints. There were relatively few of these and they were mostly concerned with

74 Interestingly, we subsequently discovered that Brighton had just such a publication. The *Blue Guide* was free and could be picked up anywhere in the city. It was paid for by the advertisers: sex workers, strip clubs, sex shops, etc. For the sex workers, the cost was far less than the cost of carding. Always a very liberal place, Brighton Library has a display of classic call box vice cards.

the lewdness of the imagery. The text on the cards was fairly inoffensive, being written in a form of coded language with services like 'In/Out Calls', 'A and O levels', 'Greek' and 'School Medicals' being offered. Sex was rarely mentioned overtly although obviously implied. However, we couldn't negotiate a toning down of the images because, by law, the acceptable number of cards in boxes was now zero. By suggesting that they could stay if they were less graphic we could be seen as condoning their continued use. Therefore, the best we could suggest was replacing the cards with some kind of directory. It was the best solution for the sex workers, for the general public and, if it cut the incidence of carding, it was also best for the people who'd asked us to look at the problem.

Our conclusions proved to be about as popular as the idea of tiger farms. The man from Westminster Council looked at me in genuine horror. The representatives of the telecommunications companies, and my own senior officers, shook their heads in dismay. What I realised, at this point, was that nothing less than elimination would do for them. That was their only goal. As far as they were concerned, the sex industry was the problem and the cards reminded those opposed to it that sex work was going on, behind closed doors, every minute of every day. The carders' constant reminders fanned the fires of their moral outrage. And so they went back to their never-ending quest to eliminate the problem, employing ever more staff and volunteers to help clear the cards out of the phone boxes and working with the police to conduct more raids.

People will do what their consciences – and their gut – drives them to do even though it may blind them to the reality of the situation. As Steven D. Levitt and Stephen J. Dubner, authors of the bestselling *Freakonomics* books, point out: 'When it comes to solving problems, one of the best ways to start is by putting away your moral compass. When you are consumed with the rightness or wrongness of a given issue […] it's easy to lose track of what the issue actually is.'

The law that made phone box carding illegal is now over

15 years old. I'm a frequent visitor to London and, to be fair, there do seem to be far fewer cards in phone boxes these days. But, then, there are far fewer phone boxes. On a recent visit to Soho, I opened the door to a box in Dean Street and found just one card for a 'young ex-model' that used quite a coy image with black stars placed over strategic anatomical details. The stench of stale urine was so overpowering, however, that it made my eyes water. I don't know who uses phone boxes to make phone calls anymore but good luck to them.

The police and the council are still chasing the carders, of course,[75] although the Crown Prosecution Service (CPS) doesn't appear to see off-street sex work as any kind of priority. Their public interest considerations are focused on 'encouraging prostitutes to find routes out of prostitution and to deter those who create the demand for it', which is much better because it's tackling the cause of the problem and not the symptoms.[76]

And, as it happens, something like *Harris's List* has evolved all by itself. Following in the wake of successful dating websites, there are now any number of sites where people can meet for the purpose of sex – paid for or otherwise – and dozens of website directories of sex workers.[77]

But the vice cards persist for the moment, even though their numbers are decreasing. One day soon, they may be as endangered as the wild tiger.

---

75 Leaving a QI production meeting in April 2015, I grabbed all of the cards from a phone box on the Strand to use as possible illustrations for this chapter. I passed by the same box an hour later and a new set of cards had already been placed in there. In some areas it seems that the carders are still very active. Ironically, the box in question was directly opposite the largest police station in the UK.

76 Meanwhile, there is a push going on within government circles to adopt the so-called 'Swedish Model' which involves criminalising the purchase of sex, rather than the sale.

77 And also many sites that support sex workers such as www.t-ess.org.uk and www.SAAFE.info, to name just two. Also worthy of note is the National Ugly Mugs site at www.uknswp.org/um/ which allows sex workers to share photographs of known violent or dangerous individuals.

5

Somewhat ironically, one of the first problems we encountered in the Problem Solving Unit was being given the name of 'Problem Solving Unit' by our bosses. Presumably they thought that it was the simplest description of what we were set up to do but the problem, if you'll pardon the clumsy prose, was that most of the time we didn't actually solve problems: at least not in the way that many people interpret the word 'solve'.

Dictionaries will tell you that *problem solving* means something like, 'the process of working through details of a problem to reach a solution'. However, it's been my experience that, if you ask people what a 'solution' is, most will equate it with elimination of a problem and that's pretty much an impossibility. What works as a solution for one person or group of people, doesn't necessarily work for others, because we all see the world through different eyes. That's why there was no such thing in our office as an off-the-shelf solution because there's no such thing as an off-the-shelf problem. Like Banksy's art, or the curious species-ism that says it's okay to farm sheep and salmon but not tigers, vice carding wasn't a simple black-and-white issue. We stood no chance of solving the problem because any solution other than elimination was unpalatable to those opposed to the sex industry in general.

Elimination of a problem isn't always possible. But you can do your damnedest to make people's lives better than they currently are. Therefore, I'd suggest that the best definition for problem solving is one coined by change management expert Michael Stevens:

Problem solving means transforming one set of circumstances into another, preferred state.

We adopted that as our team motto.

4: THE WIZARD OF WALTHAM FOREST

Problems cannot be resolved all at once. Slowly untie the knots. Divide to conquer.

Lao Tzu

Research is creating new knowledge.

Neil Armstrong

1

'Roll up! Try your luck! Find the lady and win big money!'

I followed the voice. I wasn't familiar enough with the various accents of Eastern Europe to tell if the speaker was Polish, Romanian, or from the Ukraine. Maybe he was Russian? He sounded like an affable Bond villain delivering an expository soliloquy before yanking the secret handle that sends 007 sliding down into the shark tank below.

'All you have to do is find the lady! Try your luck, sir! Madam!'

He was standing behind a makeshift table made from two stacked milk crates and a sheet of corrugated cardboard. On the desktop lay three playing cards face up: two low denomination red suit cards and the queen of spades. He deftly flipped the cards face down and shuffled them about. There was a big toothy nicotine-stained grin that came with the voice.

'All you have to do is find the Queen,' he explained to the

crowd. 'Simple, yes? There are only three cards. You have one-in-three chance!'

But then our eyes met and something sent alarm bells ringing inside him. I was trying to look like a punter but maybe my interest wasn't sufficiently focused on the cards. Or maybe he sensed that I was checking him out just a little too thoroughly. In an instant, the cards were whipped off the table and he was off, running pell-mell into the crowd of Wembley Market. I circulated a description on my radio but I knew that there would be little chance of catching him. The market was a maze of alleyways and hiding places created by the hundreds of stalls. And, like every street gambler I'd seen that morning, he was wearing the same kind of nondescript clothing as most of the market traders. There was nothing standout about any of them. They knew what they were doing, which is what you'd expect from masters of deceit.

It was 1996 which, I realise, is a big jump in the narrative

Photo: Wendy Fair

from playing hide-and-seek with my colleagues in mid-1980s Hillingdon. However, street gamblers are a perfect example for this chapter and, back in the 1980s, they weren't so much of a problem. Most of them back then were almost likeable rogues – like Del Boy and Rodney in *Only Fools and Horses* – just trying to make a dishonest bob to pay for their beer and fags and playing catch-me-if-you-can with the local rozzers. But, by the 1990s, things had changed significantly. For a start, very few now seemed to work in isolation.[78] They operated in organised teams and many were part of larger crime syndicates. The money they earned was used to fund other, more serious crimes; I've known teams that were bankrolling pirate DVD factories, the illegal drugs trade, and worse. The saddest aspect of it all was that we, the great British public, were helping them.

Street gambling is an easy way to earn big money for little outlay. Using variations on the classic Three Card Trick – also known as Chase the Lady or Three Card Monte – or the three cups and ball game, a talented operator can fleece thousands of pounds from the punters on a good day. All tax-free, of course. And they're difficult to catch because they're canny and they pick pitches with plenty of escape routes. They can disappear in an instant, having little or no equipment with them. But, frustratingly, even if you do catch them, there's not much incentive for them to quit. The fines they receive are easily affordable and just a small percentage of how much they can make on the street. Even short prison sentences don't deter them. The risks are hugely outweighed by the spoils.

Wembley Market was a large, sprawling sea of stalls and tents that covered the car parks in the shadow of the twin towers of the old Empire Stadium. There had been lots of complaints about street gambling from traders and the market organisers; certainly enough to justify swamping the area with cops. Our briefing had been simple: be visible, scare them

---

78   There are still a few solo street gamblers but they tend to get bullied off prime pitches by the organised teams.

off, catch them if you can. But catch them we couldn't. And, even more annoyingly, we knew that we were only having a temporary and minimal impact on the problem. Assigning so many officers to police the market was expensive and unsustainable and the bad guys knew it. All they had to do was wait us out. The senior management team at Wembley nick knew it too but they had to be seen to be doing something about the problem even if they knew, deep down, that it probably wouldn't generate any kind of lasting result. The whole situation left me feeling more than a little frustrated (and my superiors too, no doubt), because I knew that if we could find a smarter way to cut off these very lucrative revenue streams, we'd be helping to prevent more serious crimes in the future. But putting the street gamblers out of business meant more than just preventing illegal activity. I wanted them shut down because I can't stand people who take advantage of others. After all, there is a reason why the Three Card Trick is called the Three Card *Trick* and not the Three Card *Game*.

It's a scam. And I really hate scammers.

2

Through trial and error, and reading about the experiences of others, I'd discovered that there was a process to problem solving. It begins with demand – someone asking you to solve their problem. Then, you need to find out exactly what the problem is. As discussed in the previous chapter, the demand can sometimes be misleading; strong emotions such as fear and anger or a sense of injustice can skew people's perceptions and lead them to imagine problems where there aren't any, or to demand action against the symptoms of a problem rather than the cause. Therefore, to stand any chance of solving a problem with any degree of permanency, you have to dig deeper. And that means taking the next step in the process – research.

When I first started my problem-solving journey nearly all the research that police officers did was labelled 'investigation', and it mostly only happened after a crime was committed or when we'd had a tip-off that a crime was going to be committed. It was all very 'stimulus–response' and the primary focus was entirely upon finding evidence to catch and convict the bad guys. Intelligence gathering went on all the time, of course, but it was somewhat haphazard unless there was a specific target in mind. Once that target had been reached – e.g. a person was arrested and charged – the case was closed and the problem was deemed to be solved. Except that it often wasn't. Arresting and convicting a street robber didn't stop robberies unless they were the only robber operating in the area, which they never were. The police service didn't seem to be looking to the future and asking, 'What can we do to stop *all* robbers from robbing?'

But there were people asking those questions elsewhere. I was discovering the work of academics such as Nick Tilley, Gloria Laycock, Mike Scott, Karen Bullock, Mike Hoare, Gary Cordner, Robin Fletcher, Mike Maguire, Ken Pease, Rana Sampson, Ronald Clarke and the aforementioned Herman Goldstein; brilliant, clever people who were tirelessly crunching the numbers and working the data to figure out how and why crime happened.[79] What's more, they were developing new strategies to help bring crime figures down and to prevent crime from occurring. The field of crime science was rapidly expanding … but none of it was being taught to police officers. I had to find things out for myself. But the reward for doing so was finding tools and techniques that could help me to solve problems and prevent crime.

For example, something called 'Routine Activity Theory' – developed during the 1970s by two criminology professors called Lawrence Cohen and Marcus Felson – proved to be very useful. At its most basic, RAT states that crime can only

---

79 And that's by no means a comprehensive list of names. There are many people working behind the scenes, and outside of law enforcement agencies, trying to solve crime. I consider myself lucky that I got to meet, and sometimes work with, many of these brilliant men and women. Lots of them are listed at the back of the book.

occur when there is: (a) a motivated offender, (b) a suitable victim/target available, and (c) there is no 'capable guardian' to stop one from preying upon the other. Therefore, it suggests that if you can remove the motivation, or make a victim/target less attractive or accessible, or provide a guardian – such as police, security, CCTV, etc. – the crime can't happen. In the 1980s, Professors William Spelman and John Eck distilled RAT into a research tool called the 'Crime Triangle',[80] which encourages people to explore crimes by looking at them from three different perspectives – offender, victim and location.

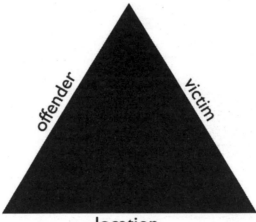

Traditionally, police investigation had given 99 per cent of its attention to just one side of the triangle – the offender. However, Cohen, Felson, Spelman and Eck argued that solving problems with any degree of permanency meant looking at all three.

Once I began to use the Crime Triangle I found it much

---

80 Also sometimes called the 'Problem Analysis Triangle' (PAT) or the 'Wolf, Duck and Den model'.

easier to identify the component parts of any problem. So I introduced it to colleagues, both inside and outside the police, and because I wanted to use it for all problems (e.g. quality of life and social issues such as litter disposal, dangerous dogs, or fear of crime) it seemed appropriate to replace the police jargon. So the offender became the *cause*, the victim the *effect*, and location became *time and place*.[81] And, after I'd been using it for a while, it occurred to me that the triangle was actually a kind of jigsaw puzzle, albeit one that wouldn't tax most people to complete.

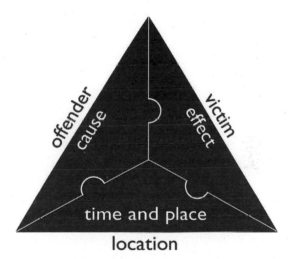

Like all jigsaws, it is only complete when you have all the pieces. So, if you remove any one of those pieces, the problem is less likely to occur.[82] Take away two pieces (and prevent

81 Not all crimes have a victim in terms of loss or harm – fly-tipping, for instance, has an effect of spoiling the environment and costing money for clear-up but few people could be said to be 'victims' of the crime so 'effect' is a suitable catch-all.

82 The Fire Service uses a similar diagnostic tool called the 'Fire Triangle'. The three sides represent fuel, heat source and oxygen. Remove any one and a fire cannot start/can be extinguished.

them from coming back) and you may have found a way to permanently stop the problem from returning, or even preventing something from becoming a problem in the first place.

Let's apply the 'Problem Solving Jigsaw' model, as we'll call it, to burglaries in our imaginary Hardy Street. If we arrest the burglar, is the problem of burglary solved?

The reality is that, for every bad guy locked up, there are plenty of motivated offenders ready to replace them. So, while we may have removed the cause, we've also created a gap in the jigsaw for a different burglar to fill. If we want to prevent burglary with any degree of permanency, we need to look at the other two pieces of the jigsaw too.

We can make changes to the houses in our street – our 'time and place'. Burglars like an easy life – they don't like double-glazing, window locks, alarms, CCTV, security lights, gravel paths, time switches, good door locks, fences and other crime prevention measures. The more obstructions and inconveniences you can put in the burglar's way, the less inclined they'll be to burgle you. This is called 'Target

Hardening'. Here's another example: which of these bikes is the least attractive to a bike thief?

There are no clues here are there (and imagine if all the bikes were covered in the same way)? The opportunistic thief has no idea what's under the cover. A great bike? Or a crappy bike? Just that one obstacle means that the bad guy has to decide whether it's worth their time and effort to remove the cover or peer underneath. It's an unwanted delay that could give witnesses a chance to note that someone is acting a bit suspiciously. It's a lot less hassle to simply steal a more obvious, identifiable target. A bike cover is a cheap and simple piece of Target Hardening. And you'll have a dry bum on the ride home.

Meanwhile, on the 'effect' piece of the jigsaw, we can also do preventative things. Burglars will go for objects that are visible, can be moved easily, have value and which are accessible, so we can encourage our potential victims to not advertise all of the great stuff they have.[83] Having blinds or net curtains will obscure the view into the house, but just simply not putting desirable objects in view of the windows is good too. We can tell people not to leave their house and car keys within reach of the letterbox (burglars can fish them out with wire coat hangers), to make sure that windows are shut and doors are fastened when they go out, and not to leave keys under mats or plant pots; getting to know the neighbours and leaving a spare key with them is much safer and much more sociable.[84] And we can encourage neighbours to look out for one another (including pulling each other's bins off the street on bin day). None of these things have to make people feel like they're living inside oppressive fortresses and none of them will have much impact upon the way they live their lives, other than to possibly improve them. But the message it sends to the burglars is: 'This house is too difficult for you. Look elsewhere.'

The Problem Solving Jigsaw allows us to see which piece or pieces we should remove in order to have the maximum impact on the problem. It encourages us to look beyond simply 'catching the culprit' and to research the mechanics of the problem: who or what is causing it and how they are causing it; how the problem affects people; and how the time and place makes it easier for the offender to operate. It helps

---

83 Which, if we use 'inertia' to mean 'easily moved', makes the handy acronym of VIVA – Visible, (has) Inertia. Valuable, Accessible. Another acronym for the types of things criminals prefer to steal is CRAVED: Concealable, Removable, Available, Valuable, Enjoyable, Disposable.

84 In January 2016, Coventry police officers engaged on anti-burglary patrols tweeted photos they'd taken inside empty premises they'd found with open ground floor windows and unlocked doors. The initiative met with mixed reactions. Some people claimed it was trespassing and a gross invasion of privacy. Others said that the owners should be thankful that it was the police and not a burglar or 'some loon with a knife'. West Midlands Police promised to review the tactic but pointed out that in excess of 25% of burglaries in that area of Coventry were 'walk-in' offences committed by opportunists taking advantage of insecure properties. They hoped, at least, that they'd increased public awareness.

us to develop effective and sustainable ways of stopping bad things from happening.

3

During 1854, the Golden Square area of Soho in London was ravaged by cholera. The first case was reported in Broad Street on August 31st and, within just seven days, 127 local people were dead. By September 10th, over 500 had been killed by the disease.

It was widely believed at the time that diseases were spread by foul air or *miasma*.[85] Social reformer and prominent miasmatist Edwin Chadwick spoke for the scientific community of the day when he told a parliamentary committee in 1846 that, 'All smell is disease.' People would carry nosegays of flowers or perfumed pomanders in order to ward it off,[86] roads were dusted with lime, and hospitals would leave out open dishes of chlorine and sulphuric acid to 'purify the air'. But for local doctor and pioneering anaesthetist, John Snow, the miasmatic theory made no sense. During the course of his daily work visiting the residents of Soho, he regularly found healthy people living among the dead and dying, all breathing the same air as, indeed, was he. He was convinced that there must be another cause. The concept of 'germs' – tiny disease-bearing organisms – was very new and there was, as yet, no consensus of opinion among physicians

---

85 This was a theory that had persisted since ancient times; a linguistic leftover from this is the name 'malaria' – *mala aria* meaning 'bad air' – because that's how people believed the disease was spread before they discovered that mosquitoes were to blame. The term 'miasma' has its origin in the ancient Greek word for pollution.

86 However, the idea that the children's nursery rhyme 'Ring a Ring o' Roses' contains references to nosegays being employed to ward off the symptoms of bubonic plague is an easily-disproved urban myth.

as to their existence.[87] But even if Snow had believed that they were responsible, he had neither the technology nor the resources to prove or disprove that they were. What he did have, however, was an enquiring mind. He believed that the methods being used to tackle cholera were wrong because the cause(s) of cholera had not been correctly identified. People's beliefs were pushing all investigation and subsequent action in the wrong direction. He decided to set established medical orthodoxy to one side and find out for himself what the causal factors were.

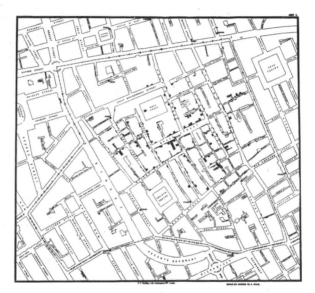

Image: John Snow

87 When you think about it, the theory of miasma is not so wild a notion. Rotten food smells nasty and if we eat rotten food it can make us ill. Therefore, if the air smells equally nasty, might we not become ill by breathing it? No less a person than Florence Nightingale was a strong believer in miasmatic theory and she spent much of her time as a nurse in the Crimea ensuring that field hospitals had good airflow and used chemicals and unguents to purify the air. It's quite scary to consider that, like most medical practitioners of that age, Nightingale probably didn't wash her hands between patients. It took over 30 years for doctors to accept Pasteur's 'radical' new germ theory of disease.

He started to map the outbreak, plotting the deaths victim by victim. He was aided in his work by a local curate, the Reverend Henry Whitehead, who was initially opposed to Snow's theory but soon came to see the truth of it. Whitehead's help proved to be invaluable as he knew his parishioners well and could provide Snow with a wealth of data. As each new death – represented by a black dot – was added to Snow's map of Soho, a pattern began to emerge.

His research revealed that the one common factor shared by all casualties was that they had drunk water from the public pump in Broad Street. In support of this theory, Snow and Whitehead discovered that local people who didn't drink Broad Street water, such as the workers at the nearby Lion Brewery, weren't getting ill at all. They habitually drank ale as they were allocated a free supply. Other disease-free areas, such as the Poland Street Workhouse, took their water from a different pump or had their own wells. Convinced, therefore, that the disease carrying agent must be in the local water supply, Snow petitioned successfully to have the handle removed from the Broad Street pump, effectively disabling it. His reasoning was that if people stopped dying, his case was proven. They did, and it was.

We now know that cholera got into the water supply because it was common practice in the mid-nineteenth century to empty chamber pots into gutters that fed into a river,[88] or into cesspools or cesspits, many of which seeped into the local water table that fed public fresh water pumps.[89] To make matters worse, the cholera bacterium *Vibrio cholerae* causes sickness and diarrhoea, which meant that infected

---

88 London had a lot of rivers at one time, most now sadly buried under concrete and tarmac. Among them were the Fleet, Tyburn, Lea, Walbrook, Effra, Neckinger, Peck and Moselle. Extraordinarily, the River Westbourne flows through Sloane Square tube station in a pipe above the heads of people waiting on the platforms.

89 Contrary to many TV and film depictions people didn't usually throw human waste out of the window. In fact, it was illegal to do so. Of course, some people would have flouted the law but, if caught, the fines could be crippling. This means that the word 'loo' almost certainly doesn't have an origin in people shouting 'Gardez l'eau!' (Look out! Water!) as they threw waste out of the window.

faeces and vomit being added to the cesspools perpetuated the vicious cycle. The disease causes potentially fatal dehydration and is commonly treated by giving the victim fluids. Ironically, in drinking more water, the victims were sealing their own fates. Snow broke the cycle and his work contributed to the decision to invest in an effective sewer system under central London. As an unexpected secondary benefit, he kick-started the science of epidemiology.

It's sad to note that the most damning evidence against the prevailing miasma theory came a month after John Snow died. The 'Great Stink' of July 1858 was caused by pollution of the River Thames – by human and animal sewage, dead animals, blood and entrails from the slaughterhouses, rotten food and industrial waste – and was so foul that people fainted in the street and Parliament was forced to evacuate the building. Michael Faraday wrote that 'the whole of the river was an opaque pale brown fluid', and the Prime Minister of the day, Henry John Temple, 3rd Viscount Palmerston, described the river as 'a Stygian pool reeking with ineffable and unbearable horror'. But, despite the smell being so foul that people living near the river were forced to hang perfume or disinfectant-soaked hessian sheets in their windows, no one was killed by it. The miasmatists were wrong. Snow's theory was proven beyond a shadow of a doubt.[90]

He is commemorated by a memorial in Broadwick Street (formerly Broad Street) shaped like a pump with no handle and in the name of the John Snow pub, built on the site of the offending pump.

---

90 Well, I say that. People still doubted it, despite the evidence. In 1849 Snow self-published the first edition of *On the Mode of Communication of Cholera* at a huge personal cost of £200 (his income was only £3 12s per month). One peer review in the *London Medical Gazette* said: 'There is, in our view, an entire failure of proof that the occurrence of any one case could be clearly and unambiguously assigned to water.'

John Snow began his investigations by interviewing cholera victims in an effort to find out what they all had in common. But these were working class people with limited educations and little knowledge of medicine. Therefore, the potential victims demanding that John Snow take action would probably have asked him to do something about the smell. We know, in hindsight, that if he'd relied on the complainant group – and that includes his peers in the medical profession – he'd have tackled the wrong problem. Instead, Snow researched the problem, gathering all the evidence he could find. He was then able to form a reasoned hypothesis about the cause – that the effect was the result of all of the victims using the same water pump. He then tested this by discouraging the pump's use and by eventually having it decommissioned. People stopped dying. His theory was proven and the problem was solved.[91]

91 A few specific problems can be solved by simply removing the cause/offender. Unlike burglary, where there are other potential burglars waiting in the wings, cholera has a single, unique cause. However, changing the location by improving access to clean water would help prevent it returning, as would changing victim behaviour: boiling water before use for example.

4

In 2008, over a decade after my experiences at Wembley Market, the problem of illegal street gambling came bounding back into my life. Information had come to light to suggest that at least one group of street gamblers, maybe more, were affiliated with people suspected of involvement in a number of more serious crimes, including drug production and distribution. The borough in question wanted the gambling market shut down and was preparing to run a series of sting operations. They asked us in the Problem Solving Unit if we had any suggestions. Remembering my past experiences with street gamblers, I knew that something smarter than just temporarily scaring them away was needed. So I began to research the whole subject of street gambling. And I came across some very interesting people who proved to be of immense help.

Glenn Hester from the Glynn County Police Department in Brunswick, Georgia, USA is both a police officer and an expert magician. He's been studying con artists and scams for many years and has written three books on the subject. He was exactly the sort of expert I needed to speak to. 'In gambling, there is a chance you can win. With this [the Three Card Trick], there is no chance of your winning,' he explained to me. 'Anyone found winning this game can be considered a secret player or a shill.[92] And it's a much more common crime than you'd think. A lot of people feel ashamed and stupid for having been conned and therefore don't report it. That's frustrating because the crime goes unpunished. Even when people do report it they often lie about the details to save face. I remember one person reporting that they were robbed, but their story didn't check out when we looked into it. It turned out that the victim was taken in by a Three Card Monte scam and had lost all of the company's money.'

---

92 A shill is a person who pretends to be a member of the crowd and gives onlookers the impression that he or she is an enthusiastic customer, seemingly enjoying small wins and encouraging the audience to bet higher.

Photo: Janice Staines

The scam is loaded 100 per cent on the side of the operator. Whatever you think, you are *never* going to win. However, the fact there are just three cards and all you have to do is pick the right one makes it look like the easiest game imaginable. We are taken in by its apparent simplicity.

Traditional policing methods had a poor success rate when it came to catching street gamblers, so I approached the problem by stripping away the rumour, innuendo, supposition, and guesswork, and honing in on the root cause(s) of the problem. I used the Problem Solving Jigsaw and asked myself 'what pieces need to be removed?' I knew from bitter experience that it was very difficult – without access to expensive resources – to catch the bad guys. And, even if I did, they'd simply go and do it again. They were highly motivated by big profits, and the frankly pitiful penalties they received if they got caught made the risks acceptable, so there wasn't much I could do about the 'cause' side of the Jigsaw. I also knew that it was unlikely that I could change the location in any way; gamblers choose pitches that are open and unrestricted with clear lines of sight and plenty of escape routes. Therefore, the only piece of the Jigsaw left for me to work with was 'effect'. And in looking into that, I realised an uncomfortable truth: street gambling only happens where

93

there are willing victims. And, tragically, many of the people queuing up to play were on desperately low incomes and hoping against hope for a big win to lift them out of debt.[93] I wanted to stop the street gamblers preying on these people. Some were suffering devastating losses. But in order to do so I'd need to convince those same people to stop gambling, which would not be an easy task.

There is a theory that every idea has its day. It's called the 'Multiple Discovery Hypothesis' and it says that very similar but entirely independent discoveries tend to happen around the same time. Or, as Farkas Bolyai, the eighteenth century mathematician once said: 'When the time is ripe for certain things, they appear at different places in the manner of violets coming to light in early spring.' For example, chloroform was discovered in the same year – 1831 – by three different scientists in three different countries, all working independently.[94] And Charles Darwin was pushed into publishing *On the Origin of Species* in 1859 because he found out that Alfred Russell Wallace had formulated the same theory at the same time.[95] Why do I mention this? It's because, when I was researching street gambling, I found a police sergeant from Waltham Forest called Jonathan Clack,

93 There are many studies that show that gambling is more prevalent in low-income areas. It stands to reason; affluent people don't need to. One 2014 study by the Research Institute on Addictions at Buffalo University interviewed nearly 5,000 individuals aged 14 to 90 and found more than 11 per cent of residents in low-income neighbourhoods were problem gamblers compared to five per cent in areas of greater economic advantage.

94 Samuel Guthrie in the USA, Eugène Soubeiran in France, and Justus von Liebig in Germany. Coincidentally, John Snow became something of an expert in its use and eventually rose to the giddy heights of administering pain relief to Queen Victoria during the births of Prince Leopold and Princess Beatrice.

95 Wallace is somewhat overshadowed by Darwin but does have recognition at last. However, almost completely forgotten is the Scottish arboriculturalist Patrick Matthew who had formulated the idea of natural selection (and coined the phrase) in a book published in 1831, nearly 30 years before. When Darwin became aware of it, he wrote that Matthew 'completely anticipates the theory of Natural Selection', and in subsequent editions of *On the Origin of Species* he acknowledged Matthew's claim to priority.

who had reached the same conclusions as I had. That's another great advantage of research; it can save you a great deal of time if you discover that someone has already found a way to solve your problem for you. And Jonathan had done just that. He'd discovered a powerful, magical way to discourage people from gambling. He'd employed a wizard.

Emanuele 'Manny' Faja is an extraordinary young man. Originally from Venice in Italy, his family moved to the UK when he was 10 but you'd never guess that from his pristine English accent. The reason I call him extraordinary is that he is so annoyingly good at so many things for someone so young. When I first met him in 2008, he wasn't quite 20 years old but he was already an accomplished musician, a talented photographer and a deep thinker. But it was his skill at sleight of hand that was a wonder to behold. After hearing about him from Jonathan, I'd arranged to meet him at a coffee shop in Leytonstone for a chat about the Three Card Trick. But first, I asked him to demonstrate his skill which he happily did, firstly with the traditional playing cards and then with three black coasters, one of which had a white dot on it. He proved to be almost supernaturally good at it. We played for close to an hour and I failed on every single attempt to 'find the lady'. Had we been betting at standard street gambling rates I'd have lost around £500. It was quite humbling to see how easily I could be manipulated by a nineteen-year-old, and it made me appreciate how good professional card sharps are; some of the ones I'd been trying to catch had been doing it for longer than Manny had been outside the womb.

The reason we were meeting was because, a few months previously, Manny had received a surprising letter from Waltham Forest Council asking if he would publicly demonstrate the Three Card Trick to shoppers at Leyton Mills Retail Park – a very large and very open-plan shopping centre in north-east London. 'It came completely out of the blue,' he told me. 'Apparently a police officer had seen me doing table magic in a pub and was impressed enough to suggest to the council that I demonstrate to shoppers that the Three Card Trick is a con.'

Things didn't go terribly smoothly on the first attempt. Flanked by council staff and uniformed Community Support Officers giving out leaflets, Manny had spent an entire day at Leyton Mills dressed as a wizard and proving to people that they couldn't win. Unfortunately, however, no one had thought to tell the afternoon shift at the local police station so there was some confusion at first. And the arrival of camera crews and reporters eager to find out why a wizard was doing card tricks in a shopping centre only added to the chaos.[96]

Despite a shaky start, the day went on to be a big success. Manny didn't once reveal to the shoppers how the trick was done, of course. But he did demonstrate very clearly that the whole thing is a scam. 'People thought they could get one over on me but they couldn't,' he told me. 'If I don't want you to win, you never will. I guess if you shut your eyes you could win by blind one-in-three chance. But, even then, I can usually steer you towards choosing the wrong card or disk. Even when people are shown how it's done they still think that they can win because there are only three choices. Nobody thinks they can be fooled every time. But they can ... which is great news for magicians like me. You've effectively handed your money over before I even start.'

Working with Jonathan Clack, he had since repeated the same performance (in less exotic attire) at a number of other popular street gambling venues. Everywhere he'd performed there had been a significant drop in the number of street gamblers and, more importantly, fewer embarrassed punters gambling money away that they could scarce afford to lose. Therefore, it seemed that the obvious thing to do in my case was to swamp the area with wizards. Or some magicians at least. Which is exactly what I did. And it proved to be just as successful as Manny's efforts.

---

96 It probably didn't help that Manny wears fairly large spectacles. Harry Potter fever was running high.

Photo: BBC News

Glenn Hester told me that a similar action took place in New York City back in the 1990s. On 42nd Street and Times Square as many as 120 Three Card Montes would set up shop every morning to fleece passing commuters. Eventually, a group of angry professional magicians decided that enough was enough. They set up their own stalls and, working alongside the NYPD, set out to educate the public. Local businesses funded the printing and distribution of some 50,000 leaflets warning people not to throw their money away. At the same time, a banner was hung from lampposts bearing the same message as the leaflets: 'You can't win, you won't win, you will never win, so don't play the game.'

This educative approach to preventing crime can be used in a variety of ways. In 2013, a campaign called 'Put-Pockets', developed by Crimestoppers and advertising giant Ogilvy One[97], saw Rob James and James Brown, professional

---

[97] As you'll discover throughout this book, marketing and advertising people have much to teach us about influencing people and I've been keen to learn as much from them as I can. It's proven to be mutually beneficial; Rory Sutherland (he of the homeopathic seahorse story mentioned in the previous chapter) was in the process of creating a branch of his company called Ogilvy Change when I first met him. The idea was to explore ways of using the skills he'd learned in advertising to do good for society. I learned much from him and, I think, he got something back from me. Certainly, he went on to write a book called *The Wiki Man* and, I'm proud to say, several pages of the book feature the work that I did with the Problem Solving Unit.

magicians, and Richard Young, an ex-pickpocket, spending their working days in busy Bristol streets discreetly popping leaflets into shoppers' bags, jackets and even trousers.

Photo: OgilvyOne London

Later in the day these 'victims' would discover the leaflets – deliberately printed to look like life-sized smartphones – which said, 'If someone can get a smartphone into your pocket they can get a smartphone out.' Similar leaflets were later created for tablets and mini-tablets too.[98]

Photo: OgilvyOne London

98 The leaflets encouraged people to visit a website for crime prevention advice. Over 93 per cent of people who found a leaflet did so and, on average, spent over three minutes viewing the online content. Within four hours of the campaign appearing on TV news, Kent Police had contacted Crimestoppers about launching the activity in Dover. The campaign has now been used all over the UK and overseas.

It was a clever campaign that undermines something called 'normalcy bias': the thing that causes us to underestimate the possibility of an event occurring and its possible effects on us. It's that 'it'll never happen to me' thought that goes through our heads as we take the next puff on a cigarette, or engage in dangerous sports, or download something illegally from the internet.[99] Good crime prevention affects our normalcy bias by making us realise that anyone – including ourselves – can fall victim to a pickpocket.

Or, for that matter, to a wizard with some playing cards.

5

John Tyndall, the Irish scientist who, among his many accomplishments, was the man who first explained why the sky is blue, once said: 'There is no genius so gifted as not to need control and verification. The brightest flashes in the world of thought are incomplete until they have been proved to have their counterparts in the world of fact.' All research has two components: information gathering and verification. The two tend to happen concurrently but as long as we do both, we can be reasonably sure that the facts we have are good facts.

One good method of verification is to get your data from multiple sources. Data obtained from a single source, particularly one that you're not entirely convinced is correct, is not much better than no data at all, and could actually be damaging.

An ex-colleague of mine called Peter Kirkham, was working on the London Borough of Lambeth around the time that his local intelligence unit had just installed some new

---

99 Conversely, there is 'worst-case bias', where a catastrophe is anticipated even though we have no idea if there will be one, and there isn't a great deal of evidence to support our belief. It's this second form of bias that leads to over-zealous safety regulations and focuses people on areas of the law that, perhaps, aren't necessarily the areas that need most looking at.

analysis software. The program collated reported crimes and generated 'hotspots' in order to show where police officers should be posted to have the maximum impact on preventing crime and catching offenders.

'One particular location was flagged up by the software as a street robbery hotspot,' Peter explains. 'The inspector responsible for that area didn't think that sounded right so he decided to investigate. He dug into the crime records and found that there were, indeed, robberies recorded. However there were some unusual features to them. Firstly, most street robberies occur in the evenings and especially at weekends, but these were nearly all at midday-ish. Secondly, all of the alleged perpetrators and all of the victims were teenagers. Therefore, rather than go marching straight in with a squad of plain clothes officers, he decided to do some further research. And he discovered that it was all about chips.'

A nearby school had recently embarked on a healthy-eating campaign and chips had been taken off the lunchtime menu. This encouraged many of the kids to go out to local fast-food shops in their lunch breaks. Outside the relative safety of the school premises, some were then being preyed upon by bullies who took their dinner money. When the victims reported this to their parents, the parents reported it to police and each offence was recorded as a robbery. 'This was, by legal definition, a spate of robberies,' says Peter, 'but the reality is that it was bullying.' [100]

The inspector's solution was to talk to the school and chips were put back on the menu. As the result, robbery figures dropped dramatically. However, the actual problem of bullying also needed to be dealt with as a matter of some priority – but

---

100 Say the word 'robbery' and many people will imagine knife-wielding thugs demanding their wallets. But what was happening here was quite different. It's an upsetting thing for any child to go through, of course, but having your dinner money taken isn't what most people would consider as a robbery. The problem of having an all-encompassing term like 'robbery' means that there is no distinction between levels of seriousness. Consequently, even dinner money theft adds to the creation of a 'robbery hotspot' and that is going to affect people's perception of the area. It's going to make people fearful. It might even affect house prices.

not just by the police. This was an issue that needed to involve the school, the parents and the kids themselves.

This story is a perfect example of why it's so important to get your facts from multiple sources. Data is plastic and easily bent, altered, destroyed or corrupted, and if you don't have all of the correct facts you'll find yourself tackling the wrong problem or missing important indicators of how your project is progressing. Or, in a worst-case scenario, failing catastrophically.

Meanwhile, the war on the street gamblers goes on and educating the public that it's a scam is one way of preventing crime. But it's an uphill struggle. The 'wizard' option was very effective and did result in a substantial drop in gambling for a number of weeks after each police operation. But the turnover of shoppers and visitors to street markets is huge and the effect of the campaign soon dissipated and people were once again queuing up to be ripped off. Sadly, I suspect that no matter how many people we educated about the Three Card Trick, normalcy bias means that there will always be some people who keep trying, hoping for that big win. Perhaps a national TV or press campaign might provide a more permanent solution? Or video displays showing people like Manny doing their thing?[101]

However, smart-thinking cops have found other innovative ways to tackle the problem. In 2012, Met Police officers used a borrowed No. 2 London bus to sneak up on a gang of street gamblers on Westminster Bridge. Normally, the lookouts alert the street gamblers well in advance but, on this occasion, they hadn't anticipated the 30-plus officers who jumped out on them as the bus came alongside. More than 25 gamblers were detained and 12 were charged with gaming offences.

---

101 In December 2015, myself and *Freakonomics* co-creator Stephen J Dubner visited some street gamblers on Westminster Bridge while gathering content for a podcast. They are just as prolific as ever, we noted, and no one appeared to be policing them, even remotely. We did wonder why CCTV and loud speakers were not being used to disperse them or, at least, to record evidential material. We are both pretty sure that there may be a technological solution here.

One of the most important lessons I ever learned was that solving problems means focusing on the actual problem, not the perceived problem – they can be two very different things. You have to explore the problem as far as you can; research and analysis are hugely important.

You have to understand what the problem is before you can have any decent chance of solving it.

5: THE APE THAT MOVED A PLANET

I can prove anything by statistics except the truth.
George Canning

If a given problem still exists, you can bet that a lot of people have already come along and failed to solve it. Easy problems evaporate; it's the hard ones that linger. Furthermore, it takes a lot of time to track down, organise, and analyse the data to answer even one small question well.
Steven D Levitt and Stephen J Dubner

1

I was watching the triumphant first-ever space shuttle landing on a black-and-white portable television set when suddenly someone shouted: 'De-bus! De-bus!' It was a word, military in origin, that I'd never heard before joining the police. Now it was a word that filled me with dread. My colleagues and I grabbed our helmets, fastened our chinstraps and piled out of our riot coach. Upon hitting the street, we were all handed a tall riot shield and we formed up into a thin blue line of tired and scared young police officers. 'Forward!' came the barked command and we slowly trudged our way towards an angry mob that began throwing bricks and bottles and petrol bombs at us. All that stood between us and them was a centimetre thick sheet of scratched and dented Perspex and some vaguely phallic lumps of wood we called truncheons. Someone started to beat his shield – we were all men because female officers weren't sent into riot situations back then – with his truncheon. Within seconds, others had joined in. Bang. Bang. Bang. Bang.

'What are we doing?' I asked as I blindly followed suit, picking up the rhythm.

'There are more of them than us. A lot more', said the officer next to me. 'This might just scare them off and then no one gets hurt. It worked in that film *Zulu Dawn*.'

'Yes it did', I said. 'But that was the Zulus. It was the guys in uniform who were massacred.'

It was April 1981 and the Brixton Uprising was in full swing. My shield serial – the officers on my coach – and I had been on duty for over 24 hours, sleeping fitfully on the Green Goddess riot coach between bursts of intense physical activity as we fended off attacks or became part of arrest teams. Three or four of my colleagues had been sufficiently badly injured that they'd been taken off to hospital, reducing our numbers. Many of those who remained – myself included – had minor cuts and scuffs and the bright red of our blood stood out starkly against the white of our uniform shirts. In the last sortie, half a brick had hit my helmet so hard that it had turned the silver badge into a concave bowl and given me a headache that lasted for two days.[102] Or maybe it was exacerbated by dehydration; we were reliant on a van bringing us meals and snacks – jokingly known as 'force feeding' – every four hours or so and fluids were limited to an occasional orange drink packaged in a curious cardboard pyramid.

The riots only lasted for 72 hours but, in that time, 280 police officers and 45 members of the public were injured, over 100 vehicles were set alight (56 of them police), and nearly 150 buildings were damaged, six burnt to the ground.

---

102 We were still several years away from the crash helmets and flame-retardant overalls that riot cops wear these days. We'd only just got riot shields in 1981. At my first Notting Hill Carnival in 1980, my colleagues and I used traffic cones and dustbin lids to defend ourselves when the bricks and bottles started to fly.

Some reports estimated that up to 5,000 people were involved in the disorder.

A bottle smashed at my feet and my suddenly petrol-soaked trousers burst into flame. As I stood there, frozen into immobility by panic, a colleague bravely ran forward through the hail of masonry and smothered the flames with a thick grey blanket. The bravado drumming of shields had stopped as soon as the first projectiles started to fly. It hadn't made us feel any braver or stronger. And as every brick smacked into my shield I can remember thinking, 'Why do these people want to hurt me? I've done them no harm. They don't even know me.' Alright, so my thoughts may not have been quite so lucid at the time but, nevertheless, for the first time in my young life, I understood what prejudice felt like. I knew what it was like to be hated solely because I belonged to a particular 'tribe'.

Photo: Kim Aldis

It was all a bit confusing for a naïve young West Country lad like me who had only recently had his first-ever Indian meal (my colleagues tricked me into having a lamb *phall* – I thought I was going to die). I'd grown up in an almost 100 per cent white community in Cornwall;

my final school photograph from 1979 features the 150-plus kids who made up the sixth form and there's just one mixed-race lad among the sea of Caucasian faces. So when I arrived in London in 1980, the idea that people could dislike, or even hate, each other solely because of a difference in skin colour or religion wasn't really on my radar. And I wasn't alone; the Met attracts applicants from all over the UK and most of my colleagues weren't Londoners – we seemed to have a very high proportion of Scots at the time as I recall – which is maybe why, despite popular belief, I didn't see very much racism among my colleagues. What I saw and heard was no worse than I'd once been guilty of myself: inappropriate language and ignorance. It was certainly no worse than you'd see on TV or in films at the time – not that that's a viable excuse.[103] But then again, I was never posted to an area of London where police and minority communities were at loggerheads, so just because I didn't see very much overt racism, it doesn't mean that there weren't any racist cops. Any large organisation is going to harbour a proportion of people with extreme views. There will be racists in the NHS, in the education system, in the civil service. There will be racist bankers, plumbers, street cleaners, MPs, retail managers, miners, postal workers, footballers and farmers. The police service was no different; it would be blinkered and naïve to claim otherwise. However, where a police officer and a plumber differ is that the cop is in a position of power. He or she has a warrant from the Queen that says that they can deprive you of your liberty. They can stop you in the street and they can search you for

---

103 And I'm not just talking about the obvious candidates here like *Mind Your Language*, *Curry and Chips* and *Love Thy Neighbour*. What we would now deem to be inappropriate language was used all over the place, even in classic shows like *Monty Python*. The *Carry On* films had white actors blacked up as Africans and Indians. And then there was *The Black And White Minstrel Show*. Were they racist shows? Maybe. But it's hard to be objective looking at them through twenty-first century eyes.

things you shouldn't have with you. When a few officers abused these powers it made the rest of us look guilty by association. I'm proud to report that in 30 years of policing I only ever saw a handful of instances of blatantly racist behaviour by colleagues. Most cops are good people. And I'd like to believe that I never treated anyone unfairly just because they were 'different' from me.

So why then was I standing shaky-legged behind a riot shield and being pelted with bricks and Molotov cocktails? I hadn't done anything to deserve this treatment. But the whole of the group I represented – every officer in the Met Police – was being held culpable for the actions of a handful of officers who had abused their authority. We were all scapegoats for the actions of a few racist oafs.

Generalisation can cause upset and damage but there's no escaping it; pattern recognition is natural and innate and clustering data helps us to make sense of a big and complex world. One obvious example of this is the way we associate danger with certain colours because Nature uses those colours as a warning. It's something called 'aposematism' – the opposite of camouflage – and the living things that blatantly advertise themselves as dangerous, poisonous, or unpalatable, tend to use striking colours like black, yellow, red and white: think wasps, toadstools, ladybirds, skunks, or certain species of frogs, beetles and caterpillars. It's why we use those same colours when we want to put up warning signs; we're pre-programmed to understand that they mean 'danger'. Pattern recognition is part of our deep-rooted and ancient System One thinking which creates shortcuts to help keep us alive and safe.[104] As Oliver Payne says in his book *Inspiring Sustainable Behaviour*: 'We jump a mile at snakes, but rarely fear electrical cable; we get spooked in the dark, but cross the road without looking. We are still imprinted with the mores of a short, brutal, provincial life.'

But our reliance on pattern recognition can lead us astray. The first mistake we can make is failing to spot a pattern, like thinking that a red and white mushroom is pretty and fairy tale-like rather than poisonous. The second is seeing a pattern that isn't there. This can manifest itself in something harmless like seeing Jesus in a slice of toast, a face in the knots of a wooden fence or a wickedly grinning Mickey Mouse in a urinal.[105]

104 Baby chicks just a few days old will tend to avoid black and yellow food, even if they have never come into contact with it before. German scientists Werner Schuler and Elke Hesse painted some mealworms with a striped yellow and black pattern, and others a drab uniform colour made by mixing the same yellow and black paints. Although the chicks would peck at the black and yellow mealworms they did not eat many. However, they ate most of the drab mealworms. Since the mealworms were otherwise identical in every way, the chicks had no reason to ignore the black and yellow ones other than an inbuilt aversion to the colours and/or patterns.

105 This is a phenomenon called 'pareidolia'.

But it can also lead to generalisation and prejudice. If a cop has mostly negative interactions with people from a particular group, they might start to see every individual from that group in a bad light. It's a form of cognitive bias that is reinforced by the fact that most of the people that cops interact with on a daily basis are either doing something wrong or are suspected of it. I had to constantly guard against sliding down that particular slippery slope, as it's worryingly easy to do so. Conversely, when people feel that they are being unfairly treated or disproportionately targeted by police officers, they will start to believe that all coppers are bastards. This is surely another strong case for community-based policing. If cops spend all of their time interacting with the worst people in society or with people who, for whatever reason, dislike or distrust the police, it's bound to have an effect on perceptions. But if a significant proportion of their working day is spent among decent, law-abiding, good and honest people, it can only serve to redress that balance. And vice versa.

Pattern recognition can have some negative effects. But when channelled in a positive way, the ability to find form and order among the chaos is what we call analysis.

2

We are an inquisitive and resourceful species; the apes who figure things out. Since we began to migrate out of Africa some 65–70,000 years ago, we've learned how to keep warm, how to ensure we have food through the leaner months, and how to domesticate animals. We've used the things we've found around us to make tools and weapons. We've extracted metals from the ground and combined chemicals to make medicines, fuel, and new materials that don't exist in nature. As we speak, scientists are unravelling the very fabric of reality from which you, I and everything in the universe – or multiverse possibly – are made. We've travelled to the depths of the ocean and walked on the Moon.[106] We've even slowed the rotation of our own planet.

Dr Benjamin Fong Chao of the Goddard Space Flight Center recently identified that the earth's rotation has slowed by 0.2 millionths of a second per day for the last 40 years solely because of the weight of water being concentrated in reservoirs between the equator and the poles. Just building one hydroelectric power station – the Three Gorges Dam in China – has increased the length of a day by 0.06 microseconds and has shifted the position of the Earth's poles by about three-quarters of an inch.[107] The effects are minimal, admittedly – earthquakes and other natural disasters have a much greater impact – but remember that this is a *planet* we're talking about; a giant ball of rock 24,900 miles in circumference, with a surface area of around 197,000,000 square miles and weighing around 6.6 sextillion tons.[108] For us fragile little humans to have moved it at all is staggeringly impressive.

For the largest part of human history, finding solutions was a clumsy and often dangerous process of trial and error. How many people plunged to their deaths before someone figured out the rules of aerodynamics? How many people inflicted terrible injuries on themselves in the quest to understand chemistry? Francis Bacon, one of the founding fathers of the modern scientific method, died from pneumonia after stuffing

---

106 Yes, we have. Don't believe all that silly conspiracy nonsense. I was lucky enough to get to hang out with Buzz Aldrin for a day back in 2012 and I asked him if he could give me one good reason why the conspiracy theories are wrong. 'They always seem to be young people who say we didn't go,' he told me. 'They weren't there during the Cold War. They don't understand the politics. The Russians and the Chinese were looking for any reason to discredit us and, believe me, they were watching us every inch of the way to the Moon. If we'd faked it, they would have spotted it and told the world. And if we faked Apollo 11 ... why did we bother to go back to the Moon five more times? Or do people believe we faked all of those missions as well? Tens of thousands of people were involved in the Apollo programme over 11 years. Are they all lying?'

107 The reservoir covers 650 square miles and holds about five trillion gallons of water weighing more than 42 billion tons.

108 And its weight increases by around 100,000lbs each year due to dust and meteoric material falling from the skies.

snow into a chicken to explore the cold preservation of food. And when Thomas Edison was asked why so many of his prototypes for the light bulb had failed he allegedly answered, 'I have not failed 700 times. I have succeeded in proving that those 700 ways will not work.' Appropriately, he was also supposedly the man who gave us the quote that 'genius is one per cent inspiration and 99 per cent perspiration.'[109] Thankfully, since the Wright Brothers, there's been no further need to jump off church towers on, quite literally, a wing and a prayer. These days, people can test their designs with computer modelling, flow tanks and wind tunnels.[110] Science has eliminated a great deal of the risk. Edison could have found his solution much quicker by chatting to all of the best brains in the world by phone or email or Skype. And Bacon could have tested his theories with the aid of a thermometer, insulating gloves and a bacteria counter. The chicken, sadly, still draws the short straw to this day. But the scientific method remains at the heart of all good research and analysis:

- Ask a question
- Do your research
- Construct a hypothesis
- Test your hypothesis
- Analyse your data
  And only then,
- Draw a conclusion.

109 There are many quotes that have no definite source and so what tends to happen is that they become attached to a well-known person. Another thing that happens is that a quote, originally said by someone not so famous, gets re-assigned to a more notable person. Popular candidates include Albert Einstein, Mark Twain, Benjamin Franklin and Britain's most revered prime minister, which is why the phenomenon has earned the name 'Churchillian Drift' (coined by Nigel Rees).

110 I realise that their claim on the first powered flight is hotly disputed by New Zealand's Richard Pearce and the UK's John Stringfellow, to name but two. However, the Wright Brothers are the best known claimants. Incidentally, they are often erroneously credited with inventing the wind tunnel too. They made pioneering use of one but the earliest wind tunnels can be traced back to Benjamin Robins and Sir George Cayley in the 18th century.

Before I got involved in problem solving and crime prevention it hadn't occurred to me that there was a 'science' behind it. But, of course, there was. The same method applies. You ask a question (What's the problem?). You research (What's causing the problem?). You test your hypothesis (Is X the cause?). You analyse (Was the cause what we thought it was?). Then the conclusion is what you act upon. It may mean going out and tackling the identified cause of the problem. But it could also mean discovering that what you thought was the cause is wrong, in which case you loop back to the research phase and run through the method again.

Analysis is about making inferences and decisions based upon knowledge; some that you already have and other material that you uncover during your research. It's about honing the information down into a usable form, sifting the wheat from the chaff and concentrating your efforts on the information that will be most useful. And it can totally change your perceptions of a problem.

3

In 2006, I travelled to Scotland several times to look at local problems and to conduct some training sessions with the police, fire and rescue services, NHS staff, community leaders, council officers and others. At the time, the Scottish Parliament was keen to bring in the same POP-style[111] of policing that we'd been advocating in the Problem Solving Unit and, rather than reinvent the wheel, they'd asked if we could come and share our experience.

Over the course of three months I travelled the length and breadth of Scotland, to large cities like Edinburgh and Glasgow, and to smaller communities in the Highlands and the Outer Hebrides. The list of local problems I discussed with people ranged from fatal stabbings,[112] to sheep rustling, to 'an invasion of Goths' – but the most common issue was antisocial behaviour by 'neds', the Scottish equivalent of the much execrated English 'chav'.[113]

On one occasion, I was told about a housing estate in western Scotland that was a hot spot for antisocial behaviour by youths who claimed that they were bored and had nothing to do.[114] The alleged antisocial behaviour consisted mostly of petty crime such as graffiti and nuisance behaviour like littering, noise, binge drinking and setting small fires. A great many of the kids would also kick footballs around in 'no ball games' areas and annoy the residents, despite the fact

---

111 Problem Oriented Policing. Remember?

112 Scotland did, for some time, have a serious problem with knife crime. Despite hitting an all-time low in 2013, Scotland still had around 48 per cent more homicides than England and Wales, of which half were committed with a blade or knife of some kind. In terms of European ranking, Scotland was 12 places ahead of England and Wales and ranked 7th after Lithuania, Estonia, Finland, Bulgaria, Romania and Belgium. However, do check out the extraordinary work of Karyn McLuskey and her Violence Reduction Unit who, over the course of the last decade, have halved the number of knife crimes in Glasgow. It is an amazing story and I wish I had room in this book to tell it. She's an inspiration.

113 If ever you needed evidence of tribalism, here it was; they all dressed the same way and they acted the same way and almost any press about them was negative.

114 I really dislike the term 'antisocial behaviour' but we've got stuck with it because of legislation; specifically the Anti-Social Behaviour Act 2003. It's a very vague and nebulous term and ripe for challenge or abuse. In my opinion, breaking wind in a lift is ASB but I doubt the perpetrator would qualify for an ASBO (Anti-Social Behaviour Order).

that there were two perfectly good council-owned football pitches nearby.

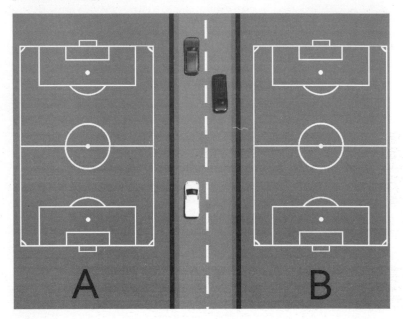

The pitches were regulation-sized and well-maintained. Pitch A was closest to the housing estate and was separated from Pitch B by a modestly busy road. Tall mesh fences were in place to stop footballs bouncing into traffic. Pitch B was getting hardly any use at all, while fights regularly broke out between groups all wanting to use Pitch A. To get to Pitch B from the estate, the kids had to walk to a pedestrian tunnel less than quarter of a mile away. Historically, they'd torn holes in the fences and run the gauntlet of the traffic, but the installation of CCTV had stopped that.[115] Meanwhile, the drinking and the antisocial behaviour around the estate continued. Residents, quite legitimately, demanded that something be done about it.

115 This is called a 'Desire Line'. The psychology of urban design is a fascinating subject which we will talk about at length later in the book.

Among the suggestions being considered when we arrived were increased police patrols and the use of Antisocial Behaviour Orders (ASBOs). There was also some talk of building a footbridge or a new underpass or a pedestrian crossing because 'the kids are too lazy to walk to the existing subway'. Some people suggested doing away with the pitches altogether because the kids didn't 'deserve them' and almost everyone blamed the parents. So we looked at those suggestions: we researched and we analysed our data.

Removing the football pitches was an expensive scorched earth solution that punished everyone for the bad behaviour of a few individuals and which would make the well-behaved football-loving kids resentful. It might also increase complaints; no amount of extra signage will stop kids playing football if they have no alternative place to play.[116] So we parked that suggestion for the time being. Besides which, the council said that they didn't have the money to develop the site into something else.

Additional police patrols might work, provided there were enough of them. However, it's another expensive option and it could be argued that, while the police are monitoring the

---

116 I chuckled when I spotted this in *Viz* magazine's 'Top Tips' section: 'COUNCILS: Putting another NO BALL GAMES sign eight yards to the left of the current one will save us having to use jumpers for goalposts.'

behaviour of a few children, more serious crimes could be happening elsewhere. The arrival of Community Support Officers has helped to take some of the burden off police officers and, when they are tasked properly, they can be hugely helpful in reducing bad behaviour and in dealing with quality of life issues. [117] However, because CSOs don't have the same powers as police officers, they are not always taken as seriously or treated with the respect they deserve. A Police CSO (PCSO) in North London once told me that she felt she was making some headway in engaging with local kids because the things they threw at her were getting softer. 'The kids still need to show off to their mates,' she told me, 'but they know me now and they don't want to hurt me. It's gone from stones to eggs to grapes. It's progress.' Of course, CCTV could be seen as a passive alternative to police patrols, but CCTV can't see everywhere. Nor can it identify people in hats and hoods very easily.

We figured that we could also forget ASBOs because the evidence is that they simply don't work. They were originally designed to be used as a preventative tool; by setting a series of conditions for a person to adhere to, it gave them a chance to change their behaviour before more serious penalties needed to be dished out. But, as time passed, ASBOs mutated into a kind of penalty in their own right and their impact was diminished. I once met a lad in Croydon who had a tattoo done every time he got issued with one, like some Don Juan carving notches in his bedpost. For him (and he's certainly not alone), the ASBO had become a badge to be worn with pride. To make matters worse, exponents of Labelling Theory will tell you that ASBOs can actually cause further bad behaviour.[118] In the past, if you

---

117 This is particularly true in Scotland where the CSOs were funded and employed by the local authority, rather than the police. Somehow, they seemed to be more effective than English PCSOs. Maybe they engendered more trust as they didn't wear police-style uniforms and because they worked within their own communities?

118 Labelling Theory studies the way in which terms used to describe or classify individuals may influence self-identity and behaviour, rather like a self-fulfilling prophecy.

misbehaved, you got a verbal warning or a caution and that was the end of the matter. But now you get an ASBO and the label stays with you on official records. Consequently, the person with the ASBO believes – often with justification – that the police and other authority figures will view them in a negative light even though they've never been convicted of an actual crime. For some, it can cause a build-up of anger and resentment resulting in them living up to their supposed reputation.

ASBOs have also been criticised for criminalising otherwise lawful behaviour; being noisy and looking a bit threatening by gathering together in groups has suddenly become punishable by curfews and exclusions. To add to the controversy, a 2002 Home Office study revealed that 44 per cent of people with ASBOs had substance abuse problems or learning disabilities and a further 16 per cent were living with psychological or behaviour difficulties within their family. In Scotland things were even worse with 55 per cent of all ASBO holders having some form of substance abuse, mental health issue or learning difficulty.[119] So it's perhaps no surprise to discover that, by 2007, the percentage of ASBOs being breached nationally was 70.3 per cent (in Manchester alone, that figure was 90.2 per cent). ASBOs are ineffective and, more importantly, they don't tackle the underlying causes of bad behaviour. So, why would they be an effective tool in this instance?[120]

Blaming the parents has always been an easy option. And it isn't a new thing. In my office I have a copy of an 1898 report called *Juvenile Offenders*, in which the Howard Association (forerunner of the Howard League for Penal Reform) blamed the 'rising tide of mischief and violence and ruffianism' on 'irresponsible parents, working mothers and lax discipline

119 It's also notable that Scotland's substance abuse problem also fuels a lot of violence. In 43 per cent of all murders in 2013, the perpetrator had taken alcohol or hard drugs prior to the attack.

120 At the time of writing, the ASBOs is in the process of being replaced by the Injunction to Prevent Nuisance and Annoyance (IPNA). IPNAs delegate more responsibilities and powers to local communities and practitioners. Time will tell if the new system is any more effective.

in schools.' I also have a book called *Children of the Nation*, written in 1907 by Sir John Eldon Gorst in which he blames everything bad in society upon the breakdown of parental influence. And there is a succession of books and reports that go on to find scapegoat after scapegoat for young people's behaviour. After the First World War, it was the lack of male role models because so many fathers, grandfathers and older siblings had died on the battlefields of Europe; in the 1930s and 40s blame fell on the rise of council estates; after the Second World War, it was once again single parents; then, in the 1960s, it was female emancipation and the influence of American movies and culture. And still the moral outrage continues with new causal factors being identified every year – glue sniffing, GM foods, rap music, video games, heavy metal, Goth culture, food additives, etc. – and, as always, the parents get the lion's share of the vitriol. In a recent poll by 'Rethinking Crime and Punishment', people were asked what single thing would be most effective in reducing crime. The most common response was 'better parenting'.[121] But while no one can deny that there are some bad parents out there, it's been my experience that the majority of mums and dads are often horrified when they discover what their kids get up to. (Did your parents know everything that you got up to?) In fact, many refuse to believe it until you provide them with concrete evidence. And, contrary to popular belief, some of the worst kids come from the best homes. Binge drinking culture is as much driven by middle-class kids – who, let's face it, are more likely to be able to afford it – as it is by kids from poor backgrounds. And kids under 18 from relatively wealthy homes are just as likely to drink (and girls drink more than boys) and to indulge in other 'risky behaviours' such as drug taking, smoking and shoplifting.

Blame the parents if you want to, but blaming them before you're sure that they're even aware of the issue will simply put them off wanting to help you. And demonising them if

---

121 Other responses included more police, better schools, and constructive activities for young people.

they have tried but failed, is hardly fair either. There is no job tougher than bringing up kids and most parents do the best that they can.

Then there were the building options: a footbridge might make a difference but it would also cost approximately £500,000. A new subway would be a similar price. Even a simple pedestrian crossing is surprisingly expensive, the average cost being around £100,000 to £120,000.[122] Is anyone going to write those kinds of cheques for an issue of antisocial behaviour? Of course not. They're going to say, 'Why don't the police sort it out – that's their job.' Or 'I blame the parents.'

We were back at Square One and, while we hadn't necessarily abandoned any of those options, we were pretty convinced that they were unlikely to work or were unlikely to happen due to cost. So we thought about sources of data for our research. And we realised that the only group of people who hadn't had a say in how to solve the problem were the kids themselves. Now, there could have been all sorts of reasons why this was: fear, shyness, insecurity, language or cultural barriers, etc. Or maybe, like the underpass example in chapter 3 the kids believed that everyone hated them. You can make all kinds of assumptions and predictions about why people are acting the way they are, but the simplest and most direct way of finding out is to ask. After all, they are the one group of people guaranteed to know. It also means that they may be able to tell you what it would take for them to stop behaving antisocially. These kinds of discussions aren't always easy to arrange; meetings between young people and adults are often difficult because the two groups rarely see eye to eye and, when those adults are in police uniform, the problem is magnified enormously. But it is still possible to

---

122 I was surprised by the cost of this so I asked a local authority for a breakdown. Their reply stated that the cost has to take into account such things as design, labour costs, traffic management whilst the crossing is under construction, drainage, excavation of existing pavement, disposal of material, new kerbing and paving, anti-skid surfacing, road markings and studs, new traffic signs, electrical connection, supply pillars and new signal heads and poles.

open a dialogue – you just have to find people who can act as impartial go-betweens.

In this instance it was the Scottish Fire and Rescue Service who stepped up and performed that role brilliantly for us. Firefighters are perfect for this kind of work; they're authority figures, they're great role models, and people trust them.[123] And they're not a threat; they can't arrest you, confiscate your booze or search your pockets for knives or drugs. Of course, if you use someone as a go-between, you should never ask them to break any confidences as that will destroy the trust. But there is no problem with them letting you know what the kids think in general terms. And you can use them to relay your thoughts back.

In this particular case, consultations produced a wealth of information which, when analysed, provided us with a solution that cost not half a million, but £180.96 (including delivery) plus £650 labour costs. And here it is:

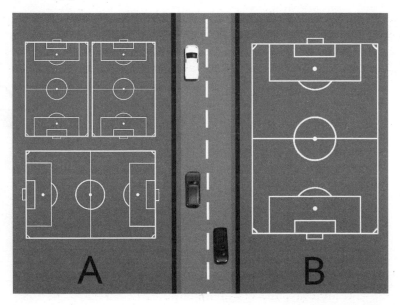

123 In recent years the Scottish Fire and Rescue Service has opened youth clubs and run junior citizenship courses that have proven to be hugely popular and very effective. It's been a brilliant initiative.

Using a couple of 30-litre drums of white pitch-marking paint and a man with a line-painting machine, Pitch A was subdivided into three smaller pitches. And antisocial behaviour on the estate dropped by an average, month on month, of around 35–45 per cent. Here's why it worked:

Talking to the kids had revealed lots of new information. Firstly, it identified that younger children from the estate (aged 9–12) were frequently bullied off Pitch A by older children (aged 13–16). Not being allowed (by their anything but uncaring parents) to cross the road, these younger kids would then find something else to do which often led to nuisance behaviour. The 13–16 year olds were, in turn, bullied off Pitch A by young adults aged 17–24 keen to assert their authority. The 13–16 year olds would then wander around the estate getting drunk and leery. The reason that they, and the youngest group of kids, didn't use the existing pedestrian underpass was not laziness; it was because the kids from the 17–24 age group had claimed it as their place to hang out.

It was no surprise to discover that all three groups were crazy about football but it turned out that there were degrees of crazy. The youngest group just wanted somewhere to kick a ball around where they wouldn't get moaned at by adults. The middle-sized kids wanted a properly marked-out football pitch but weren't that bothered about the size. However, the oldest of the three groups took their football very seriously and wouldn't play on anything less than a regulation-sized pitch so they didn't want the former Pitch A anymore and stuck solely to Pitch B. The clashes therefore ended because the three age groups had distinct 'cliques' and would not play football with each other. Therefore, more pitches were needed, not fewer. And, because that's what they got, the clashes ended.

Kids engaged in meaningful activity don't get involved in antisocial behaviour anywhere near as much as bored kids do and although the complaints didn't disappear – there are always a few kids who won't toe the line and whose behaviour will need to be controlled or modified by other means – they dropped to a much more acceptable level. Two CSOs, along with some willing parents, even started a local five-a-side *futsal* competition. Everyone was happy with the results.

Sub-dividing the pitches wasn't the only way to tackle the problem but, in this instance, it was smart, cheap, effective and sustainable. All it took was asking questions, forming hypotheses, testing those hypotheses and analysing the results.

4

'Look before you leap' has been a constant theme running through this book, whether we've been discussing killer snakes in African maize fields or cholera epidemics in Soho. The purpose of analysis is to ensure that you fully understand the 'why' of your problem. It's easy to be led astray by opinion, prejudice or by seeing patterns that simply aren't there.

Harvard law graduate Tyler Vigen runs a fantastic website called 'Spurious Correlations' in which he demonstrates just how easy it is to be fooled by patterns. For example, if you plot the amount that the US spends on science, space and technology, you get an almost identical graph to one mapping US deaths from strangulation, hanging and suffocation. Lay the two graphs over each other and the data are almost identical. But, of course, there is no link whatsoever between the two data sets. It's just coincidence. Here's my favourite example that Tyler found:

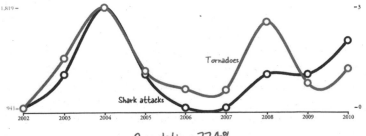

Correlation: 77.4%

Image: Tyler Vigen

Using data from the Florida Museum of Natural History and the US Weather Service, he found a 77.4 per cent correlation between the incidences of tornadoes and shark attacks. Yes indeed, the plot of that incredibly silly 2013 film *Sharknado* appears to have statistical evidence behind it. Except, of course, it hasn't. Like the previous example, the only thing that these two data sets have in common is a similar-looking pattern of peaks and troughs.

Elsewhere on Tyler's website (and in his excellent book of the same name) you'll find many more spurious correlations between such things as: crude oil imports from Norway and drivers killed in collisions with trains; and the number of maths doctorates awarded and the amount of uranium stored at US nuclear plants. Some skirt alarmingly close to a perfect correlation: there's a 99.7 per cent match between chlamydia rates per 100,000 American males between 1997 and 2006, and the number of males taking High School Advanced Placement (AP) statistics tests. It's nonsense, of course. But there is something oddly persuasive about the data when you see it laid out so convincingly on a graph; our natural propensity for pattern recognition can subvert reality.

Within the police service it wasn't uncommon to see colleagues making assumptions about the causes of problems based upon poor data or guesswork. For example, there are more burglaries than usual during school holidays. Therefore, it might (and did) lead some to think that the extra summertime burglaries were being committed by kids. But it's not necessarily the case. Yes, some might be committed by kids. But the other thing that also happens during the summer is that lots of families go away on holiday for a week or two, so there are lots more empty houses for the burglars to pick from. Plus, it's a big jump from bored schoolkid to burglar when you think about it. Correlation isn't always causation.

I recall one particular incident whenever I think about the necessity of understanding the causes of a problem before taking action. The Problem Solving Unit was told about a large number of drug dealers operating in and around a particular busy street market. So, we said we'd look into the problem. Presumably frustrated or annoyed by the fact that we hadn't immediately sprung into action with a potential solution, one local Chief Inspector decided that he couldn't wait for us to 'faff around' with research and analysis and flooded the area with uniformed officers ... and the traffic in drugs actually appeared to increase.[124]

Meanwhile, we were looking for data from as many different sources as we could find, including speaking to ex-users and ex-dealers. And it was from them that we learned the surprising reason why putting extra cops in the area had made things worse. We were told that dealers were quite often mugged by desperate users in the mistaken belief that they were carrying supplies (they almost never were) or because they carried large amounts of untraceable cash (they almost always did).[125] Therefore, the visible extra police staff had resulted in a drop in the number of robberies at the market, making the public feel safer but also inadvertently preventing the dealers getting robbed too. Consequently, they were able to do more business.

Because we took the time to find out how the dealers operated, we were able to develop more effective ways to disrupt their activity than filling the market with uniforms.

---

124 This is something called 'The Cobra Effect' after a story – possibly apocryphal – from Delhi during the days of British rule. When the colonial governors of the city placed a bounty on cobras, money was paid out for every cobra skin presented. However, cobra numbers didn't diminish and it was eventually discovered that local people had started breeding them to collect on the bounty. Once the British learned of this, they cancelled the reward and the now worthless cobras were set free, making the problem much worse than it had originally been. Another example that springs to mind involves pencils that were issued to New York school kids in 1998 and printed along their length with a strong anti-drugs message: 'Too cool to do drugs'. Unfortunately, what the suppliers – the Bureau for At-Risk Youth – hadn't anticipated was what happened when students sharpened the pencils. After a couple of turns in a sharpener the message quickly became 'Cool to do drugs'. A few more turns and it became the imperative 'Do Drugs'.

125 This was a fact we only learned at a later date; drug dealers don't tend to report these robberies to police for obvious reasons.

My Problem Solving Unit colleague Neil Henson developed a method for dismantling the infrastructure of their business. He called it 'Nimitz' after US Admiral Chester Nimitz who, during the Pacific War of 1945, defeated the mighty Japanese Navy despite having far fewer ships and planes at his disposal. Nimitz knew that he'd be unlikely to defeat the enemy in open battle as much of the US fleet had been lost or damaged at Pearl Harbour, but he knew that the Imperial Navy relied upon various islands for the storage and supply of things like fresh water, food, aircraft support, fuel, etc. By identifying and isolating the vital supply islands and mining the seas around them, the appropriately-named 'Operation Starvation' disrupted 35 of the 47 most essential Japanese convoy routes and sank or damaged more ships – 670 of them – in the last six months of the war than all of the Allied military forces combined.[126] Criminal operations like drugs markets also have an infrastructure. Neil's brilliant idea was to 'mine' the various pillars that supported the market – supply, transport, cash flow, etc. – thus making drug dealing harder or impossible.

Photo: Wendy Fair

---

126 Neil has developed his Nimitz Principle into a complete strategic package for problem-solvers. If it sounds like the sort of thing you'd use, do contact him at www.SixthSenseTraining.co.uk.

We knew that the most successful dealers weren't stupid enough to carry drugs on them; that's why they didn't get arrested even if stopped and searched by police. The drugs were stashed somewhere safe not too far away and the dealers would employ runners to fetch and deliver them to the buyer once a deal was done. So we put some effort into identifying the runners and finding the stash sites. We also looked for potential new stash sites and found ways of stopping them from being used in future. A popular site back then was the decorative metal grills that councils placed around the bases of trees. They were easy to lift, no one really looked at them too closely and it was easy to scoop out a hidey-hole underneath. Replacing them with locked covers, decorative gravel or removing them altogether made them unusable.

Analysing how the drugs markets operated made them easier to bring down. There's an old saying that goes, 'Kill the head and the body will die.' But it's equally true that if you pull all the legs off a spider, it can't operate as a spider any more.

5

Virgin Atlantic gives its 'Upper Class' airline passengers a cruet to use during in-flight meals. The salt and pepper shakers look like chunky little airplanes with feet and almost everyone seeing them is gripped with the urge to pop them into their pocket as a cute keepsake ... which you'd think would be a problem. But Virgin didn't see it that way. Their analysis revealed that it was an opportunity rather than a threat.

There is no escaping the fact that Virgin was losing lots of salt and pepper shakers to petty pilfering. An unimaginative company would have simply taken the shakers away or factored the loss into the ticket price, like hotels do with shampoo, or burger chains do with free gifts and 'premiums'. However, when the analysts asked *why* people were taking them home, they found out that it was because (a) they're cute little objects, and (b) people like to show them off to their friends – 'Look, I've travelled Upper Class!' So they cleverly turned the cruet into a cheap and effective marketing tool by embossing 'Pinched from Virgin Atlantic' on the bottom of every single shaker (*and* built the cost into the ticket price, of course). Now everyone who nabs a cruet is advertising not only the fact that they've flown business class, but also that Virgin Atlantic are fun people to fly with.

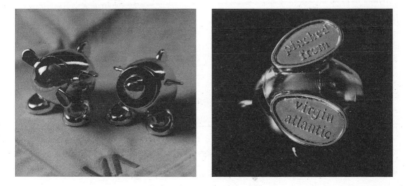

I was first told about this by Rory Sutherland, who you've already heard mention of in this book. Rory – who was voted the 22nd most influential person in the British media in 2010 (and the worst-dressed man in advertising) – says that we should be paying more attention to what he calls 'things with intangible value', and that one of the best ways to create value in the world may not be designing or investing in new things, but looking at things that already exist in a new way. He gives an interesting example of this in one of his very popular TED Talks, when he discusses the Eurostar train link from London to the coast: 'Eurostar wanted suggestions on how to improve the service. Engineers came up with a £6 billion solution that involved laying a whole new set of tracks and faster trains that got you to the coast 40 minutes earlier. It strikes me that it's a pretty unimaginative way of improving a train journey just to make it faster,' he says. 'They could have put on decent wi-fi and had all of the world's top male and female supermodels wandering up and down the carriages serving *Château Pétrus* for the entire journey instead and they'd have saved around £3 billion. I'm pretty sure passengers would see this as an improvement and people would actually be asking for the trains to go slower.'

It's very easy to be seduced by numbers, but data should always be viewed in a human context; it's a measurement of things in the real world that have an impact upon people's lives. If Virgin had only counted their losses in monetary terms, they'd have missed the human story and a great opportunity.[127] Meanwhile, Eurostar didn't take the human element into account and potentially ended up spending far more than they needed to. It's a common problem. As Rory points out, having a large budget often blinds people to cheaper and simpler solutions that might be available: 'Our own sense of self-aggrandisement feels that big important problems need big and, most importantly, expensive solutions attached to them. And yet what behavioural economics shows us time and again, is that what changes our behaviour and what changes our attitudes to things is not actually proportionate to the expense or the amount of force applied.'[128]

In the police service, and certainly during my time in the Problem Solving Unit, we rarely had any budget at all to work with. Therefore, understanding the problem and finding those

---

127 And it's an opportunity that keeps on giving. The human story is so good that Rory told it to me and I'm telling it to you. You may choose to pass it on in turn.

128 You will be hearing a lot more about behavioural economics later in the book. Suffice to say, it's a science based upon research and analysis.

'intangibles' became paramount. In the case of the Scottish football pitches, very few of the assumptions made about the kids were right. Consequently, none of the 'knee-jerk' proposed responses were going to be right. Every problem has unique features that determine the most suitable response and this example reinforces the importance of research and analysis – that you shouldn't start assigning money and resources to solving a problem until you fully understand what the problem is.

You may find that the right solution requires nothing more than a different way of looking at existing circumstances.[129]

---

129 My Problem Solving Unit colleague Neil Henson was a master of this. I was once behind him waiting in line for a carvery lunch when he whispered conspiratorially: 'When you get to the guy carving the meat, don't ask for 'a bit of both' because you'll only get one slice of turkey and one slice of ham. That's what everyone does. What you do is this ... when you get to him, say, "Turkey please", and wait until he's put two slices on your plate. Then say, "Ooh, could I have some ham too?" Trust me. It works.' He was absolutely right. That's the power of analysis.

6: NO ONE EVER GOT SENT ON A LINEAR THINKING COURSE

If everyone is thinking alike, then somebody isn't thinking.

George S. Patton

I think one of the keys to leadership is recognising that everybody has gifts and talents. A good leader will learn how to harness those gifts toward the same goal.

Ben Carson

1

One curious fact I know about the standard Monopoly board is that the orange set, located between Free Parking and Marylebone Station, contains one street that is barely a street at all and another street that doesn't exist.

In 1935 Victor Watson, director of Leeds-based toy manufacturers Waddingtons, and his secretary Marge Phillips, arrived in London to scout out possible locations for the first British version of the game. How they made some of their decisions is still a mystery. Some sets, like the greens (Oxford Street, Regent Street and Bond Street), are obvious as they are all famous shopping streets located right next to each other. But why did they choose railway stations like Marylebone and Fenchurch Street over bigger, busier and much better-known stations like Paddington, Victoria, Euston or Waterloo? And equally puzzling is the aforementioned orange set because there is no obvious link between the three sites – they're not even that close to each other in real life. However, in his book *Do Not Pass Go*, Tim Moore suggests that they are connected by a theme: law and order. The best known of the three is Bow Street in Covent Garden which was, famously, the home of the Bow Street Runners, the forerunners of the modern police. Bow Street Police Station and the adjacent magistrates' court saw many famous names pass through their doors, including Dr Crippen, Casanova, the Kray Twins, Emmeline Pankhurst, General Pinochet and Oscar Wilde, before they both closed for business in 2006.

There was also a magistrates' court, until it closed in 1990, in *Great* Marlborough Street just off Regent Street and opposite the Liberty store and Carnaby Street. The fact that its name was often shortened to 'Marlborough Street Magistrates', by locals is possibly why Vic and Marge got the name wrong on the Monopoly board. There is no Marlborough Street in the whole of London.

The final orange stop is Vine Street, little more than an alleyway off Swallow Street, near Piccadilly Circus. There is almost nothing in tiny Vine Street except the rear entrances to several buildings on Piccadilly. But there used to be a police station there; the oldest operational police station in London, as it happens, and, at one time, the capital's busiest. But like Bow Street Police Station and the two magistrates' courts, Vine Street is now gone – it shut in 1997. So if Tim Moore is right, the curious choices made for the orange Monopoly set all relate to premises that represented law and order in the West End back in 1935. They were all still operational in 1986 – I know this because, in that year, Met Police Commissioner Sir Kenneth Newman sent me to work on the orange set.

He had recently introduced something called Inter-District Transfer (IDT), a scheme supposedly designed to prevent police corruption. His thinking, as I understand it, was that people who work together for too long and become too close could be more inclined to cover each other's mistakes or turn a blind eye to bad behaviour. That may be true – I never saw any research to support the assertion – but Newman decided that 'too long' meant five years and, in the spirit of fairness, stated that IDT should apply to every officer in the Met.[130]

It backfired horribly. Quite apart from upsetting the majority of good, decent cops who were suddenly wrenched away from roles they loved and places they enjoyed working, an enormous amount of useful local intelligence was lost. An officer who had worked at the same station for five years or more, would suddenly find him/herself uprooted and having to start all over again somewhere new. All of the contacts and knowledge that they'd accrued regarding local villains, crime patterns and MOs suddenly became worthless to them and, just as importantly, were no longer available to colleagues on their former divisions.[131] Community ties were similarly broken. And officers who had become specialists in certain fields found themselves in roles where that knowledge wasn't needed while their former team or unit lost a great deal of experience. As problem solving goes, it's a great example of a 'scorched earth' solution badly applied. Unsurprisingly, IDT didn't last for very long. But it lasted long enough to catch me.

I was told that I was being transferred to Vine Street, a place I'd only ever heard of as a name on the Monopoly board. And I'll admit that I was annoyed by the fact that I would now have to commute into central London every day when I'd just got the hang of the London Borough of Hillingdon. But this isn't sour grapes; I enjoyed my time in the West End very much, even if the move did hit me with almost as big a culture shock as had my move from Cornwall to London. Back in suburban, residential Uxbridge my day-to-day work had been reporting thefts and burglaries, arresting shoplifters

---

130 Was the senior command of the Met suggesting that only police officers can be corrupt? It's worth noting that IDT only affected police officers. Support staff were left alone. Probably because they had unions who would fight such a policy (police officers have no union and no job description – so it's illegal for them to strike and they can't 'work to rule'). I'd be interested to hear of any other profession that dictates that people can't work together for longer than five years in case they 'go bad'.

131 This issue was resolved when local knowledge was replaced by Borough Intelligence Units. However, by then IDT was dead.

and dealing with motor vehicle accidents. Plus, of course, all of the community safety and preventative work I'd done. Here at Vine Street, it was street robbery, vice crimes and offences I'd never even heard of like 'van-dragging'.[132] But the bread-and-butter work of West End cops was tackling drunkenness and disorderliness. The night shift in central London – especially at weekends – was a world away from sleepy Hillingdon where everything had stopped at midnight. In Westminster, midnight was when things were just getting started.[133]

Friday and Saturday nights were so busy that we often drafted extra cops into the area. There were usually a few special constables to bolster our numbers as well, and officers on 'rowdyism patrol', an unpopular additional 7pm to 3am shift that borrowed officers from other teams and occasionally pulled them out of their nine-to-five office jobs. SPG officers would sometimes be drafted into the area too.[134]

Our task was to wander around the streets smiling benignly at the drunks and breaking up disturbances. Fights were common but, just recently, they had become more frequent and the injuries more serious. It seemed to me, looking at it with a freshman's eyes, that what was needed was a response that was less a show of force and more a show of smart thinking.

132 Van-dragging meant stealing goods from the back of a truck while the delivery guys were away or not looking. The lack of mobile phones back then meant there was ample getaway time before police were alerted. It's a crime that's been around ever since vehicle deliveries began; the Old Bailey's website tells the story of one Michael William Hickey, one of two men whose MO was to jump up on the tailboard of moving horse drawn delivery carts to steal goods. Hickey was caught in the City Road in 1899 while pilfering mailbags.

133 Community work wasn't really something that West End cops got involved with. The communities within our small patch of London were tight-knit and tended to look after themselves: the Chinese in Chinatown, the vice clubs and sex workers in Soho, the frighteningly rich denizens of Mayfair.

134 The SPG – the Special Patrol Group – was a mobile reserve of police officers who patrolled in 'carriers' (armoured minibuses) that could be called in if extra cops were needed to control a situation, or help with searches or door-to-door enquiries, etc. They were often employed as the first wave of riot control. The SPG was disbanded in 1987 and replaced by the Territorial Support Group (TSG), which still exists today.

2

The term 'groupthink' was first coined by sociologist William H Whyte in 1952 and later defined by Professor Irving L Janis as 'a mode of thinking that people engage in when they are deeply involved in a cohesive in-group, when the members' strivings for unanimity override their motivation to realistically appraise alternative courses of action.'

It doesn't take a major stretch of the imagination to see that groupthink might exist within an organisation like the police.[135] But that isn't necessarily a negative thing. A team works much more efficiently if all of its members are on the same wavelength, and targets are easier to reach if everyone

---

135 I suspect that this was very much in Sir Kenneth Newman's mind when he introduced the IDT scheme. It is true that teams of officers form strong bonds of mutual trust, forged by shared adversity. After all, they often spend more waking hours with their colleagues per week than with their own families. They face dangerous, even life-threatening, situations together and rely on each other to watch their backs. Cops are human, just like you and me, with all of the same needs and frailties, so being excluded from such a group – to be ousted from the 'tribe' – would be upsetting and demoralising. But that still doesn't mean that cops would turn a blind eye to a colleague's misdemeanours any more than someone in any other profession would.

is focused on the same goals.[136] Conformity can lead to faster decision-making too. However, the one big disadvantage of even moderate groupthink is that it can stifle innovation and originality.

The simple way to avoid this is to regularly involve people in your work who think differently. I wasn't immune to the effects of groupthink – no one truly is – and I knew that if I asked only police colleagues for ideas about how to tackle a problem, they would probably come up with solutions based on previous policing experience, legislation, and/or established enforcement tactics. So, instead, I often looked beyond the police service to people who didn't 'think like cops'. It was yet another excellent opportunity to involve the community in policing; people who had a stake in the problem but who weren't hampered by police constraints and perceptions. They often came up with refreshingly new ideas. They could *think outside the box.*

One of my Problem Solving Unit colleagues, Paul Scott, liked to hold problem solving think tanks where people from all sorts of backgrounds were brought together to discuss a range of problems. On occasions, he invited members of youth groups, such as the UK Youth Parliament.[137] At one such meeting we discussed how to improve the lives of people living in a road where soliciting was rife. The problem had existed for so long that the name of the area had become synonymous with prostitution. The people around the table – police officers, people from partner agencies, community advocates, residents, etc. – suggested using plain-clothes

---

136 It was certainly policy during the two World Wars to draft people from the same family and/or town/village into the same regiment as it was believed, quite rightly, that they'd function better together as a unit. Tragically, it also meant that they died together which is why war memorials the length and breadth of the country often record the loss of entire families.

137 I should just say that the young people at this meeting were all over 17 and very mature for their age. The UK Youth Parliament provides opportunities for 11–18 year olds to use their voice in creative ways to bring about social change. It is run by young people for young people and is a brilliant resource. You can find out more at www.ukyouthparliament.org.uk.

officers as 'Johns' to catch the sex workers. They talked about installing hi-res CCTV and brighter street lighting. One creative person wondered whether green street lighting would work as the women would all 'look like monsters' and put the punters off.[138] And then one of the lads from the Youth Parliament said, 'Why don't you just change the name of the road?'

Kids are great at thinking outside the box because they don't yet recognise that the box, or boxes, exist. Changing the name of the road was a blisteringly simple idea and, the more I thought about it, the cleverer it got. Could changing the name wipe out its association with vice? I suspect it might. Would people still visit Carnaby Street if the name was changed? The name resonates with the Swinging Sixties and trendy fashion boutiques but those things have all long since gone. The only reason anyone visits any more is the name.[139]

It was a great idea but, unfortunately, changing a street name is a complex and time-consuming matter; the costs of public consultation, official changes of address, notifying all of the relevant agencies, signage, re-drawing of maps, etc. far outweighed the nuisance caused by a few sex workers. And that's often the problem with thinking outside the box; it's all very well when you're as rich as Croesus, but for most of us, the world is a place of finite resources, constant scrutiny by penny-pinching accounts departments and bosses whose promotion prospects are heightened if they save money. We all have restrictions and limitations placed upon us that dictate what we are able to do and how far we can go; they are all 'boxes' within which we have to work. But that doesn't mean that we're helpless. Thinking outside the box is great for

---

138 It wouldn't work – for reasons we'll discuss in Chapter 10.

139 On the flip-side, locations often take their names with them when they move even though the name is no longer accurate. Covent Garden Flower Market is no longer in Covent Garden (it's moved to Nine Elms and is called 'New Covent Garden'). Some brands move on but their name betrays their past. The Carphone Warehouse chain of stores hasn't sold a car phone in 20 years and despite their vehicle being made by the *Svenska Aeroplan Aaktiebolag* (Swedish Aeroplane Company), most SAAB owners don't own a jet fighter.

generating ideas but it's been my experience that some of the best problem solving happens by thinking *inside the box*.

Do you remember that BBC TV series *Ready, Steady, Cook?* Contestants were told to buy £5 worth of groceries and then celebrity chefs had to make the best meal they could in 20 minutes with their purchases. It meant that the chefs had to be endlessly inventive 'inside the boxes' of time, personal knowledge and the availability of ingredients and equipment. And they often turned out amazing results; necessity really is the mother of invention. I would argue that if you challenged someone to make the best meal they could using any ingredients they liked and with no time limit, they would probably fall back on something familiar which they have cooked many times before. Freed from all restrictions, they'd probably demonstrate far less innovation and take fewer risks.

I often found myself being tasked to solve a problem with nothing, or next to nothing, in terms of resources – but it was still possible to get results, especially if I involved people who thought in a different way from me. The wider the range of personal and work experience I had around the table, the less chance there was of the group becoming fixed upon inflexible 'groupthink-ish' patterns of thinking. And the more ideas we generated, the better chance we had of success. Bringing people together who all think in different ways is what I call smart thinking. And with smart thinking, people can do an awful lot with very little.

3

Back in 1986 I spent a lot of time wondering if there was a smarter way to tackle the West End's drink-related issues. My guiding star, as always, was prevention. It wasn't likely that I could have any impact on people's drinking habits but maybe I could prevent some of the fights, injuries, sexual assaults and other problems that resulted from them.

Research and analysis revealed that there were easily identifiable pinch points. These were places or situations where violence was most likely to flare up due to trigger factors like blocked access routes, queues for limited transport facilities, and overcrowding in the street. Unsurprisingly, cops were either told to patrol these areas or they naturally gravitated towards them. These were also the places that generated the most complaints about noise.[140] But breaking up the groups created animosity. And, because most weren't drunk enough to warrant being arrested, they would drift around the streets like gangs of squiffy ghosts, generating noise complaints. The problem was keeping them calm and quiet while they waited for cabs and night buses to get them out of central London. But how? Police officers have no specific powers to deal with noise. Without any actual offences being committed all we could do was arrest someone for Breach of the Peace. We could hardly gag people ... or could we?

One afternoon I was discussing the issue with a friend, a West End cinema projectionist with no connections to police work at all, when he said, 'Why not give them all gobstoppers? That would shut them up.'[141] It was an interesting idea. An original idea. And it certainly wasn't the kind of solution that a police officer would be likely to suggest at a strategy meeting. I reckoned it was worth a shot.

I used my own money to buy some toffees (they came in big bags and were significantly cheaper than gobstoppers) and, in my first few experiments, I had some success. It's really hard to make a lot of noise when you're chewing a sticky toffee, and offering them out among boozy crowds kept the mood light and made the police seem more friendly and human. Of course, I soon realised that their reaction was probably more to do with the fact that cops were being friendly rather than oppressive or strict – it did make me wonder whether putting

---

140 Although there were far fewer residents in the West End than in outlying boroughs, they still quite reasonably demanded that things quieten down after a certain time. Unfortunately, some clubs didn't kick out until 2am or even later so this was always a problem.

141 Also known in other countries as 'jawbreakers'.

lots of extra police on the streets had actually been seen as provocative and may have inadvertently inspired violence.[142] I didn't get to test that theory but, when I was ordered to stop dishing out toffees after a complaint that someone had lost a filling, I did find that being friendly and helpful while patrolling the pinch points led to fewer fights and complaints of noise. Meanwhile, (and in accordance with the 'Multiple Discovery Hypothesis' mentioned in Chapter 3) people elsewhere had found an even better solution than toffees or gobstoppers.

Photo: Gord Webster

I've never been able to trace the very first time that lollipops and nightclubs met; the first recorded incidence I've found dates from 1999,[143] more than 10 years after my toffee experiments, but it was already good practice by then.

---

142 As I was editing this chapter, the 5p charge for plastic carrier bags was introduced. And it seemed to make a lot of people very angry. But, as a psychologist friend suggested to me, 'They're not cross about 5p. They couldn't care less about 5p. They're kicking back against authority ordering them to do something they've always enjoyed for free.' Brits don't like being told what to do, a subject we'll discuss in greater length in Chapter 9. And it may explain why violence increased when there were more police on the streets.

143 At the Students' Union Bar at the University of London in Bloomsbury.

Certainly, I'd heard stories of their use before 1999 and by 2001 the Devon and Cornwall Constabulary were trying it in Bideford after 'hearing about successes in Canada', so it had already gone global. As local PC Paul Dawe explained to BBC News at the time, 'The people leaving the club are calmer, and there has been a reduction in the fights and the general noise from that particular club.' Just like toffees, it's almost impossible to shout when you've got a lollipop in your mouth.[144] But unlike toffees, there is something childlike and silly about sucking on a lollipop that can't help but reduce tensions. Some have suggested that the calming effect may be Freudian with clubbers unconsciously recalling the first few years of life. Or maybe it's the sugar hit helping to stabilise moods. Whatever the reason, lollipops really do reduce antisocial behaviour and are infinitely preferable to threats of arrest. You could say that carrots, or lollipops, work better than sticks. Boiled sweets are also a popular choice and in 2011, police in Durham started giving out 10,000 of them on the busiest nights of the year. Each sweet, rather like candy *Lovehearts*, bore a message such as 'Quiet please' or 'Shush!'

Other innovations I've seen include door staff giving out water to stop noise and to help people rehydrate,[145] and staff distributing condoms in areas where 'a night on the tiles' was being linked to unwanted pregnancies. The introduction of Street Pastors has also been very effective. These are inter-denominational non-police Christian adults who volunteer to patrol the streets at night in recognisable blue uniforms, helping and caring for people. Their presence is often very calming. At the time of writing there are some 9,000 trained volunteers in 250-plus teams around the UK and the initiative is now spreading to other countries. There are also Street Angels who perform much the same function (and regularly give out lollipops) and many other support organisations and

---

144 And they won't pull your fillings out. Why didn't I think of that?

145 Not so good an idea in the depths of winter though, as a colleague of mine from Cardiff discovered one year when spilled water created small ice slicks outside the clubs.

initiatives, such as 'Love Your Streets' and 'Wash My Pink Jumper', that help people to break out of their binge drinking and antisocial lifestyles.[146] I've also seen schemes in operation, such as the Devon and Cornwall Constabulary's RU2Drunk initiative, where door staff breathalyse people before allowing entry to licensed premises. The idea is to prevent offences (it is illegal to serve alcohol to people who are drunk) and to put people off 'pre-loading' by drinking excess alcohol before they go out. The breathalysers also provide security staff with additional evidence if they decide to eject someone who has had too much.

However, as noble as all of these solutions are, they are tackling the symptoms of the problem and not the causes of bad behaviour, which may possibly be more to do with attitude than how much people have drunk.

Social anthropologist Kate Fox, author of the bestselling book *Watching the English*, asserts that bad behaviour is determined predominantly by cultural rules and norms. In a series of carefully controlled experiments, she gave people placebos instead of booze and found that the subjects exhibited the same kinds of behaviours that they'd have displayed if they'd been given alcohol. As she told BBC Radio 4's *Four Thought* programme: 'To put it very simply, when people think they are drinking alcohol, they behave according to their cultural beliefs about the behavioural effects of alcohol.' She points out that there are plenty of other societies – many of which drink far more than we

---

146 There are also culturally-focused groups like the Shomrim that patrol predominantly Jewish areas and deal with bad behaviour or breaches of religious etiquette among young Jews. However, when a group starts to 'police' people from outside of their culture, it becomes an issue, especially if the people concerned are not breaking UK laws. In recent years, so-called 'Muslim Patrols' or 'Sharia Patrols' have appeared; groups of men who confiscate alcohol without authority, tell women to 'cover up', abuse gay people and deface what they see as obscene adverts (such as women in underwear). Their actions have been condemned by many Muslim organisations, such as the Ramadhan Foundation and the East London Mosque, which campaign for peaceful co-existence among communities. Five men were arrested in January 2013 as part of an investigation into the patrols and three were given jail sentences.

do in the UK – where drinking is not associated with bad behaviour.[147] 'Our beliefs about the effects of alcohol act as self-fulfilling prophecies – if you firmly believe and expect that booze will make you aggressive, then it will do exactly that,' says Fox. 'In fact, you will be able to get roaring drunk on a non-alcoholic placebo. And our erroneous beliefs provide the perfect excuse for antisocial behaviour. You can blame the booze – 'it was the drink talking', 'I was not myself', and so on.'

Fox is adamant that it's possible to change our drinking culture and she's conducted further experiments that appear to support her assertion. 'Even when people are very drunk, if they are given an incentive (either financial reward or even just social approval), they are perfectly capable of remaining in complete control of their behaviour – of behaving as though they were totally sober,' she says. 'Alcohol education will have achieved its ultimate goal, not when young people in this country are afraid of alcohol and avoid it because it is toxic and dangerous, but when they are, frankly, just a little bit bored by it.'

If Kate Fox is right, maybe we just need to think about the alcohol problem in a different way.

4

In 1999 Dr Edward de Bono, often hailed as the father of lateral thinking, famously suggested that conflict in the Middle East could be solved by Marmite; not by bombs or diplomacy or religion, but by a thick, brown, yeasty paste that you spread on your toast. A lack of zinc, he explained, makes men aggressive and short-tempered. Yeasty products are rich in zinc but the majority of bread eaten in the Middle East is

---

147 As a nation, we're not even in the Top 10. According to the World Health Organisation, Belarus, Moldova, and Lithuania top the chart with average annual consumptions of over 15 litres of pure alcohol per person per year. The Belarus average is 17.5 litres while the UK average is around 11.6.

unleavened. Therefore, Marmite would be a way of boosting yeast intake.[148]

This is a story I've been told many times as an example of creative thinking, of 'thinking outside the box'. And, if we're to believe the hyperbole on the webpages and brochures of companies offering problem solving training, you can't solve problems without it. This may be true. However, what isn't true is that creative thinking has any bigger part to play in problem solving than any other type of thinking. Many problems can be solved despite having crushing limitations placed upon creativity, and some problems can be solved with little or no creative thinking involved at all.

Take Hospital-Acquired Infections (HAIs) as a good example. These account for a large number of deaths – 99,000 per year in the USA alone (making it the fourth most common cause of death nationally), even though 30–50 per cent of HAIs are entirely preventable and may be eliminated by simply enforcing tougher hygiene regimes. The Mayo Clinic recently published the results of a study in which it showed that 'consistent daily cleaning of all high-touch surfaces with a spore-killing bleach disinfectant wipe' had substantially reduced the incidence of superbug *Clostridium difficile* infection at a hospital in Minnesota. 'The goal was to reduce hospital-acquired *C. difficile* infection rates in two of our highest-incidence units by 30 per cent,' explained lead investigator Robert Orenstein. 'Our data shows we far exceeded that. When the study concluded, one unit had gone 137 days without a hospital-acquired *C. difficile* infection.' There's no creative thinking involved here – just discipline,

---

148 Zinc deficiency causes a number of health issues including a rise in blood copper levels that can lead to hyperactivity and schizophrenia. A number of clinical reports have found a strong relationship between violence and abnormal zinc and copper imbalances.

routine and maybe a *soupçon* of understanding about how to motivate people to do the right thing.[149]

Here's another example: in World War II, US paratroopers had a problem with the fact that, allegedly, one in twenty chutes failed in some way. The solution was to require the packers and inspectors to regularly jump out of airplanes using parachutes chosen at random from the store. The quality of packing then rose to 100 per cent and stayed there. 'The packers are all jumpers,' explained one NCO to *Stars and Stripes* magazine: 'We try to have each man jump once a month. That's a pretty good way to keep them honest on the tables.'[150]

And here's another. You may not have heard of Dr David Nalin. Or Dr Richard Cash. Or Dr Norbert Hirschhorn. Most people haven't. And yet, they have saved an estimated 50 million lives between them. There should be statues of them on every continent. All three doctors were working in Bangladesh in the mid-1960s during a cholera epidemic in which 40 per cent of all untreated people were dying. Attempts had been made – notably by Doctors Robert Phillips and David Sachar – to find a way of replacing expensive intravenous rehydration therapy with something affordable that could be taken orally. Somehow, they needed to get water and salts into the body to counter the fatal dehydration caused by disease. But giving people the level of salts they needed orally could, perversely, cause vomiting and further dehydration. What Nain, Cash and Hirschhorn worked out

---

149 Hand hygiene improved 100 per cent at Cedars-Sinai Medical Center after the hospital started using pictures of the bacteria found on the palm prints of medical staff as screensavers. A more subtle approach can be tried using a lemon scent in the air. The association with cleanliness is so strong that it can encourage a 10–15 per cent increase in hand washing. Copper door handles and touch surfaces work too as copper and copper alloys are antimicrobial.

150 I recently found a similar example in Dave Trott's book *Predatory Thinking*, where he reveals that the flight attendants who check baggage for the El Al airline have to travel on the same plane as the baggage they've checked. It's one of the reasons why El Al has such a strong reputation for safety; the staff literally bet their lives on the quality of their work.

was that, by adding glucose, salts could be more effectively absorbed through the intestinal wall so smaller, safer amounts could be used. Dedicated analytical work provided the right solution. And by widely publicising the results of their studies and the proportions of each chemical to use, ordinary people could easily make up solutions using ingredients found in the home. Medical journal *The Lancet* has described Oral Rehydration Therapy (ORT) as 'potentially the most important medical advance of the twentieth century' and UNICEF has stated that no other medical innovation of the century prevented so many deaths over such a short period of time and at such little cost.[151]

Ironically, anyone who thinks that creative thinking is the only kind of thinking you need to solve problems is not thinking very creatively.

A sudden, unexpected and left-field idea seems so much more exciting than one that's been arrived at by slow, methodical research and testing, but it doesn't necessarily follow that 'unexpected' and 'left-field' is a guarantee of success. Creative thinking is important but don't put all of your eggs in one basket; think about other types of thinkers and what they can bring to the problem.

If it seems that I'm being harsh on creative thinking, then I'm not explaining myself clearly. I'm considered a creative thinker myself, but I know for a fact that I could never have solved many of the problems I was asked to look at without surrounding myself with people who think very differently from me: tactical and strategic thinkers, analytical and critical thinkers, practical and emotional thinkers, and more.

---

151 The World Health Organisation (WHO) reports that diarrhoeal disease is the second leading cause of death in children under five, and is responsible for killing around 760,000 children every year. UNICEF produces and distributes around 500 million rehydration sachets a year, each costing less than 10p each. Education programmes are also showing mothers in developing countries how to make up the life-saving solution at home using household ingredients.

Photo: Pexels

Let's go back to Edward de Bono's Marmite idea. It's a great creative insight, but how do you get an entire male population to change their eating habits?[152] You use smart thinking.

An analytical thinker could test other commonly-eaten foods and work out which could have their zinc levels increased without changing appearance or flavour. A strategic thinker would be able to work out the logistics of getting hold of the ingredients and transporting them to where they are needed. A persuasive thinker could work on convincing politicians and manufacturers to increase zinc levels in commonly-bought foods. A critical thinker would anticipate pitfalls and blockages, and an emotional thinker could work with a behavioural thinker to consider the 'hearts and minds' aspect; how to persuade people to accept a slight change to their diet that will benefit them all.

My oldest friend, a chap named Huw Williams, has been working as an advertising creative for over 30 years. He told me: 'There's a phrase – *linear thinking* – that gets used as a catchall for people who aren't predominantly creative thinkers and I think it's very insulting. It makes that kind of person

---

152 I wonder if it wouldn't spark a new conflict between the 'love it' and 'hate it' factions?

sound somehow one-dimensional. You never hear of anyone being sent on a linear thinking course, do you? That's because it doesn't exist. Everyone is creative to some degree but some people are predominantly creative so they end up in creative jobs. Meanwhile, brilliantly strategic people become project managers or military leaders or TV producers, and naturally emotional and empathic thinkers become counsellors, life-coaches, nurses and therapists. They are, arguably, much more important jobs than mine. It's all very well us creatives coming up with ideas, but someone has to ground those ideas in reality.'

He also points out that some of the best ideas don't come from creatives but from people who bring a new perspective to bear on a problem. He points to people like Kevin May who owns the Sticks Agency in Seattle as an example. 'He holds "brainstorm salons" where he invites groups of smart people along who have nothing to do with the brand campaigns they will be talking about,' he explains. 'He has a group of about 200 people he can pick from, all with very different knowledge and skills from each other. He says it's amazing what an engineer has to say about lingerie or an artist has to say about accountancy problems. You just get amazingly different insights and reframed approaches; other ways of looking at problems that people immersed in the problem would never come up with because they're blinkered by being too close.'

Believe me, if the zombie apocalypse happens tomorrow it will be the strategists and the tacticians and the other 'doers' who will survive, while the creatives like me and Huw and Kevin huddle in a corner trying to remember how Six Hat Thinking works and wondering whether Marmite will placate the ravenous undead.

5

In February 2014, the government announced that it would be banning deep discount supermarket booze.

However, even the Home Office's own impact assessment acknowledged that this is only likely to hit 1.3 per cent of all alcohol sales. And Eric Appleby, chief executive of Alcohol Concern, dismissed the move: 'The idea that banning below-cost sales will help tackle our problem with alcohol is laughable,' he told the *Daily Telegraph*. 'It's confusing and close to impossible to implement.' Whether it works or not, it's now over two years later and it hasn't happened yet.

Meanwhile there are plenty of other suggestions being put forward as ways to reduce consumption. One is to subtly reduce the alcohol content of popular drinks or to tax stronger drinks at a higher rate. Another is to encourage a return to using pubs by removing the legal requirement to add 20 per cent VAT to food and drink. At present pubs cannot compete with supermarket prices. There are also suggestions to raise the drinking age to 21, like it is in

America and some other countries, to ban alcohol marketing, or even to legalise drugs such as cannabis and ecstasy as alternatives to booze.[153]

In 2009, Dr David Nutt, former chair of the government's Drugs Advisory Committee,[154] published a report in which he ranked 20 drugs – based on their negative effects on users and society. Tobacco and cocaine were described as being equally harmful, while ecstasy and LSD, were listed among the least damaging. Most controversially, alcohol was reported to be more dangerous than heroin. As he told the BBC at the time: 'In Britain today, alcohol is a leading cause of death in men between the ages of 16 and 50. It has overtaken traffic accidents, suicide and cancer. It is, therefore, the most harmful drug there is in terms of life expectancy, family disruption and road traffic accidents.' Meanwhile, as he pointed out in an article for the *Journal of Psychopharmacology*, statistically ecstasy is less dangerous than horse riding, which causes around 10 deaths and more than 100 road traffic accidents a year. He wrote that the risks of horse riding showed that society 'does not adequately balance the relative risks of drugs against their harms'. It's estimated that there are around 1.6 million problem drinkers in England, more than five times the number of problem drug-users. Yet we spend just £91 million

---

153 The legalisation of cannabis could possibly result in a reduction in road deaths. Since Colorado decriminalised cannabis use in 2012, there has been a dramatic drop in road fatalities to a record low. Other states have reported similar effects. However, it's too early to say whether the decriminalisation has had a positive or negative impact. For example, the number of drivers testing positive for drugs has dramatically risen, something that anti-drugs campaigners are keen to point out. However, as the test looks for evidence of cannabis use rather than evidence of intoxication, the statistics aren't, at the moment, much help. Evidence of cannabis use can remain in the bloodstream long after any effects of the drug have worn off. It will be interesting to see how things develop. Watch this space.

154 He was famously sacked after disagreeing with the government's decision to re-classify cannabis as a restricted drug. He argued that alcohol consumption would drop by 25 per cent if we legalised cannabis and that the cost of policing cannabis use was only £500m a year compared with the £6bn a year bill for policing the use of alcohol.

per year on treatments for alcoholism, compared with the £2 billion we spend on drug-users.

Nutt's solution to the problem, therefore, is to create a safe, harmless, non-addictive alternative to alcohol; a drug that gives the user the same effects as drinking but which doesn't cause any medical side effects. An obvious parallel here is the electronic cigarette as a replacement for tobacco. It delivers a nicotine hit but doesn't generate cancer-inducing toxins, or cause passive smoking or litter. But Dr Nutt has gone one better: he says that it's possible to create a 'sober-up pill' that cancels out the effects of his alcohol alternative. You simply pop a pill at the end of the evening – or maybe suck on a suitably treated lollipop – and there's no more hangovers, no more drunken drivers, no more lost days at work, no more expense to the NHS and, maybe, just maybe, fewer crimes.[155] 'It all boils down to the question of what we are trying to do when we make drugs illegal,' he explains. 'We should be trying to reduce harm for people, but in order to decide on whether to make something illegal we need to have a good appreciation of what the relative harms are.'[156]

So how close is the idea to reality? The answer is … pretty close. Nutt has already isolated the appropriate chemicals and says that they just need 'tweaking' to make them more palatable; at present, adding them to beer and wine in place of alcohol would adversely affect the flavour. However, once

155 If you think this is a city problem, think again. The aforementioned RU2Drunk scheme was part of a package of initiatives aimed at tackling alcohol-related violence in supposedly 'sleepy' rural Cornwall, where 30.6% of all violent crime reported in the 12 months prior to the initiative involved alcohol.

156 The current UK legal status of certain drugs does not equate in any way to the evidence and risk assessments of the relative harms they do. If they did, alcohol would be illegal. Incidentally, the history of why cannabis was made illegal is complex and includes a degree of apathy, misunderstanding, corporate greed (anti-hemp lobbyists) and some small degree of racism (especially in the USA). One thing I've become sure of is that there were no concrete medical or crime-related grounds for criminalising its use. But don't take my word for it. Research the topic yourselves and draw your own conclusions.

he gets it right, he plans to release it in the form of a non-alcoholic cocktail. 'The intoxicating effect of the first three "doses" will be cumulative,' he says, 'but subsequent shots will have no effect.' Once you reach a certain plateau of 'drunkenness', you stay there.

Like any creative idea that has worth, it'll be the strategic thinkers and the analytical thinkers and the emotional thinkers who will help Nutt's idea to become a reality. Governments will need to be persuaded that it is safe. And so will drinks companies. 'The drinks companies know that their product kills [almost] three million people a year. They would like a safer alcohol, but [...] we need to incentivise them to change,' says Nutt. 'What we need is for the public to say "we need this", and for governments to encourage it as a healthy substitute. The tobacco industry eventually came to accept the worth of electronic cigarettes. The alcohol industry will come to accept that an alcohol substitute has a place too.'

It's curious to think that someone who was conceived during a drunken leg-over in 1986, back when I was stationed at one of the orange stops on the Monopoly board, will be 30 now. They'll have never known anything other than the ubiquity of booze, in their paper shops, in their petrol stations and in their supermarkets. They'll have grown up in a world where employers look through photo albums full of drunk selfies on social media platforms like *Facebook* and make decisions about whether or not to employ them; a world of reality TV shows where drunk people are displayed as 'entertainment', where liquor advertising is all about having fun, fun, fun, and where doing the job they're paid to do somehow means that they 'deserve' a bottle of wine at the end of the day.[157] The local

---

157 An idea that was invented by the brewery trade in the 1980s and promoted through commercials. A 2010 Australian road safety campaign lampooned the 'You deserve it' beer commercials with a narrative over scenes of people having fun after work and then drinking and driving. 'After a hard day's work – you deserve it,' it said 'Catching up with your mates – you deserve it. Grabbing a bite with the missus – you deserve it.' You then see a driver being breathalysed by a police officer and the narrator says: 'But drive after a few ... you deserve it.'

pub that their parents drank in may well have closed down and been converted into a small supermarket where, ironically, it sells beer at a far cheaper price than the pub could ever have done. In some supermarkets a bottle of beer is now cheaper than a bottle of water.

But maybe, if people like David Nutt get their way, their kids will grow up in a world where alcohol is something that 'they did in the olden days'; back when the silly sods really didn't know any better. Of course, replacing one drug for another won't make any difference to the bad behaviour if, as Kate Fox suggests, it's actually the social norms of the British that are the problem. It may be that the answer lies in us adopting a more mature attitude to alcohol like they have in many other countries.

What I do know for sure is that you will always increase your chances of solving a problem if you surround yourself with people who view the world in different ways from you and to each other. It's my firm belief that involving the community in policing – not just homeowners and tenants, but shopkeepers, schoolkids, doctors, college students, postal workers, teachers, bus drivers, beauticians and anyone who can bring fresh eyes to a problem – will result in smarter thinking. Thinking outside the box and inside the box will maximise what you can do with those ideas. And they will help to ensure that a lack of resources won't necessarily bog you down.

Like the staff at Strathclyde Fire and Rescue HQ who solved the problem of their officers not realising that they were dangerously dehydrated by putting pee colour charts above the urinals and on the inside of cubicle doors (for female staff) to remind the firefighters to self-monitor; the chart helps them to identify how hydrated they are.[158]

---

158 The hydration charts go from a clear bar to a dark yellow/orange bar but some wags had added extra levels above. A green bar said 'see doctor'. A red bar said 'pox'. And a black bar said, simply, 'Guinness'. Interestingly, mediaeval doctors used a similar technique to diagnose illness by comparing colour, smell and even taste (urp) against a 'urine wheel' colour chart. The wheel consisted of 20 colours ranging from 'white as wellwater' to 'ruddy as pure intense gold' and lastly 'black as very dark horn'. Did they have Guinness back then? You can get your very own pee colour chart at www.urinecolours.com. No, really.

Or the groundskeeper at a London public gardens who discouraged drinkers from hanging around near closing time by setting off the irrigation system a quarter of an hour before locking up, soaking the lawns and benches.

Or retired cop Bill Angus who – fed up with people regularly doing speeds of 70mph or more on the 30mph road outside his house in Newbottle, near Sunderland – built a bird box, painted it fluorescent yellow ('to attract blue tits') and attached it to a pole where it would be clearly visible to road users. The speeding soon stopped and, to Bill's delight, he got the blessing of the authorities. A spokesman for the Northumbria Safer Roads Initiative said: 'If he wants to have a bird box that looks like a speed camera then that's up to the gentleman concerned. If it's slowing traffic down, as far as we're concerned, it's a good thing'.

Or a colleague of mine who worked on a troubled housing estate and who started a word-of-mouth rumour that DNA samples were being taken from urine and drugs paraphernalia left in stairwells in order to identify the culprits. Within just a few days, the stairwells were clean and remained so.

Smart thinking means that you can do a lot with very little and, sometimes, even with nothing at all.

7: LOBSTERNOMICS

*If you have an apple and I have an apple and we
exchange these apples then you and I will still each
have one apple. But if you have an idea and I have
an idea and we exchange these ideas, then each of
us will have two ideas.*

George Bernard Shaw

*Five guys on the [basketball] court working together
can achieve more than five talented individuals
who come and go as individuals.*

Kareem Abdul-Jabbar

1

In February 2015 I was at Euston station in London waiting
for a train to take me to Stoke-on-Trent to give a talk. This
book was very much on my mind as the talk I was giving,
called 'The Skeptical Bobby', was all about policing and
problem solving. It was going to be the ninety-eighth time I'd
performed the talk in 14 months so I was always looking for
new material to freshen up my slide show.[159]

---

159 I do realise that some of you will be throwing your arms in the air in despair at
this 'Americanisation' of sceptical. However, the global science-based scepticism
movement favours the K spelling because in most words that start with 'sc',
the C is silent (e.g. science, scene, scent, sceptre, scissors etc.) so there's
less ambiguity about pronunciation for non-English speakers. This is reflected in
publications like *The Skeptic* magazine (British) and the worldwide *Skeptics In The
Pub* network of social groups.

A few days previously I'd photographed these bins (below) at Oxford train station which, like the bins at many stations these days, consist of transparent bags so that staff can see what's in them.

Euston, I noted, also had transparent bins but they were of a different, rigid design. Like the Oxford bin bags they were introduced as a way to prevent terrorist attacks. Thankfully, terrorism is very low on the list of things that are likely to kill you, especially if you don't live in a major city.[160] But that doesn't mean we should drop our guard. We don't have to live

---

160 At the risk of sounding controversial, terrorists are not terribly good at what they do, and the police and security services are very good at foiling them. That's why there are so few incidents. Since 2000, 52 people have died in terrorism incidents on UK soil (all on one day – July 7th, 2005). In that same 15-year period around two million Brits have been killed by cancer and over 30,000 have been killed on the roads. So which should you be most worried about – terrorists, that cigarette you're smoking, or your car?

in constant fear but keeping an eye open for suspicious people and objects is a good thing.[161] There was a time when there were no litter bins in central London because of the frequency of IRA bomb attacks but this created a massive litter problem. Transparent bins are a good compromise; plus they flip two fingers to the terrorists by saying; 'You're not having an impact on our lives – we win'.

As I was thinking about this, I photographed the litter bin. I figured that it would be useful if I decided to write about counter-terrorism measures and whether things like see-through bins and postboxes (they have them at some airports) are an effective deterrent or not. And almost immediately I realised that I'd made a big mistake. The figure in black you can see approaching from the right is one of a brace of British Transport Police officers, both heavily armed with machine guns and tasers, who walked up to me and said: 'Excuse me sir, may we have a word with you?'

161 In 2001, *Police*, the journal of the Police Federation, reported that a suspicious box was found outside a Territorial Army centre in Bristol. The TA called the police, who called an army bomb-disposal unit, which blew up the box – only to discover that it was full of leaflets on how to deal with suspicious packages. Irony klaxon.

They were, it must be said, very polite and professional and it was an interesting experience for me, as an ex-cop, to be on the receiving end of a police stop. After the formalities were complete I revealed that I used to be a police officer myself and asked why I'd been stopped – as everyone is entitled to do. 'A member of the public notified us of a man acting suspiciously,' said one of the officers. 'You were photographing the bins and CCTV cameras.' There were indeed CCTV cameras above the bin and they were in the periphery of a couple of my photos. I hadn't actually been photographing them but, even if I had, I couldn't quite understand why photographing them 'looked suspicious'. I showed the officers the photos I'd taken and told them I wanted to use the photos in my talks and possibly in a book.[162] I also offered to delete them if there was anything in them that they felt was a security risk. But they were quite happy with the photos and went on their way.

As I sat on my train, rattling towards The Potteries, I deconstructed the incident in my mind. Did I look like a potential terrorist? I'm overweight, blonde, beardy and over 50, and I was wearing a *Wacky Races* T-shirt. Not, you'll agree, the 'mad bomber' stereotype and not exactly hard to spot either. For a short time, I admit, I felt a little annoyed at being viewed as 'a suspicious person'. But then I looked at the whole incident more objectively and asked myself, what does a terrorist look like? There may have been a spike in recent years of young Arabic and South Asian men committing these atrocities but, not so long ago, it was middle-aged Irishmen doing it in the name of the Provisional IRA and the Real IRA. And then there were the unpredictable terrorists like neo-Nazi militant David Copeland who, in 1999, set off a series of nail bombs in London, killing three people and injuring 139 others. Or what about the 'Unabomber', Theodore 'Ted' Kaczynski, who, between 1978 and 1995, engaged in a nationwide bombing campaign across the USA, killing three

---

162 If they'd asked to see the photos it would have constituted a search and created more paperwork for them. I made their lives a little easier by volunteering to show them – I have been in their shoes, after all.

people and injuring 23 others. Annoyingly, he looks a bit like me. The fact is, there is no terrorist 'type' against which to make comparisons.[163] A terrorist could look like you, me or anyone. And then I realised something else; it was a member of the public that had spotted me – not CCTV, not police officers and not the staff of the train station – and they had alerted the authorities.

In the wake of the January 2015 *Charlie Hebdo* shootings in Paris, Prime Minister David Cameron promised tighter security controls and increased surveillance. But, as several social commentators and security experts pointed out at the time, we already have mass surveillance in the UK.[164] France also has mass surveillance, and ID cards too, but it didn't stop the shootings. It just allowed us to watch the events in horror. Ray Corrigan, a senior lecturer at the Open University, has pointed out that it would take 20 intelligence and security staff to properly monitor a single suspect 24/7. Meanwhile, any kind of serious surveillance would mean figuring out where to find the 1.2 billion staff and associated resources you'd need to keep tabs on the UK's population. CCTV isn't the answer.

But what if we all worked together and kept an eye out for each other, like the anonymous member of the public did when they saw me acting suspiciously? That's 60 million pairs of eyes, a huge resource by anyone's reckoning. It's yet another example of how we could all be involved in policing. If the police and the community work together in partnership the bad guys don't have a chance. And what if public agencies

---

163 Another example here of our natural tendency to form patterns which, if unchecked, can become prejudices.

164 A 2013 study by the British Security Industry Association (BSIA) revealed that there are maybe six million CCTV cameras operating in Britain – that's one camera for every 11 persons – the majority of which are under private control. The police and local authorities control around 70,000 of them – less than two per cent of the overall number. The fact is that no one seems to know the precise number and what they are used for. It's been estimated by the UK Surveillance Commissioner that someone living in a British city will be filmed by CCTV cameras around 300 times per day.

shared information with each other to help to root out wrongdoers and prevent crime from happening? Wouldn't working together in partnership be a powerful way to solve crime and other social problems?

2

Imagine living in a place where you daren't go out after dark, where people engage openly in drug deals and drug taking, where drunks try to molest you and women offer you sex for money so that they can feed their drug habit. Now imagine this place is the street where you live and the drunks are your neighbours, the sex worker lives opposite and the drug dealer lives next door. Every few nights your windows get egged and local kids regularly set fire to your wheelie bin and push it down the street. Life is hell.

Just a few years ago, this could quite easily have been a resident describing their life in a street called Welland Crescent in the village of Elsecar, South Yorkshire. It was built in the 1950s as temporary housing for Scottish miners who had migrated to Barnsley to work in the local coal mines but, when the mines closed, the Scots returned home leaving 120 properties ripe for use as social housing. Over a period of time the houses were bought by private landlords, some less responsible than others, and a few houses soon fell into an extremely poor state of repair, while others became derelict and suffered frequent arson damage. Fly-tipping and dog fouling became endemic, along with graffiti and vandalism. It was known that some residents had broken into their electricity and gas supplies by bypassing their meters, and very few TV licences were registered in the area. If you visited Welland Crescent, you were four times more likely to become a victim of crime than in adjacent areas. The crescent began to grow the reputation of being a 'no-go area' for members of the public and the name of Welland Crescent became synonymous with criminal activity and disorder.

Posts on community and local newspaper websites read like the script of a Ken Loach drama. 'There are houses that have no windows or roofs and have been repeatedly set on fire,' wrote one resident. 'It is terrible to live with this outside of your own home. We are fed up of being intimidated by youths and the fear of our property being vandalised. The village of Elsecar is considered by some to be prestigious. They have obviously not visited Welland Crescent.' Another wrote, 'There is rubbish everywhere, not to mention the burning of wheelie bins, and a strange woman that walks around in a bra and jogger bottoms who is obviously on drugs.' The general sentiments of the decent residents were summed up by someone called, appropriately, 'FedUp': 'When my tenancy has finished I am running a mile.' The police were frequent visitors to the crescent but, as soon as they were called away to deal with other matters, the problems came straight back.

In 2007 the decent folk of Welland Crescent formed a Neighbourhood Watch group, nicknamed the 'Welland Rangers', and began to keep diaries of incidents in the crescent and passed the information on to local police officers and the council. It was the start of a partnership that quickly grew and grew, bringing in more and more agencies as the problems of Welland Crescent, and the causes of those problems, were identified.

Two years later, in October 2009, all of this good work culminated in 'Operation Bagley', a partnership of 12 agencies – including the Police, the Fire Service, the local NHS Trust, Housing Department, Social Services and others – who descended upon the street over three consecutive days and dealt with all of its problems in one massive hit. Having gathered as much intelligence as they could over 12 months, and in a perfectly coordinated effort, the police executed warrants and made arrests, issued fixed penalty notices, and seized contraband including two vehicles and 7,500 cigarettes; the power companies found nine fraudulently 'cracked' electricity meters and either made them secure or replaced them; the Fire Service fitted 42 smoke alarms and made 101 people safer; the TV licensing people issued summonses; the Education Authority identified truanting children and the Police and Youth Services dealt with misbehaving kids and established engagement programmes. Benefit fraudsters were caught, troubled families were referred to Social Services and medical treatment and other support was given to those who needed it. Most impressive of all, the local Waste Management team took away over 100 tons of refuse in a convoy of trucks and bulldozers. Approximately 1,000 man-hours were invested in the three-day blitz on Welland Crescent, but the result was that the decent citizens got their street back. It was now up to them to decide if they wanted to keep it that way.

Following the operation, crime dropped immediately by 43 per cent (there was a 100 per cent decrease in arson – a particular problem in the area), and 999 and other calls for service fell by 58 per cent. Residents reported that they now felt safer in their homes. A follow-up operation, called 'Bagley II', took place in April 2010 to check that things had not regressed to their previous state. They hadn't. Constant vigilance is needed as a handful of people have invariably reverted to their old ways. Changing the bad habits of a lifetime doesn't happen overnight.

In October 2011, a mini 'Bagley' took place where staff from South Yorkshire Police, the Fire Service, the council's environmental regulatory services, dog wardens, addiction support workers and local volunteers organised a clear-up of litter, advised people about benefit entitlement, and offered counselling for those with addiction issues. As one of the organisers, PC Paul Davies, told local newspapers: 'It's so easy for people to say "It's a run-down area", but you can't just forget about it and leave it. There are a lot of good people here. We have to bring the standard up on the street and things are improving. Even some of the bad people appreciate what's being done for them.'

The story of Welland Crescent is no fairy tale with an unrealistically happy ending. It remains an area of high unemployment and bleak prospects, and has higher than the national average level of drug and alcohol dependent residents. However, things really are improving. The price of a three-bedroom semi-detached house in the area is now four to five times higher than it was six years ago and prestigious new houses costing over £200,000 are being built in cul-de-sacs off the Crescent. Crime rates have continued to fall but, although the street still has its problems, it's no longer seen as the unsolvable problem that it once was.

Whichever way you look at it, the more people who are looking out for you and the place you call home, the better. A functional community enjoys less crime, less disorder and fewer disturbances. And the nicer your environment, the safer you feel. Just ask the residents of Welland Crescent. Or the people of Lingard Road, Manchester where Jay Crawford and his neighbours happily pull each other's wheelie bins off the street. Or Brighton where people involved in Zocalo all look out for each other's houses when they're empty.

Persuading people to take a stake in crime prevention and community safety is always easier if you can demonstrate to them that they will benefit from doing so. All of the agencies who took part in Operation Bagley needed to understand that it was in their best interests to be involved and 12 months of evidence gathering provided what was needed to convince them. Much later in my career, during my Problem Solving Unit days, we would coin the phrase; 'Who shares your problem?' for exactly these kinds of circumstances. Identifying the people and organisations that have a stake in making a situation better – even if they are sometimes unaware of it – is vital if you want to have the maximum impact on that problem.

It can lead to the most fruitful, and surprising, partnerships.

3

If you ask schoolboys what they want to be when they grow up, you won't often hear them say 'a fisherman'.[165] I grew up in west Cornwall and I knew kids whose dads crewed the beam trawlers that came and went from nearby Newlyn Harbour. They would go away to sea for a week to 10 days at a time, with just a couple of days in port before setting out again. Even when they were home, the work didn't end. The fish had to be unloaded and sent to market, there were nets to repair and boats to be cleaned and maintained. And once back at sea, the crews worked three hours on, three hours off, for the duration of each trip – the marine radio their only link to their loved ones. Even today, mobile phones often can't get a signal when out at sea. Every three hours the nets were hauled in and the fish were cleaned, gutted and frozen. In-between hauls, the crew ate, played cards or tried to catch a couple of hours sleep before going through the same routine all over again.

Once a month the crews would meet in a local pub to share out the spoils. Once the cost of fuel, food and other necessities had been subtracted, all that most of them were left with was something approximating a minimum wage. And these were people working in one of the world's most dangerous professions. They didn't have pensions, they didn't get sick pay and when the weather was too bad to put to sea, no one earned any money except the publicans. The fishermen's kids were always the poorest kids at my school.

Some 40 years on and things are, if anything, worse for the fishermen. According to Dr Stephen Roberts of Oxford University, they top the league for work-based mortality. 'They have to contend with unique occupational and weather-related hazards,' he explains. 'These, together with

---

165 I'm not using the terms 'schoolboy' or 'fisherman' in any pejorative or sexist sense here. The industry was, and still is, dominated by men due to the intense physical nature of the job. And because women probably have more sense.

economic pressures, often make this industry unreceptive to the introduction of safety measures.' According to his analysis of official cause of death (at work) statistics between 1976 and 1995, fishermen are over 50 times more likely to die at work than most of the rest of us. Around 103 per 100,000 fishermen die on the job compared to a national average of 2 per 100,000.[166] Their insurance premiums are outrageously high.

Photo: Dawn Colgan

Life is a little better for the specialist lobster fishermen. Usually working more closely to shore, they do, at least, come home to warm beds most nights. But they face the same quotas, the same restrictions, the same heavily-taxed fuel prices, insurance, mooring fees, weather, rough seas and much more. And, during the 1990s, they faced another potentially disastrous problem when catches off the Cornish coast began

166 And this is a vast improvement on how things used to be. In 1885, a Royal Commission reported that around 10,000 seamen (1 in 63) died at work every year. It was hard to find more up-to-date statistics for UK fishermen but, as an indicator that the problem still exists, I found out that the 2012 fatality rate per 100,000 American fishermen was 121 - even higher than the UK's 1995 figures and despite a reduction in the number of working fishermen

to drastically fall off. Almost immediately, people started looking for someone or something to blame. Was it global warming? Was it pollution? Or were the fishermen taking more lobsters than they should?

Discussions began about how to preserve stocks. In 1994 the minimum size that could be kept and sold was raised to 90mm and a complete ban was placed on landing egg-bearing female lobsters (known as 'berried hens'). But still the numbers dropped and fingers continued to point at the fishermen who, despite doing one of the toughest and most dangerous jobs imaginable, were now also being accused of scuppering their own ailing industry.

The fishermen fought back, pointing out that they could not be the cause as they were themselves an 'endangered species'. As one ex-fisherman said to me, 'We were losing numbers faster than the bloody lobsters.' The Cornish fishing fleet has been in decline for two decades; in Newlyn, once home to the largest fleet in the UK, the number of fishing boats has more than halved since 1985. When the government offered generous terms for decommissioning in the early 1990s, more than 40 owners jumped at the chance. Many boats are old and in desperate need of repair but the industry doesn't generate large enough profits to allow this. There is also a shortage of people to man the boats. The next generation of potential fishermen are more interested in warm offices, computers, pension schemes and having social lives – than in entering one of the most dangerous and demanding professions on earth. 'They go down to the quay and they see these old rust bucket vessels and it must frighten them to death,' Newlyn fish trader Robin Turner told *The Guardian*. 'They look and think to themselves that they don't want to be working on those boats for the next 40 years, and you can't blame them. It's their necks they are putting on the line. The sea doesn't take any prisoners; I attend enough bloody funerals to know that.'

Photo: Si Colgan

In 1971, British fishing vessels landed catches totalling 913,000 tonnes. By 1990 that figure had fallen to 528,000 tonnes. The fishing industry is just a shadow of its former size ... so was it really possible that the shrinking Cornish fleet was responsible for the decline in lobster numbers? Unsurprisingly, it wasn't. The lobster's plight was being caused, in large part, by you and me due to a number of factors including the British obsession with one particular species of fish.

For some reason no one can quite explain, over the past three decades Britons have fallen head over heels in love with cod. Our little island consumes fully one-third of all the cod eaten in the world and 85 per cent of cod caught in European waters.[167] If we ate nothing but fish caught in UK waters, based on current levels of consumption, we would run out on August 3rd each year. The result has been a rapid depletion of cod stocks to the point that strict quotas had to be brought in to protect the species. In 2006, the official quota was just 23,000 tonnes: a 70 per cent reduction on the amount fished in the 1970s. The International Council for the Exploration

---

167 The overwhelming percentage (around 80 per cent) of all fish sold in the UK comes down to just three species: tuna, salmon and cod.

of the Sea has warned for many years that a complete fishing ban is the only way to revive North Sea stocks. And as Mark Kurlansky points out in his excellent book *Cod*, 'It is harder to kill off fish than mammals [because they lay millions of eggs]. But after 1,000 years of hunting the Atlantic cod, we know that it can be done.'

Cod are the vacuum cleaners of the sea and will eat almost anything. More than 150 different species of fish and other organisms have been found in cod stomachs, including clams, cockles, mussels, crabs, lobsters, sea urchins and small fish such as herring, capelin, shad, mackerel and young haddock (researchers have also found such things as jewellery, rope, shoes and, bizarrely, ducks). So, as cod stocks have been crashing due to overfishing, smaller fish like herring have enjoyed a population boom. And this has happened at a time when British people no longer eat these small fish in the huge numbers that they used to. There are billions more small fish than ever before. And guess what small fish eat? The tiny, tasty infant lobsters that form part of the plankton population. By eating too many cod we, the British consumer, have been helping to seal the lobster's fate. And our other activities may also be contributing to their decline. As Cornwall's Sea Fisheries Officer Eddy Derriman explained at the time, 'less than five baby lobsters in every thousand currently survive to adulthood in the wild, and the problems caused by pollution and climate change mean that lobster stocks in Cornwall are only a fraction of what they were.'

For a long time, the people most loudly bemoaning the ever-decreasing numbers of lobsters were the fishermen and environmentalists who, at first glance, appear to be on opposite sides. However, asking the question, 'Who shares your problem?' led to a surprising realisation. There are lots of people out there who want there to be more lobsters; retailers, chefs, restaurateurs and seafood lovers. The people who catch them, sell them, cook them and eat them share the problem. And the more agencies you have onside, the more resources you have to tackle a problem.

Suddenly, a partnership of over 40 agencies – universities,

supermarkets and restaurants, fishmongers, TV chefs and environmentalists among them – came together to save the lobster, albeit for different, and occasionally conflicting, reasons. And the result was the National Lobster Hatchery in Padstow, which opened in 2000.

Photo: Bernie Pettersen

Funded by charitable donations, Cornwall Council and various business partners, the Hatchery's job is to develop new ways to increase lobster numbers. One method, involving local fishermen, is that berried hens, which were traditionally returned to the sea, are now kept in a safe environment until their eggs have hatched. The larvae then have a chance to develop without being eaten and, once they've reached their third moult, they are then large enough and tough enough to be released back into the sea, where they will stand a good chance of seeing off a hungry herring. Since the hatchery was set up, the lobster larvae have been released at regular intervals in batches of hundreds at a time; Over 200,000 juveniles have been released since the Hatchery opened - that's £2 million worth of lobsters. And releases continue to grow with up to 50,000 larvae being released each season. Coincidentally that's around how many visitors the Hatchery gets per year; it has become something of a tourist attraction which regularly attracts school parties and marine biology undergraduates. It also works in partnership with universities to look at nutritional and environmental issues and new academic qualifications in aquaculture have been created. General Manager Dom Boothroyd has stated that: 'We need more space, we need to expand our work and I have a dream that we will become a National Centre for Sustainable Fisheries and Aquaculture.'

Success is already being seen in the lobster pots; in some cases, up to 30 per cent of the catch has to be returned to the sea because they are under-sized. It proves that the young lobsters are surviving and, indeed, thriving, which means that more are reaching adulthood.

And there's good news for the cod industry as well; new analysis in 2015 suggests that North Sea stocks could be back to sustainability levels within 10 years, possibly even five.

Quotas have been drastically slashed to help revive numbers. Meanwhile, retailers, restaurants and fast food outlets are being encouraged to push alternatives like haddock, coley, pollack, hoki and basa, all of which taste very much like cod, or other fish like mackerel, pouting, gurnard or dogfish ('rock cod'). Or a battered sausage now and again, just for a change.

By tackling the causes – reviving the cod stocks and stopping tiny lobsters being eaten by a glut of small fish – and by involving everyone who 'shares the problem' rather than trying to pin the blame on anyone or any one thing, real results are being achieved. Everyone is happy. And, if they were smart enough to realise it, the lobsters would be happy too.

4

Agencies and/or individuals working in partnership can often achieve much more than agencies/individuals working in isolation. As we discussed in the last chapter, having a mixed group of thinkers is useful for generating ideas. But it's also hugely useful when considering how to tackle a problem. Remember the Problem Solving Jigsaw from Chapter 3?

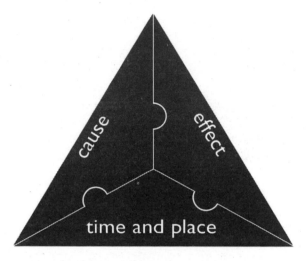

Let's consider, for a moment, a common crime like theft of bicycles, or parts of bicycles. Around 25,000 bicycles are stolen in London every year. It may be many more; a lot of people don't bother to report the crime because of the unlikelihood of getting their bike back. It works out that, nationally, there's one bike stolen every minute and the recovery rate is very poor: some estimates suggest that it's as low as four per cent. There are good reasons for that: firstly, there are no forensics as the items that may bear fingerprints or DNA are the items stolen; secondly, there is usually little or no relationship between the victim and the offender so it's difficult to identify suspects; thirdly, it's a stealthy kind of theft and largely goes unnoticed or unchallenged; and, fourthly, even when the victims do report the crime to police many cannot supply sufficient details to assist in an investigation. Even if the cops do catch the thief, he or she could walk free if the owner can't identify their cycle if it's recovered. At any one time, the Met Police has around 2,000 cycles in storage as lost or possibly stolen property that people either don't claim or cannot identify.

But there are a few things that every cyclist can do to decrease their chances of it happening to them. Firstly, invest in some good bike locks; not some cheap and flimsy rope/chain thing with a tumbler lock because, while they may deter an opportunistic amateur scallywag, they are ridiculously easy to crack. Get the best you can afford and two locks are always better than one; remember that the more obstructions you put in the bad guys' way, the better. And pick a good location, well-lit with plenty of footfall and a good, solid bike rack to attach the bike to.

This person did it right:

These owners didn't:

Property marking is useful too. In Portsmouth in 2003, a multi-agency project led by Hampshire Constabulary called 'Operation Mullion' was put in place to tackle the problems surrounding a particularly troublesome secondary school. Among the aims of the operation was a scheme to reduce bicycle theft. The partnership, which included local media and the council, started a bicycle-marking scheme using ultraviolet pens[168] or acid etching, ran theft prevention roadshows, and created a 24-hour telephone database for cyclists to log details about themselves and their bikes. Reported cycle thefts decreased by 39 per cent in the year following the operation. The target aimed for was 15 per cent. You could also register the bike with the national property register[169] so that, if you are unlucky enough to suffer a loss, you have a better chance of getting it back.

So, thinking back to the Jigsaw, how can we help stop bicycles being stolen? The owner – the potential victim – can do their part, certainly. But what about the offenders, the cause of the problem? What can be done to put them off? I was once told about a cycle hire firm that painted all of their cycles pink, which put a lot of thieves off because it lowered the chances of their making a quick sale. Although colours can generate some interesting behavioural effects (as we'll discuss in chapter 10), I've never been able to pin the story down. However, there has been some success with another initiative – the use of 'Big Brother' posters and signage.

A 'Big Brother' poster is one that features a pair of eyes that seem to be watching you. It's long been known that if people feel that they are being watched, even if only by a photo or a painted figure whose 'eyes follow you around the room', they feel uncomfortable. It can also deter bad behaviour. There

---

168 I was told that kids took to stealing the UV pens but this resulted in an unexpected *diffusion of benefits* as they used them to mark other property at their homes. And, as each pen advertised the operation, it was free marketing – just like the Virgin Atlantic salt and pepper pots.

169 www.immobilise.com. There are others such as bikeregister.com, bikeshepherd.org and bikeindex.org which does create some confusion. It would be better if all bikes were on the same register.

have been a number of studies that seem to support that the effect exists. A two-year experiment run by Newcastle University between 2010 and 2012 placed Big Brother eyes watching over bike racks. During this period there were 62 per cent fewer thefts from those sites compared with the previous year, while sites without the eyes saw thefts increase by 63 per cent.[170] Meanwhile, a 2006 study by the same team found that staring eyes made people pay almost three times as much into a tea-room honesty box, and a further 2010 study showed that people were more likely to clear away their tray after a canteen meal if they felt like someone was watching them. The research was certainly convincing enough for the British Transport Police to consider trying the posters at cycle racks around the UK. Other forces use them too now, including my old employers, the Met. I spotted this one outside BBC Broadcasting House in June 2015.

170 This experiment didn't result in any kind of crime reduction as it appears that the criminal activity was displaced rather than prevented. I'd like to see a follow-up study that uses Big Brother posters on all bike racks. Perhaps the British Transport Police will have some data for us in the near future as they use them in most train stations now.

Another popular way to use 'Big Brother' psychology is using cardboard cut-outs of police officers, police cars and other authority figures. Even after you realise that they are 2D images you are still left with the impression that someone is watching you.

That's two pieces of the Problem Solving Jigsaw looked at and the ideas we've discussed here are just the tip of the iceberg. Now let's think about the place and time. Obviously, your best solution is to use a dedicated purpose-built cycle rack. Or is it? It all rather depends on whether the people who install such things have chosen a suitable design, sited the rack properly and installed it correctly. I've seen many that were placed too close to a wall or railings, or too close to the road so that cars reversing into parking spaces hit the bikes. I've seen others that get in the way of pedestrian traffic, and tethering posts positioned too closely together so that they can only accommodate half as many bikes as the rack is intended for. And I've seen many poorly-designed bike racks that are designed to be artistic but which are next to useless functionally. The point I'm making is that if you want to get it right, you need representatives from all three sides of the Jigsaw. That could include police crime prevention advisors, cyclists, cycle clubs and cycling organisations, cycle shops, local government officials, community planning organisations, traffic engineering departments, street furniture designers, insurance companies, large employers, transport providers (if bike racks at train stations or bus depots), educational establishments such as schools, colleges and universities and even former bike thieves. Everyone, in fact, who shares the problem.

How much easier could problem solving be with so many interested parties putting in time, effort, resources and ideas?

5

The Cornish lobster industry benefited hugely from the collaboration formed between universities, fishermen, retailers, environmentalists and other agencies with a vested interest in conservation. And the residents of Welland Crescent, the police and a host of other agencies were willing to pitch in together to transform what had been an increasingly dangerous and unpleasant area to live in into a place where people felt safe and crime rates dropped. Despite differences in politics, beliefs or agendas, a good partnership can achieve extraordinary things simply by focusing on the process of setting a shared target and working towards meeting it.

The problems encountered in places like Welland Crescent – and there are many places like it – don't get 'solved' overnight; there is no magic bullet. It takes time and dedication to tackle an ongoing set of problems, bit by bit, day by day, and often with some people trying to undermine the good work. I can understand why even the best, most dedicated, sensitive professionals occasionally throw their hands up in despair at the apparent futility of it all. But a strong partnership of agencies can survive all of the ups and downs by being mutually supportive. A strong partnership perseveres.

Look at the demand; research and analyse the problem; find other people who think differently from you; and identify people and agencies who share your problem ... and you're on your way to solving it.

8: REARRANGING THE DECKCHAIRS ON THE *TITANIC*

You never change things by fighting the existing reality. To change something, build a new model that makes the existing model obsolete.

Richard Buckminster Fuller

No one is asking what happened to all the homeless. No one cares, because it's easier to get on the subway and not be accosted.

Richard Linklater

1

Around the turn of the millennium the Problem Solving Unit was based at a police-owned building on the Victoria Embankment, virtually opposite the London Eye.[171] We'd

---

171 It was called Territorial Policing Headquarters or TPHQ and, as of 2015, it has become the new New Scotland Yard. Or, rather, the new new New Scotland Yard. The Met's first HQ was in Whitehall Place with a public entrance in Great Scotland Yard. The name soon became synonymous with policing and when the Met moved to a new HQ on the Embankment in 1890, it was christened New Scotland Yard (it is now the Norman Shaw Buildings). Then, in 1967, HQ moved to an office block in Broadway, St James, retaining the name (though now it should have been New New Scotland Yard) and sprouting the now iconic triangular rotating sign outside. In 2015, it moved back to the Embankment almost next door to the Norman Shaw Buildings.

been given a suite of three rooms: a main office, a smaller side office – which was claimed by our Chief Inspector – and a WC and shower room. Office space in HQ buildings is always at a premium so it seemed too good to be true. And sure enough, it was. Within a month of us settling in, a senior officer claimed the whole suite as his own and the six of us (and our Chief Inspector) were relegated to a pokey single office. That's the privilege of rank I guess; superiority over sensible apportioning of resources. However, despite the downsizing, we flourished. The office was a hothouse of great ideas, intense research and detailed analysis. Flipcharts stood covered in to-do lists, a large whiteboard was covered in hand-drawn flowcharts and one wall was festooned with scribbled self-adhesive notes, each bearing a cryptic message such as 'bubble wrap carpet?' and 'reward pooper scoopers with dog treats?' Desks were stacked high with Home Office research reports, popular business books, crime science literature, newspapers, magazines, academic papers, witness statements and crime prevention surveys. I loved going to work every day. And so did the other members of the team as we'd all finally been given free rein to explore those 'mad ideas' that had caused us so much hassle in the early years of our careers. The one big advantage of the new, smaller office was that we had a splendid view of the River Thames and across Westminster Bridge to County Hall; a real bonus on New Year's Eve when the London Eye would be the setting for the UK's biggest and best annual firework display. But it also meant that we had a splendid nose-full of Bazalgette's massive Victorian sewer[172] that ran underneath the Victoria Embankment and which, in the summer months, occasionally, made our office smell like an arse's arse.

My daily commute brought me in by train from

---

172 Which, as you know was a response to the 'Great Stink' mentioned in chapter 4. Now well over a century old, it is prone to occasional whiffy leaks. However, Bazalgette gave the city a staggering 13,000 miles (21,000km) of sewers and the fact that it still does the excellent job it does to this day is testament to his skills as an engineer.

Buckinghamshire to Marylebone and then on to Embankment Station by Tube. From there I'd walk to the office, sometimes strolling along by the river, but most days through Whitehall Gardens with its proliferation of statues and pleasantly laid-out flowerbeds. And there's a very striking, and probably very old, leaning tree that's propped up with green iron crutches so that it looks like that huge slumbering brown thing being held aloft in Salvador Dali's painting *Sleep*.

Crossing the road at Horse Guards Avenue I'd then walk through the gardens in front of the rather ugly MOD (Ministry of Defence) building, once described by architectural historian Nicholas Pevsner as 'a monument of tiredness'. Here, there were more statues: war memorials mostly, including Hamo Thornycroft's bronze of General Gordon of Khartoum, and others remembering the fallen of the Fleet Air Arm and the Chindit Campaign to name but two. In the large open space in front of these memorials there were plenty of park benches where civil servants would eat their lunchtime sandwiches in the sunshine, and where aged veterans could sit and pay their quiet respects to fallen comrades. The benches were rarely empty. And, come evening, as I left work, I'd find the benches still occupied but by an entirely different crowd.

As nearby Big Ben struck 6pm, a group of seven or eight men would arrive and greet each other warmly before making preparations for the night. It was always fascinating to watch as each of them had their own bench – the same one every evening – and a distinct routine that they went through. One chap, for instance, had a series of hinged wooden batons that he'd set up around his bench like a tent frame. He would then drape sheets of polythene over it – some clear, some opaque for privacy – and fix them with spring clamps. Next, the bench was waterproofed with bin bags and made comfortable and warm with layers of insulating cardboard. This was then topped off with a sleeping bag and more waterproof polythene. Inside this little bivouac, he'd be warm and dry all night. Another chap had something like a tent made of bits of plastic fabric, joined and hinged with gaffer tape, that he could erect on a bamboo frame around his bench. I was always struck by how organised these homeless people were. They certainly didn't fit the common and derogatory stereotype of the shambolic, filthy, drunken hobo. They were clean, sober and organised and they always left the benches pristine every morning for others to enjoy. And their choice of venue was well-considered; the area was lit at night, the MOD building was surrounded by tight security and CCTV, and there were police officers and vehicles going in and out of TPHQ – the building where I worked – at all hours of the day and night. If there was any place in London where a homeless person could sleep and feel pretty safe, this was it. And more than that; these people were obviously friends. They looked after each other within their small but tight-knit community; a real community, in the true sense of the word.

I would often exchange pleasantries with them as I passed by and they were always friendly and polite. Most seemed to be aged between 35–50 and they were all ex-servicemen, something I suspected but which was confirmed for me by a chap in his 40s whom I will call Tom.[173] The first time I had a proper conversation with him, beyond a simple 'Good evening' or a comment about the weather, he was showing a younger man how to get his bench waterproof and secure for the night. I couldn't help comparing his circumstances to those of the ministers, senior staff and civil servants in the MOD building beyond who were, at this time, enjoying the benefits of a £746 million refurbishment.[174] I also wondered how many other homeless people around London were ex-servicemen like Tom and his friends and decided to do a little bit of research. I was genuinely surprised by what I found.

173 I'm not sure that I ever actually knew his name but the name 'Tom' keeps surfacing in my memory. I do remember that he looked quite a lot like the late Richard Briers (who played Tom Good in the 1970s BBC sitcom *The Good Life*). So maybe that's it.

174 What did I say earlier about the perks of rank? But, to be fair, the building hadn't had any work done on it since 1951, was expensive to maintain and had some health and safety issues. By covering the three interior courtyards with glass, more office space was created and 700 extra staff could move in, allowing for the disposal of five other London sites which helped to fund these changes. The upgraded building houses some 3,150 staff.

In the late 1990s, homeless charity Crisis reported that at least one in four of all rough sleepers were ex-armed forces personnel.[175] They found that 55 per cent of homeless ex-servicemen[176] had been homeless for more than five years (many for over 10 years) compared to just 30 per cent of other homeless people. They were also less likely than other homeless people to stay in a hostel and over half of those surveyed (51 per cent) said they were not looking for alternative accommodation. 'Ex-servicemen are more likely to be successful at surviving on

---

175 In 2008, research by the University of York's Centre for Housing Policy found that the number of homeless ex-servicemen in London had dropped to six per cent of the total homeless population; a substantial reduction from the 25 per cent reported in the mid-1990s when this story is set. However, that is still approximately 1,100 'non-statutory single homeless' ex-servicemen living in London on any given night. 'Non-statutory' means that the local authority is under no obligation to find housing for them unless they have dependents or can demonstrate specific vulnerability.

176 Homeless ex-armed forces personnel are almost exclusively male, which is why *Crisis*, and I, feel justified in using the term 'servicemen'.

the streets – squaddies, after all, are trained to sleep rough – and less likely to take advantage of the support on offer,' stated the report. 'Over one in five (21 per cent) of those questioned … did not require help, compared to only seven per cent of non-service homeless people.' However, research by The British Legion and others had found that an ex-serviceman's self-belief in their ability to survive was often over-optimistic and that many also had psychological issues to contend with such as post-traumatic stress disorder, chaotic childhoods or a history of abuse, which added to their difficulties.

When I told Tom about these findings, he wasn't at all surprised. 'A lot of guys sign up when they're really young. Then, when they're demobbed, they have no idea how the world works,' he explained. 'They got housed, fed, paid, told what to do and how to live. Without that, some guys can't cope and they end up falling back on what they've been trained to do – survive. Most of us don't need help. We just need a safe place to sleep at night. People don't usually bother to ask us who we are or what we want. To be honest, most people simply ignore us.'

Around six months after I'd first starting speaking to Tom and his friends, something terrible happened. A reporter told their story. This should have been a good thing but, unfortunately, the aim of the piece seemed to be less about highlighting the plight of the veterans and more about attacking the government spending millions on 'posher offices' when ex-servicemen were sleeping rough on benches outside. The MOD responded by removing the benches, which seemed petty and counter-productive. Were they really so embarrassed by the situation? So I called the Ministry to ask why the benches had been removed and was told by a spokeswoman that the clearance was to do with 'heightened security'. That may be true; shortly afterwards, a whole new set of steel and concrete barriers was erected around the outside of the building to protect it from car bombs being placed too close or driven into the building. However, the benches were not replaced even though there was ample room for them and they posed no terrorism threat. (Note: the benches did eventually return but they now sported armrests so that people cannot lie on them). Meanwhile, Tom and his friends were forced to move on. As he said to me at the time, 'I don't understand why they're doing this to us. We do no harm. We sleep here because it's safe.' Homeless magazine *The Pavement* commented on the Victoria Embankment 'clear-up': 'There is irony in this move, and some do feel that it's a sharpened double-edge sword: dispersing this population across the capital, away from the shelter provided by the gardens and the mutual support of numbers surely only serves to make the homeless more vulnerable to attacks.'

Solving a problem like homelessness is difficult but moving a problem from place to place is easy and it makes it look like you're doing something positive when, actually, you're not.

2

Tokyo's Ueno Onshi is the oldest public park in Japan and is a very popular place to visit. It boasts the country's largest collection of museums and art galleries, a library and a zoo. During the blossoming of the many cherry trees the park becomes a riot of colour and the ground looks to be covered in fragrant confetti.

Photo: Bernard Gagnon

However, the park is not as welcoming as it first appears. The park benches are curiously hard and unforgiving, with metal partitions that force you to sit uncomfortably upright. Some slope forward, meaning that you have to constantly brace yourself against the ground to avoid sliding off their polished stainless steel seats; sit on one for more than a few minutes and your back starts to ache. Not that you're likely to sit there for long. Stainless steel may be easy to keep clean but it gets very hot in the summer and freezing cold in the winter. Elsewhere, grass verges and low walls are studded with regular protrusions every metre or so and thorny shrubs are planted behind low walls so that sitters get stabbed in the back.[177] None of this is an accident; everything has been designed specifically to discourage loitering. Ueno Onshi and, indeed, most of Tokyo's open spaces have embraced the concept of 'defensive architecture' and taken it to new heights.

Photo: Steve Mushero

---

177 You may recall the public furore in mid-2014 when it was revealed that a new block of luxury flats had been built in London with metal spikes on the floor to prevent homeless people sleeping in the covered area by the front door. It's not just the Japanese who do this stuff, I'm sad to say. That said, the spikes were removed after a petition attracted 130,000 signatures.

Dr Dan Lockton is a senior research associate at the Helen Hamlyn Centre for Design (part of the Royal College of Art) in London. He specialises in 'design for behaviour change', which means understanding and influencing our use of products and services for social and environmental benefit. He is also an outspoken critic of places like Ueno Onshi Park. 'Defensive architecture doesn't address the underlying problem of homelessness,' he told *The Guardian* newspaper. 'It simply shifts it from one area to another, or worst still, reduces its visibility. Many of these tactics have their origins in a more positive movement to design against crime, which aims to make public spaces feel safer. The original goal was a lot more pro-public but these new features are part of a range of strategies that perceive the public as a threat and treat everyone as a criminal.'

It's long been understood that you can use environmental design to influence behaviour – it's one of the 10 principles of crime prevention[178] and makes up a whole third of the Problem Solving Jigsaw. The high windows in older schools were placed not only to let in light but to raise the sills above the eye level of pupils to reduce distraction, for example. And an unbroken set of railings along the edge of a pavement with just a few breaks will shepherd pedestrians to specific, safer road crossing points.

178 Too detailed to list here but easily found online.

Speed humps can slow traffic to a sensible and legal speed, and irregular wall surfaces – using textured paints, unusual materials or simple wooden batons – can prevent bill-sticking and graffiti.

On a much bigger scale, much of central Paris was remodelled between 1853 and 1869 to clean up the area, to gentrify it and to prevent public protests. To this end, wide boulevards were built where once there had been narrow streets because it's much harder to build barricades across a wide thoroughfare and, on a psychological level, protestors would feel less significant and less powerful in a large space. You can, with careful planning, 'design crime out' of both private and public spaces.

In the 1970s, the late urban planner and architect Oscar Newman coined the term 'Defensible Space' to describe 'restructuring the physical layout of communities to allow residents to control the areas around their homes'.[179] This

179 You can download a free PDF of his classic guide *Creating Defensible Space* here: http://www.defensiblespace.com/book.htm

entails making changes – often inexpensive, or even cost-free, changes – to their environment in order to make it a nicer place to live and a place where crime is less likely to happen. A central thrust of this book is the power of communities so I won't labour the point, but we're talking here about subtle changes to a space that will benefit everyone; for example, keeping shrubs and trees well-trimmed and maintained so that clear lines of sight are retained. An overgrown plant could provide a mugger with something to hide behind, or shield people from view while making a drug deal. Or it could obscure the clear view left or right at a road junction. The important thing about the defensible space ideal is that it doesn't rely upon official sanction or funding. As Newman says: '[It] relies on self-help rather than on government intervention, and so it is not vulnerable to government's withdrawal of support. It depends on resident involvement to reduce crime and to remove the presence of criminals. It has the ability to bring people of different incomes and race together in a mutually beneficial union.'

It's my belief that the police service has a major role to play here; all officers – not just a select few – should be trained in crime prevention and crime science so that they are in a position to offer advice to the public about how small changes can make communities safer. In truth, it would be a return to a style of policing that would have been familiar to my late father when he joined the police in the late 1950s; while on a foot patrol he would talk to the public and advise them to shut a window here, use a better lock there, or not display high-value goods to passers-by. It's impossible to put a cop on every street corner but you don't need to if the community is doing what it can to 'defend their space' and make it difficult for criminals to operate.

However, when we talk about shared public spaces with no clear ownership – places like town centres and densely populated housing projects – the safety of lives and property now falls to landlords, stewards, urban planners and, of course, law enforcement agencies. And this is where the idea of defensive architecture has taken a twist towards the sinister. Whereas, in the past, urban planners were tasked with creating spaces with such things as clear lines of sight and safe access and exit points in order to prevent crime, now they were being asked to create features to remove 'undesirable elements' from the area by making those areas inhospitable. Suddenly, studs and spikes and cages started to appear on low walls and around buildings to prevent people sitting or lying down.

Perhaps the most obvious outward sign of this change in focus is the humble park bench. In order to discourage rough sleeping, designers began to install partitions or arm rests. But, necessity being the mother of invention, some determined people found ways around this by acts of bodily contortion, or by snapping off the arm rests, or by packing the spaces between partitions so that they were lying down above the level of the arm rests.

So the designers then made the benches too small or, in some other way (such as curved or sloping surfaces, or having no back rest), made them almost impossible to lie on. Soon, the designs had become so uncomfortable that they discouraged loitering by all but the most persistent of sitters.

The evolution of the unfriendly bench

But surely redesigning benches to the extent that no one wants to sit on them rather negates the purpose of having benches in the first place, doesn't it? And, you may just be shooting yourself in the foot. 'I recently saw some bus stops in Oxford that have a narrow sloping seat,' says Dan Lockton. 'A young child couldn't easily sit on it without sliding off. An adult has to stretch out his or her legs just to perch. A parent couldn't sit next to a young child. A shopper would have to put down his or her bags on the ground, since they'd slide off the perch. You wouldn't want to wait any longer than necessary at that bus stop. By making bus users feel unwanted – despised even – you don't enhance the image or desirability of the mode of travel. The buses themselves are great, but if the experience of using the service seems to demonstrate contempt for the user, the user may develop contempt for the service.'

3

If you look towards the centre of Ueno Onshi Park you

will find up to 300 people sleeping rough in a motley collection of tents or shelters made of blue plastic sheeting, cardboard, shopping trolleys and other street detritus. It is a community constantly in flux as new people join and others leave and, as there are some 5,000 homeless people in the greater Tokyo area, there is potential for a great many more to join this makeshift canvas village. It's these people that the benches and other unfriendly structures are aimed at.

Photo: Kok Leng Yeo

In Tokyo, many of the homeless are casualties of the 'boom and bust' Japanese economy. During the 1964 Olympics, thousands of workers came to the city to build a complex that would show the world that Japan had recovered from the Second World War. 'Labour sharks' would scout rural areas and recruit workers with promises of higher pay and a better life in the city. The men would be billeted – often many to a room – in old and decrepit properties, for which they paid exorbitant rents to their 'agents'. The agents would also charge a fee for finding them work. Often, all the workers had left, after deductions, was just enough money for food. Then, during the late 1980s, the economy collapsed and thousands of low-paid, casual labourers suddenly found themselves without work of any kind. It was around this time that Ueno Onshi's homeless village was created.[180]

But no amount of bench redesign is going to prevent people from becoming homeless or help those who already are. Nor will it stop homeless people from hanging around the city where it is warmer and where money, food and shelter are more readily available than in rural areas. The use of defensive architecture isn't being used to prevent crime; it's being used to make a problem less visible.

Similarly, removing the benches in the MoD gardens contributed nothing to solving the problem of homelessness among ex-soldiers. It just removed any embarrassment suffered by the Ministry of Defence. Meanwhile, the deliberately uncomfortable designed environments of places like Ueno Onshi Park simply make life even more hellish for the homeless. 'Does forcing the homeless to lie on the ground, or preventing people sitting comfortably and watching the world go by, really "solve" any problems?' asks Dan Lockton. Of course it doesn't. But what's the alternative? The obvious and simplest solution to the problem of homelessness is to find someone a home. However, as we've seen in earlier chapters, strong personal feelings and entrenched attitudes can get in the way of the simplest and most practical solutions.

---

180 The Tokyo Prefecture did begin an 'independence system' in 2004 in which homeless people are brought into a shelter, supplied with meals and given useful advice on how to break out of their lifestyle. However, each resident's stay is limited to two months and the facilities can only handle around 500 people at a time, a tenth of the estimated homeless population so the problem persists.

Photo: Kok Leng Yeo

In 2006, writer and social commentator Malcolm Gladwell wrote a feature for the *New Yorker* magazine about a homeless man from Reno, Nevada, called Murray Barr. Murray was an alcoholic and had been on the streets for 10 years. By the time he died, adding together all of his doctors' fees, medical and substance abuse treatment costs and other expenses, he'd achieved some notoriety as the first homeless man to accrue unpaid medical bills of over a million dollars. However, as Gladwell pointed out, a simple and cheap solution exists for people like 'Million Dollar Murray' – give homes to the homeless.

Time and again, it's been shown that giving someone stability and shelter will often break the cycle of their erratic lifestyle. A 2008 report by the Cambridge Centre for Housing and Planning Research concluded that a local residential scheme designed to get homeless people back into work had saved the state £31,000 per person per year (for 'state' read 'taxpayers'). And a self-build project run by Tyneside Cyrenians reduced the annual cost of tackling homelessness (through a reduction in criminal activity, medical interventions and dependency upon benefits) by 89 per cent as a result of training, supporting and employing homeless individuals. In the five years prior to this project, the homeless participants had cost the public purse a total of £513,779.

Housing the homeless needn't be massively expensive either. In 2013 Brighton Housing Trust, in association with Brighton and Hove City Council and QED Estates, built the Richardson's Yard project which transformed old shipping containers into affordable housing. Each 40-feet long container costs around £27,000 to buy, ship, position and convert into a self-contained studio flat of 25 square metres including a kitchen, bathroom, living and sleeping space. The containers were stacked into apartment blocks and linked together by stairs and walkways.

Photo: Brighton Housing Trust/QED Estates

The residents of Richardson's Yard are all homeless people who have demonstrated a desire to break out of their destructive lifestyle, and the project began with the realisation that one of the biggest stumbling blocks to doing so is the lack of a home address. By providing one, the Housing Trust has made it possible for the residents to open bank accounts, apply for jobs and education courses, and access medical services and benefits, all of which helps them to get back on their feet and re-enter society. Once they do that, they can leave Richardson's Yard and new people in need of help can move in. Good public consultation has led to a largely positive response to the project, which also has the knock-on effect of freeing up space in homeless shelters, so that more rough sleepers can come in off the streets. Similar schemes are now being considered in other cities using containers or even converted disused blocks of garages.

Photo: Ross Gilbert

Photo: Brighton Housing Trust/QED Estates

In 2016, the city of Medicine Hat, Alberta, Canada, became the first large conurbation (to my knowledge) to eradicate their homeless problem. And they did it by giving homes to the homeless. No one in the city spends more than 10 days in an emergency shelter or on the streets. If you've got no place to go, they'll simply provide you with housing.

Mayor Ted Clugston admits that when the project began in 2009, he was an active opponent of the plan. "I even said some dumb things like, 'Why should they have granite countertops when I don't,'" he says in an interview with CBC Radio. "However, I've come around to realise that this makes financial sense." Clugston says that it costs about $20,000 a year to house someone. If they're on the street, it can cost up to $100,000 a year. "This is the cheapest and the most humane way to treat people," he says. "It used to be, 'You want a home, get off the drugs or deal with your mental health issues'. But if you're addicted to drugs, it's going to be pretty hard to get off them if you're sleeping under a park bench."

And the strategy has worked. In Medicine Hat, emergency room visits and interactions with police have dropped. But there was one change that initially surprised Clugston — court appearances went up. "They end up dealing with their past, atoning for their sins," he says.

If we gave homes to homeless people, even temporary homes, we'd all be financially better off. But could we ever, as a society, become that philanthropic? The stark reality is that many of us work very hard to meet our rents and mortgage payments and the idea of someone bypassing that route leaves us feeling cheated. 'Social benefits are supposed to have some kind of moral justification,' says Malcolm Gladwell. 'We give them to widows and disabled veterans and poor mothers with small children. Giving the homeless guy passed out on the sidewalk an apartment has a different rationale. It's simply about efficiency.'

But the problem is growing. According to the latest figures available from www.homeless.org.uk, 29,050 homeless people applied for housing in 2015, 68,500 people were in temporary accommodation and around 3,600 people were sleeping rough in the UK every night. The problem is getting worse and it's costing the taxpayer an increasingly large amount of money every year. Is it time to give efficiency and compassion a go at solving the issue? As an old Greek proverb goes: 'A society grows great when old men plant trees under whose shade they know they will never sit'.

4

In 2010 a large number of newspapers, magazines and websites reported that people visiting the Yantai Park in Shangdong province in eastern China were being discouraged from hanging about for too long by the installation of pay-per-use park benches. Overstay your paid welcome and the bench gently asks you to leave by pushing spikes up into your bottom. The British newspaper *Metro* carried a quote, supposedly from a park official, which stated, 'This seems like a fair way to stop people grabbing a bench at dawn and staying there all day.'

Photo: CEN

The bench shown in press photos was almost identical to one designed back in 2008 by German sculptor Fabian Brunsing. Ironically, his 'Pay & Sit' installation was a protest against the commercialisation of modern life.[181] As to whether it's 'fair' depends on whom you ask; the homeless probably can't afford to sit there at all.

The debasement of the concept of defensive architecture has now reached a point where we can more realistically call it 'disciplinary architecture', but the problems it is supposedly intended to solve aren't getting solved: they're just being moved around.

A solution isn't a solution if it doesn't work, no matter how many times you apply it. It's like 're-arranging the deckchairs on the Titanic' – it gives the impression of activity but achieves nothing useful in the long-term. Or how about that other expression: 'It's like painting the Forth Bridge'. For decades that was a metaphor for a never-ending task because the bridge is so huge; by the time you finished painting it, it was time to go back and start again, over and over, year after year. It was a never-ending problem. But it isn't any more. In 2010, someone found a new, incredibly hard-wearing, glass flake epoxy paint with a life of 15–25 years. Which is why, although the most recent paint job was completed in December 2011, no one has to worry about painting the Forth Bridge this year. Or next year. Or the year after. Or, maybe even for a whole quarter of a century. The problem hasn't been entirely eliminated but things are better than they were because they're tackling the root cause of the problem – the longevity of the paint – rather than constantly responding to the symptoms. What an excellent metaphor for how homelessness should be tackled.

When I first put on my police uniform, the constable's

---

181 You can see a video of Brunsing's 'Pay & Sit' bench at https://vimeo.com/1665301. However, it's an idea that had already been explored in 2001 by Dr Steve Mann, an electrical engineering specialist at the University of Toronto, who created a similar art installation called 'SeatSale'. You can see it here: http://wearcam.org/seatsale/

oath I swore said that I would do my job 'with fairness, integrity, diligence and impartiality, upholding fundamental human rights and according equal respect to all people'. The poorest and least advantaged members of society need help more than most and it's my belief that police officers have a part to play: firstly, by recognising that the homeless are people, not merely a nuisance; secondly, by appreciating that they are more frequently the victims of crime than other members of society; and thirdly, by getting involved in projects – like Brighton's Richardson's Yard – that actively seek to get people off the streets. But, more importantly, we all can do more to help the homeless by just being understanding and compassionate. It does no harm to stop and chat to someone who has probably spent their day feeling cold, hungry, lonely and shunned. A kind word can do a great deal of good. As Mother Teresa of Calcutta once said: 'We think sometimes that poverty is only being hungry, naked and homeless. The poverty of being unwanted, unloved and uncared for is the greatest poverty.'

While police officers are not expected to be social workers, they do have a responsibility to protect everyone from harm, regardless of social status – the job isn't just about prosecuting offenders.

It's also a fact that merely moving a problem from place to place is an exercise in futility and solves nothing.

9: THE PHANTOM BUS STOPS OF DÜSSELDORF

We can't solve problems by using the same kind of thinking we used when we created them.

Albert Einstein

The world is full of nice people. If you can't find one, be one.

Bill Murray

1

In March 2009, musician and comedian Tim Minchin appeared on an episode of the BBC Radio 4 show, *The Museum of Curiosity*.[182] I was still a cop at the time although I was coasting towards my retirement in early 2010 and I had already begun writing parts of what would become this book. I was also going to be working on the radio show once I'd retired from the police, so I had backstage access. It was the second time I'd met Tim as I'd also appeared in an episode of Dave Gorman's TV series *Genius* with him.

After the recording, we found ourselves in the green room and discussing the notion of tempting fate: the idea that we can somehow influence events that are outside of our control

---

182 If you don't know it, it's the sister show of BBC2's *QI*. Host John Lloyd and a guest curator – a different comedian every series – invite three panellists to donate something to the impossibly large 'Museum of Curiosity' that makes them go 'Wow!'

– such as causing it to rain by washing a car. Tim told me that he'd once seen a simple experiment performed which perfectly highlighted the depths of human irrationality when it came to this kind of 'magical thinking'. 'This guy first of all sifted out all of those people in the group who were religious or superstitious until all he had left were the atheists and the logic-lovers,' he explained. 'He asked them again if they had any kind of superstitious belief. They said no. Then he asked them if they would accept anything just on faith rather than evidence supported by the scientific method. Again they said no. He then asked them to write down the sentence, "I want my family and those I love to be killed in a car crash this year". It was surprising how few would do it, despite their claims of non-superstitious belief. Of course they all knew that simply writing that sentence could not, in any possible way, affect the fates of their loved ones. But they still couldn't write it down … just in case. It's like it's something so deeply ingrained in us that we can't completely overcome it.'

What separates us from every other life form on earth, possibly from every other living thing in the universe, is our capacity for advanced thought. We're the apes that figure things out: like the creative thinking that turns the petty thefts of airline customers into a marketing ploy, or the analytical reasoning that dissects the business structure of a drugs market so that it can be undermined and closed down, we're good at thinking our way through to solutions. However, while we've come a long way very quickly, in evolutionary terms, we're still a very young species and there are ancient parts of our wonderful brains, down deep in the dark where our System One thinking resides, that haven't yet caught up. These areas can influence our behaviour no matter how much logic we apply to counter the silliness of things like 'tempting fate'. That's why we can't write 'I want my family and those I love to be killed in a car crash this year' on a piece of paper. And also why we sometimes avoid saying things that, even though they are actually positive and caring, perversely make us think the opposite. Actors won't say 'Good luck' to each other because that might 'jinx' the performance, so they say

'Break a leg!' instead. And when Tim and I parted after the recording, he said to me, 'Hope your train doesn't crash and kill you!' It's strange how unsettling I found his genuine good wishes.

We've looked at the power of bringing together different types of thinkers to tackle problems. But understanding how people think – and especially what motivates them – is just as important. If you can discover how to positively influence people's behaviour, you can make some people less likely to offend and others less likely to become the victims of crime.

It's not a superpower. It's simply a matter of watching and listening.

2

The term 'behavioural economics' describes a mixing of disciplines: a dollop of psychology stirred into a bowl of economics and sprinkled with some neuroscience. It's essentially the study of why people make decisions and how those decisions can be influenced or 'nudged'. A great deal of behavioural economics research tells us something that we probably all know about ourselves – namely that people respond better to carrots than they do to sticks. We've seen several examples of this throughout the book: the Scottish kids and their football pitches, and Kate Fox's experiments where people were paid to behave after they'd been drinking, for example. Another is youth shelters; you can spend lots of time and money in finding ways to stop kids hanging about in groups. Or you can give them somewhere to go.

Do an internet search on 'objection to youth shelters' or words to that effect and you'll find lots of local newspaper reports full of comments from the public such as 'teenagers don't deserve anything', or 'a waste of taxpayers' money', or 'a youth shelter would become the haunt of antisocials and cause more problems'. One Lancastrian lady told the *Bolton News* that she'd objected to a shelter in a nearby park because she'd suffered 'unacceptable disturbances caused by youths gathering together' behind her house (not, you'll note, in the park) and, at a public meeting at Thame in Oxfordshire, one councillor called the idea of a youth shelter 'ludicrous' and 'something that would worsen the quality of life of people living in the area'. Interestingly, at that same meeting, another councillor reported that he'd done extensive research and 'had struggled to find any negative comments on youth shelters that had been installed elsewhere in the country'. But his argument fell on deaf ears and the shelter, in Thame at least, was not approved.

Photo: Janice Staines

What's interesting about the second councillor's comment is that he was absolutely right. It is extremely difficult to find any negative stories about youth shelters once they're installed and in use. You're far more likely to read stories about how successful they've been. In just an hour of research I found lots. For example, a story from Burnley in Lancashire reported an 87 per cent reduction in vandalism after installation. In addition to this, over a 12-month period, reports of nuisance behaviour had reduced by 29 per cent in the whole town and by 50 per cent in the streets near the park where the shelter was sited. I found reports from Lincoln and Hamilton that rejoiced in similar results, and Cirencester Town Council reported a reduction of over 50 per cent in reported nuisance incidents following the installation of a youth shelter in Chesterton. Telford Borough Council found that installing a youth shelter at the Aqueduct in Dawley Hamlets rekindled so much interest in the neighbouring old ball court that it led to redeveloping the area as a community facility. And in Aylesbury, Buckinghamshire, the building of youth shelters at four sites had a dramatic effect on damage to play areas. The cost of repairs in 1996/7 was £4,532. The total cost of repairs in 1997/8 – the year after the youth shelters were built – was 30p.[183] Youth shelters work – the evidence is there for all to see and employing positive actions to encourage good behaviour works far better than using sanctions or punishments for bad behaviour. Carrots beat sticks.

In 2010, Volkswagen ran its annual 'The Fun Theory' competition asking for ideas to prove that when people have fun they are more likely to comply with rules or respond to suggestions. The winner of that year's competition, San Francisco game producer Kevin Richardson, suggested that maybe people would be less inclined to speed if, instead of fines and penalty points, they got a reward for staying under the speed limit.[184] VW decided to test the idea in Stockholm and, working closely with ad agency DDB and the Swedish National Society for Road Safety, they set up a speed camera linked to a large roadside LED display board. When a vehicle passed the camera the board displayed the speed being driven.

---

183 In the interests of balance, I must point out that the repair bills did rise above 30p in subsequent years but never anywhere near previous totals. Overall, the reduction in repair costs has been massive.

184 Incidentally, research also suggests that a countdown system of penalty points for bad driving – like they have in Italy, for example – would be more effective than the current 'totting up' system we have in the UK. In Italy all new driving licences are issued bearing 12 points. Points are removed when you're bad. Adding points to a licence isn't as impactful as taking points away because loss is more deeply-felt than gain. A 'countdown' focuses the mind.

If the vehicle went over the limit the driver/rider got a digital image of a 'thumbs down' gesture and a fine. But if they drove under the speed limit the board displayed a 'thumbs up' and told them that they'd been automatically entered into a lottery draw for good drivers. A winner was then randomly chosen from among the good drivers and rewarded with 20,000 krona, drawn from fines paid by those caught speeding so it cost the taxpayer nothing. The 'speed camera lottery' was widely publicised and, over a three-day period 24,857 cars were counted driving past the camera and sign; a daily average of around 8,300 per day. The average speed in the street before the experiment was run was 32kph (in a 30kph zone). The average speed during the experiment was 25kph. 'All the attention seems to go on the bad apples – the people who are breaking the law – and there's really no attention given to the people obeying the law,' Richardson told *The Toronto Star*. 'I hope that this process is adopted to make things safer, better and more positive. Driving is already scary and fraught with peril as it is, so why not make it easier and safer?'

To my knowledge, the idea has never progressed beyond this one experiment and a similar one run in the USA by behaviourist Dan Pink for his National Geographic show *Crowd Control* (he got a 33 per cent reduction in speeding). Incidentally, there is also research, conducted both in the UK and the USA, which demonstrates that speed indicator displays (SIDs) – those electronic signs that tell drivers how fast they're driving – lose their effectiveness after two to three weeks because the novelty factor of seeing them has gone. But SIDs that show the vehicle's speed plus a smiley face/ sad face, depending on the speed of the car, appear to be at least 10 per cent more effective in slowing drivers down and the effect lasts a lot longer than a fortnight. In Belgium they've gone one step further. Antwerp-based agency Duval Guillaume, working with local government, has created the Selfie Speeding Sign. The public are encouraged to upload two selfies of themselves to a website; one happy, one sad. Then those selfies are used on signs in the area where the selfie-taker lives. What it means is that drivers get to see the smiling or sad faces of real people displayed and it's likely that the photos might be of someone they know locally. There's impact and motivation for you. And it's communities being empowered to do something positive to make where they live safer. They even appear on the campaign posters.[185]

Photo: www.graagtraag.be

185 'Graag traag in onze straat' literally translates as 'willingly/gladly slow in our street'. The message is asking drivers to make the decision to drive more slowly. All of the posters feature groups of people. This one is from 'the fathers of Zurenborg', a suburb of Antwerp.

208

We humans are thinking animals – but we're also emotional animals and we react to things like this. A photograph of a person in a wheelchair accompanied by a message like, 'Think of me, keep it free', has far more impact on stopping inconsiderate drivers parking in disabled spaces than the standard graphic disabled icon. People have more empathy for the story of one person than for the hundreds of thousands of people represented by an icon. Tapping into people's feelings is how you create influence. So why aren't these kinds of initiatives being used everywhere? And why hasn't anyone run with the idea of the speeding lottery and given it a proper evaluation? It's hard to find an answer to that question. All I can do is speculate, but I'm pretty sure it's because some people don't take fun very seriously.

You might recall a news story back in 2010 about a group of Thames Valley Police officers who were captured on video tobogganing down a snowy Oxfordshire hill on a riot shield. As one officer is pushed off by his colleagues one of them shouts, 'Whatever happens, keep smiling!' The footage was recorded by Rick Latham who posted it on YouTube. 'They were jovial and it was nice to see officers taking time out to get involved,' he told a BBC reporter. 'They were only there for a few minutes so I don't think they should be criticised. Since I've put the footage up lots of people have commented saying how good it is to see officers having a sense of humour. It makes a change from the image you usually read about.' Similarly, public comments attached to the YouTube video are all positive: 'It is so nice to see cops having fun! I personally don't like the police but this made me smile,' wrote Emma Miller. 'Totally ok, cops need to smile more,' said SquidCaps. 'Why can't the police be friendly like this more often?' wrote Mortablunt, a sentiment echoed by LeoRikimaru who said, 'Seriously, if the police were as cool as this usually they'd be alright.' And SnappyPenguins hit the nail on the head when he wrote: 'This is what the police should be doing! Interacting with the community!'

However, the reaction from the officers' line manager was quite different. Local area commander Supt Andrew Murray told the BBC, 'I have spoken to the officers concerned and reminded them in no uncertain terms that tobogganing on duty, on police equipment and at taxpayers' expense is a very bad idea should they wish to progress under my command.' My first reaction when I saw the video – I was still a police officer at the time – was to crack a big smile. My colleagues did the same. I completely agree with the public that officers having a few minutes' break from a tough, often distressing and dangerous job to take part in a fun activity with the public, can only be a good thing. What actual harm was being done that warranted a police reprimand? No damage was done to equipment and, if it had been, the cost would have come out of the officers' pocket. And as for 'taxpayers' expense' I'd argue that a five-minute sledge-fest is no different to the average taxpayer taking a few minutes away from their work for a tea break, to have a cigarette, to read a paper, or to play a round of *Candy Crush* on their phone. Everyone, including cops, deserves a brief respite from work every day and, on this occasion, it generated nothing but goodwill and smiles and showed police officers in a positive light. You can't put a price on that.

More recently, in October 2015, you may have seen a video of an unnamed female police officer from Washington DC who broke up a potentially violent situation by challenging a 17-year-old girl called Aaliya Taylor to a dance-off. The event was caught on a mobile phone by Antwain Bynum and the video quickly went viral. So how did people in authority react to the officer's behaviour? Better than British cop bosses did. DC Mayor Muriel Bowser tweeted, 'DC has innovative ways to keep our community safer and stronger. A DC Police Dept officer even did the Nae Nae.' And no less a person than President Barack Obama got involved: 'Who knew community policing could involve the Nae Nae? Great example of police having fun while keeping us safe.'[186] Most importantly, however, was Aaliya Taylor's

---

186 The dance-off was to the song 'Watch Me (Whip/ Nae Nae)' by US rapper Silentó.

reaction. She told the *Washington Post*, 'I thought all cops were cruel because that's how I saw them. It shows there are good cops too.' She then told a *News 4* reporter that 'She gave me a hug and I was like "yeah, we need more cops like you".' Her perception of police officers has been changed for the better. And who knows how many other young people have had their perceptions changed since? And all due to one officer choosing fun over seriousness or, as the *Sydney Morning Herald* put it, 'Humanity trumps force'.[187]

Why should the police service – and law enforcement in general – have to be seen as deadly serious and officious at all times? Frowny senior police officers should maybe read up on such things as the 'pratfall effect',[188] a curious counterintuitive phenomenon that makes people, organisations and products more attractive, likeable and accessible if they are seen to be less than perfect or they occasionally make mistakes. Imperfection and fallibility are factors that people find endearing and natural; as the expression goes 'I'm only human!' We don't trust perfection.[189] Advertisers have long known that humanising a brand sells more products. They will even go as far as to employ phrases where the grammar isn't perfect – e.g. 'I'm lovin' it' (McDonald's) or 'Every Little Helps' (Tesco) – to give a brand a kind of personality. If police officers and police forces never admit to making mistakes, people will think 'they must be covering something up' because *everyone* makes mistakes. An occasional toboggan down a snowy hill makes you look human and approachable.

---

187 Another example you might like is the Dover (Delaware) Police Department officer caught on his car's dashboard camera dancing and singing along to Taylor Swift's 'Shake it off'. His superiors, rather than telling him off, put the video online as one of a series of 'Dash Cam Confessionals'. The idea of showing their cops as human has been very popular, not least with Taylor Swift herself who commented on Twitter: 'Lolololol The Sass!' Watch the video here: https://www.youtube.com/watch?v=8XFBUM8dMqw

188 Originally described in 1966 by Elliot Aronson.

189 The ancient Greeks built imperfections into their buildings as they believed that aiming for perfection might anger the gods.

Perfection creates distance and an unattractive air of invincibility. I don't think that's the image the public want police officers to have and yet there is a general malaise within the police service that sees anything fun-based as trivial, unprofessional, and something to be stamped on. What is everyone so afraid of? Do senior officers really think that showing people that cops are people too will undermine their authority? If so, provide the evidence; I've never heard of a single case of that happening. It's been my experience that the friendliest, most approachable cops were the best cops while the *über*-serious dour cops were the ones to watch. Call me old-fashioned but I think that a police officer's job is to reassure and protect the public, not repress and frighten them. Remember what Sir Robert Peel said at the birth of modern policing about 'the police are the public and the public are the police'? His 'Principles' also stated that police officers should do their job 'by ready offering of individual service and friendship to all members of society without regard to their race or social standing, by ready exercise of courtesy and friendly good humour'. *Friendship. Courtesy. Good humour.* Cops are supposed to reflect the communities they serve. Everyone's life is a mix of light and dark, happy and sad, serious and fun. So why not cops?

London isn't Mega-City One and cops are not Judge Dredd.[190] People respond much better to kindness and friendly persuasion than they do to grim faces, shows of force, and being given orders.[191] Those things are sometimes needed of course. But carrots trump sticks every time. Even subtle, almost unnoticed carrots.

190 Yup. Cops read comics too.

191 Did you know, for example, that getting people to imagine doing something that you want them to do is far more effective then telling them why they should do it? Try it.

3

During World War II, the government asked the British people to do their part for the war effort by collecting rags, bones and metal that could be recycled into munitions, glue, weapons and vehicles. In a campaign led by Lord Beaverbrook, households gave up aluminium and cast-iron kitchen utensils for the Pans into Planes campaign. Children went from house to house collecting scrap metal in old prams. Then, in 1941, the government passed an order compulsorily requisitioning larger items; all post-1850 iron gates and railings – with a few exceptions of particular historic interest – were gathered in or cut down and taken away for smelting (in many places you can still see the stumps of the old railings where they were removed).

Photo: Craig Lewis

Rich or poor, the British public responded magnificently. Everyone felt that they were doing their bit for the war effort ... which was what the campaign was really about. The fact is that a great deal of the metal was never recycled as it was of too poor a quality. But even if it had been good enough there were simply not enough smelting plants and ironworks operating to handle that amount of metal (and with bombings and blackouts, they couldn't operate at night). Historian John Farr claims that only 26 per cent of the ironwork collected was used for munitions and by 1944 much of it was rusting in council depots or railway sidings. Many tons of iron sat in a warehouse in Durham until as late as the 1970s. One eyewitness account says that, in Glasgow, there were 'vast mounds of railings piled up in a scrapyard on Alexandra Parade in the city. They were still there well after the war was over.' And a large amount of scrap was taken out into the Thames estuary and dumped; the truth started to come to light in the late 1970s when dockers who had worked on 'lighters' (barges) during the war came forward to tell their stories. They claimed that so much was dumped at certain spots that ships needed pilots to guide them because their compasses were so strongly affected by the quantity of iron on the seabed.

But none of that mattered. The gathering of metal was important but public morale was even more so. Britain was being blitzed by bombers and V-weapons and the enemy was making plans to cross the channel. Food and other items were subject to rationing and most people had loved ones fighting at the front. Many felt disempowered and defenceless, especially those who were not fit enough for active service or who couldn't do any of the more physical volunteering work on farms and in coal mines and factories. The recycling campaign united communities; it gave everyone a chance to contribute to the war effort and took their minds off the daily danger of air raids. It also appealed to the British sense of fair play as everyone, right across the class divide from stately home to council terrace, was seen to be doing their bit.[192] Uniting a nation in adversity and giving everyone a sense of purpose was worth losing a few railings for.

Asking people to get involved resulted in a much better outcome than if they'd simply ordered people to surrender their metal (even though there was a degree of that for the metal railings). It made people feel good about themselves and it made the enemy realise who they were facing – not just a military force but a whole nation. The powerful message to Hitler and his cronies was that the Brits were all in this together.

People think that this 'hearts and minds' approach to getting people on board with solving problems is new. But, as the wartime metal campaign shows, it very much isn't. And there are people who still actively seek to change people's behaviour or perceptions of problems by winning them over.

If our lives are ruled by **fear** we will make innocent people our enemies.

If our lives are ruled by **love** we can make strangers our friends.

Photo: Craftivist Collective

192 Invariably, a few didn't. I recently found a blog post by a lady blacksmith who stated that she and her colleagues are 'fascinated by the regular occurrence of railings coming to light having been hidden behind sheds and shrubs to avoid giving them up for the war effort.' She also found 'a large ornate pair of entrance gates, thought popularly to have been sacrificed for the war effort, secreted upright behind a fake wall at the end of a large house.' Naughty.

Despite a couple of decades in London, Sarah Corbett's Evertonian lilt is still quite strong. It's a sing-song accent with a tone that rises at the ends of sentences. And she still has a habit of saying 'boss' when she thinks that something is good. Sarah is a craftivist – a person who uses arts and crafts as a form of activism[193] and, when I caught up with her on London's South Bank on a warm June day in 2015, she'd just spent the whole morning making up 'hanky kits' for an upcoming event. 'The plan is to sew bespoke messages onto the hankies and give them to senior managers at the AGM of a well-known department store chain,' she told me. 'The messages will all be focused on one thing – to make those managers think about staff wages. No threats. No violence. Just simple messages highlighting the hardships their staff have to endure on minimum wage. I was reading lots of reports by politicians, big companies and NGOs where they were saying that they weren't influenced by being bullied. So I thought about how to get messages across in a more productive and less confrontational way.'

Sarah has been involved in politics since she was three although, as she happily admits, she obviously didn't really understand what she was protesting about at the time. 'I grew up in a family of activists that were trying to make people's lives better – my mum's still a councillor to this day,' she explains. 'We were always going to demos and meetings when I was younger. But I was a quiet, introverted kid and I didn't like how a lot of it was about egos – things seemed to be more about power dynamics rather than peace and love. Then a few years ago I was doing quite a lot of travelling and I'd buy myself crafting kits – cross-stitch squares and things like that – to do on the train. And I'd find myself crafting little slogans and messages about social injustice and people would ask me what I was doing. I'd always known that art can be political and affect people's perceptions in a positive way. Or in a negative way, like propaganda posters and stuff. But this was something else.

193 The term 'craftivism' was coined by activist Betsy Greer who defined it as: 'a way of looking at life where voicing opinions through creativity makes your voice stronger, your compassion deeper and your quest for justice more infinite.'

I suddenly realised that maybe crafting could do some good. So I read up on behavioural and psychology stuff and put it all together with crafting and suddenly it felt right. I'm still figuring things out. But I know that what we're doing has an impact.'

In 2009 Sarah created the Craftivist Collective, a loose-knit (If you'll pardon the pun) network of crafty sewers, beaders, knitters, crocheters and hand-embroiderers who, as their website explains, 'use craft for critical thinking, questioning and considered creative activism'. 'That sounds a bit grand doesn't it?' she says, 'but I love the idea of making small, beautiful things to challenge big, nasty things like poverty and violence. I love the aesthetics of it. And the more I did it and the more boss feedback I got, the more I saw how useful craftivism is. It's useful because it gives creative introverted people a voice and they can get involved without confrontation or being a part of big groups; it's useful because it gets media coverage in places where the normal types of protest don't get coverage, like fashion and glamour magazines and places like that, where they wouldn't normally cover politics. It was ticking all these new boxes so I just kept going.'

Photo: Craftivist Collective

A typical craftivist stunt might involve leaving a beautifully embroidered scrap of material on a park bench with a message about homelessness. Or a cross-stitched square hanging on some railings with a suitable quote about making the world a better place. What happens to the piece doesn't matter – most are taken away by members of the public or removed by street cleaners – as long as it's been seen by people and, hopefully, raised awareness about an issue. But how do craftivists know whether they're having an impact? I asked Sarah how she measures success. 'What keeps me going – because I do have a wobble now and again – is that every day, every single day, I get letters and emails and text messages and phone calls from people telling me how much it's made them re-evaluate how they think about things. Last week I ran a workshop in Soho and a woman came along from some little village in the South-East somewhere and she told me that her husband had sent her because he thought it would do her good. Apparently she has a strong social conscience and was constantly getting angry about injustices and things on the news. And she hates her local MP and the party he represents. Anyway, I got this email from her the day after saying that it had really made her rethink the way she deals with things. She's now going to channel all that energy into something more positive than hate. That's made me so happy. That's the kind of feedback I get all the time. It may just be changing the world one person at a time but that's powerful. Weirdly, I think the more specific an issue is, the harder it is to have an impact. We could run a campaign protesting about something like fracking but behind a lot of these very specific issues – and there are so many of them – are much bigger things like greed, poverty, violence, lack of compassion; just a handful of behaviours that underpin all of the bad stuff. I want craftivists to think about their own personal values, to think about the kind of world they want to live in, to think about what's important to them and to spread those kinds of messages. We want to provoke people to think rather than preach to them. People who make up their own minds are much more likely to do the right thing than people you try to coerce.'

Sometimes all anyone needs is a gentle nudge in the right direction.

4

You've probably heard of something called 'Broken Windows Theory'. It's the idea that low-level nuisances create the impression that an area is uncared for and will therefore attract more serious nuisances and, ultimately, crime. A rundown area says to the people who live there 'No one cares'. It sends the same message to the bad guys who think, 'That's a good area for me to operate inside'. It was certainly the case for the people of Welland Crescent, for example.

The theory was popularised by social scientists James Q. Wilson and George L. Kelling in the early 1980s but the idea is a little older. Back in the late 1960s, in a well-known experiment staged by Stanford psychologist Philip Zimbardo, two identical 1969 Oldsmobiles were left parked with no number plates and their bonnets up, in two different locations. One was a Bronx ghetto neighbourhood. The other was a quite well-to-do street in Palo Alto, California (near Stanford itself). Within minutes the Bronx car had had its radiator and battery removed and, within 24 hours, everything of value had been stripped and local kids were using it as a playground. The Palo Alto car remained untouched. This was entirely in keeping with people's expectations for the two locations. However, Zimbardo then broke one of the Palo Alto car's windows. In no time at all, other people started to smash up the car and steal parts from it. But these weren't hoodlums or teenage thugs. The majority of the adults were well-dressed, respectable men. As James Q. Wilson later wrote: 'Human behaviour is strongly influenced by symbols of order and disorder. Therefore, the objective for preventing street crimes is to prevent the first window from getting broken, or prevent the first graffiti marks, or prevent the first drunkard from a public display.' In other words, to prevent that first nudge that influences other people to misbehave.

Broken Windows Theory does have its critics. Some say that it is based solely upon perception and that people used to being in areas of continual poor repair no longer feel threatened by it. However, the theory is tested fairly regularly and the results are pretty convincing. In November 2008, Professor Kees Keizer and colleagues at Groningen University in the Netherlands ran a series of experiments in which they set up two almost identical bicycle parks. Both had very visible signs prohibiting graffiti that would be seen by anyone collecting a bike. All of the bikes had a flyer attached to their handlebars advertising a sporting event. The demographic for the people visiting both sites was the same. The only difference was that one site was tidy and orderly, while the other was covered in graffiti. The researchers then observed the two areas from a hideout. What would the owners do? They could take the flyer with them, attach it to another bike, or drop it on the floor (there were no litter bins). At the site that had graffiti, 69 per cent of the riders littered compared with 33 per cent at the clean site. Keizer and his team created a whole series of similar experiments and, in each scenario, the results were similar. From personal experience (which the critics would label as 'based solely on perception' I guess), I am convinced that Broken Windows Theory is a very real phenomenon. I've seen so many examples of areas that have gone quickly downhill once urban decay sets in and how that affects the people who live there. Unchecked bad behaviour gives other people 'permission' to be bad too, just like in Zimbardo's cars experiment.[194] If enough old sofas and other rubbish get

---

194 If Zimbardo's name sounds familiar, he was also behind the infamous Stanford Prison Experiment.

fly-tipped at a particular location, the amount will quickly escalate as people think 'Well, if they're doing it, I can do it too'. We may like to believe that we are independent thinkers, utterly individual and unique, but the reality is that most of us will subconsciously follow the herd. We are creatures of habit. I don't mean that in any derogatory way and I know that people will rail against the idea that we are so easily influenced. I hate the idea myself that I'm maybe not fully in control of my decisions, but I can't deny the truth of it.

Back in the 1950s psychologist Solomon Asch ran a series of now-famous experiments to gauge the degree to which individuals conform to the behaviours of groups they are part of. A typical experiment would see a subject placed in a room with seven other people – all stooges that had been briefed by Asch. Then they would all be asked to take a simple perceptual test – to say which line of a choice of three (A, B or C) is the same length as a fourth line (X).

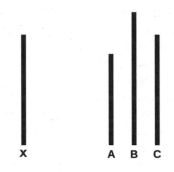

The stooges were all told to verbally give the same wrong answer (B) and the room was set up in such a way that the subject would always be the last to give their answer. On average, 76 per cent or more of the non-briefed subjects answered (B) and went along with the group answer, despite the evidence of their senses.[195]

As we discussed as far back as Chapter 2, humans have a strong, innate desire to 'fit in' – to be part of a tribe or a social group. We are naturally inclined to conform. But that isn't a bad thing; there's comfort in patterns and routines, even if this means yielding, albeit subconsciously, to group pressures or cultural norms or regular patterns of behaviour. As Pelle Hansen, behavioural philosopher at the University of Southern Denmark and chairman of the excellently named Danish Nudging Network says: 'Our brains are designed to go into autopilot once we've established a routine that works for us. This is useful because it frees us up to think about things other than day-to-day tasks.'

Understanding that fact can help save lives.

It's not uncommon for elderly residents and patients to

---

195 What's particularly interesting is that Asch set out to prove that the effect wasn't real. He had heard of experiments, most notably Muzafir Sherif's 'Robbers Cave' experiment, that suggested this innate desire to conform and wasn't convinced. Ironically, Asch's experiments are now the benchmark for conformity testing.

wander out of care homes and sheltered accommodation. It happens regularly when they have degenerative illnesses like Alzheimer's. And because they are frail and vulnerable they invariably get reported to the police as missing persons. I picked up more than a few during my police career and took them to a place of safety; where they lived if we knew where that was, or to a police station where they usually ended up in the canteen having a cup of tea with me and telling me all sorts of fascinating stuff about their lives. It was never a chore, but it was time that I probably should really have been spending on the street. I would always make a point of talking to the care home staff about ways to keep their residents on site and most did the best they could. But they were always short-staffed and they couldn't be everywhere at once.[196]

The staff at Benrath Senior Centre in Düsseldorf found a unique way to deal with the problem without constantly involving the emergency services. They looked at the history of 'walk-outs' at the home and noticed a regular pattern of behaviour; namely that their missing residents were often picked up at bus stops. 'Our members are 84 years old on average. Their short-term memory hardly works, but their long-term memory is still active,' explained Franz-Josef Goebel[197] to *The Telegraph*. 'They know the green and yellow bus sign and remember that waiting there means they will go home.' The centre therefore asked the Rheinbahn transport network to supply a fake bus stop which was set up in the street outside the home. Now, when anyone goes missing, the first place checked is the bus stop and, most of the time, the person is there waiting. 'We will approach them and say that the bus is coming later and invite them in for a coffee,' says

---

196 I have a friend who is the full-time carer for her father who has dementia. He has a tendency to wander off but she couldn't watch him all the time and didn't want him to feel like he was a prisoner in his own home. So she put bubble wrap under a thin mat on the floor by every exit so she could hear when he went on his travels. She understands his behaviours and habits and has found a simple and clever way to keep him safe

197 Goebel works with a local care association called Old Lions.

Benrath's director Richard Neureither. 'Five minutes later they have completely forgotten they wanted to leave.' The system has been so successful that it's been adopted by several other homes across Germany.[198]

5

The big focus of this chapter is the importance of understanding behaviour – why people do the things they do. If you can get to know people's needs, desires and motivations, their habits, foibles and interests, and what informs their choices and decisions, you can design solutions to problems that thwart the bad guys and support the good guys. It means that cops have to become good readers of people. Or they have to work with people who are good readers of people. It's pointless putting a solution in place if you don't have any understanding of how people are likely to react to it.

In 2007, Operation Trident – the Met Police's anti-gun crime branch – paraded a replica prison cell around several London boroughs on the back of a truck. The walls were made of Perspex and a bunk bed, stainless steel wash basin and toilet could be clearly seen inside the cramped space. It was part of a campaign called Don't Blow Your Life Away.

Detective Chief Superintendent Helen Ball, head of Trident at the time, told BBC News: 'We have designed this campaign to encourage young people to think about what really matters to them and what they would not be able to do, or have, if they ended up in a prison cell. Trident is concerned that people are starting to carry guns from an increasingly young age. That is why this campaign is aimed at 13–19 year-olds in London, especially those living in gun crime hotspots.' The 'glass cell' was backed up by an extensive radio, TV and

---

198 There is an amazing resource for police officers – or anyone else - that provides advice about mental health matters. It's https://mentalhealthcop.wordpress.com run by Inspector Michael Brown of West Midlands Police (currently seconded to the College of Policing).

online campaign and, according to the Met's own website, 63 per cent recalled seeing or hearing at least one element of the campaign'.[199]

So how did this translate to results? Like most preventative initiatives, that's very difficult to quantify. There's no easy way to find out how many kids were put off becoming involved with guns as a result of the campaign. I would hope that it opened the eyes of many who were heading in that direction. In terms of making existing offenders put their guns down, there is also scant data. But we do have gun crime statistics. In January 2008, it was reported that gun crime in London rose by four per cent during 2007 – the year when the 'glass-cell' campaign ran – while the numbers of other serious crimes fell. In January 2010, it was revealed that gun crime in 2009 rose by a staggering 48.7 per cent. Of course, that's reported crimes; the percentage may actually reflect growing trust in authority so we must always be slightly wary of numbers as evidence, especially percentages. But, whichever way you look at it, it's hard to see whether the glass cell was a success or not.

199 We've discussed statistics and percentages in a previous chapter. Without wanting to take away any of the campaign's success, for the purposes of accuracy I must point out that the site doesn't say who was canvassed – youths or the public in general – nor how big the sample was.

It would be both petty and unfair to criticise any genuine, heartfelt effort to make things better and, if just one young person didn't pick up a gun as the result of the campaign, it's money well spent as far as I'm concerned. I applaud the effort. But, that said, the figures imply very strongly that the campaign didn't reach a substantial portion of those 13–19 year olds already involved in gun crime. It made me wonder why not. And, in 2008, a year after the glass prison cells exercise, I had the opportunity to find out.

I was helping to facilitate a group discussion with some young people in Southwark, a central London borough that, at the time, had a serious problem with youths and gun and knife crime. I hoped that I'd learn some things that would help me to help them. What I got was a revealing and occasionally shocking window on their world.

Many, it seemed, had parents who were alcoholic or drug dependent and had relied on older siblings to feed and clothe them. One hadn't seen his mum in six months and thought she might be dead (she was working as a prostitute to feed her addiction). Most had no contact with their fathers. All but three (in a group of 14) knew someone who had been unlawfully killed in the previous five years. All of them knew someone who had been 'shanked' (stabbed) and three of them had been stabbed themselves. One fourteen-year-old told me that his sixteen-year-old brother wore a colostomy bag due to an abdominal wound he'd received when aged 13. One of the girls had an older sister who had been gang raped to 'teach her brother respect'. Two of the kids had handled a 'strap' (gun). None of these offences had ever been reported because of distrust of the police and fear of gang reprisals.[200]

I asked them if the glass prison had worked; had it made an

---

200 One local hospital doctor told us that he had seen a high number of stabbing victims, many of whom had numerous historic scars. Most of the patients were gang members who told him that they refused contact with the police. Because of patient confidentiality, hospitals are prevented from providing the police with the details of knife crime victims, but anonymous raw data in terms of number of admissions would show that the true number of inter-gang stabbings is much higher than reported figures.

impact on them? The consensus was no. One young lad was more specific. 'Prison isn't that hard,' he said. He'd done some time inside and said that, for him, prison was something to boast about; it gave him credibility. The group agreed. When I asked why none of the campaigns to get them into further education or employment had worked, they asked why they would work in a supermarket or a burger bar for minimum wage when they could make hundreds of pounds, tax-free, every week as drug runners and stashers? Some of them had become runners as young as nine years old. Gang culture was portrayed as desirable; the gang was seen as a family; a 'tribe' that offered protection and even a career path. Gang 'elders' could expect to earn enough to buy designer clothes, expensive cars and a champagne lifestyle.

When I asked them about their future, they were distressingly morbid. One told me that 'You don't get to live past 30' where he came from. All of them shared the same fatalistic view that when it was your time, that was it. They all expected to be victims some day. They were resigned to it. I realise that they sound almost like characters from a TV cop show but they were all too real. And very few of them had spoken to police officers before about the issues they faced. They simply didn't trust police officers. And that works both ways. When I told some of my colleagues that I was going to try to talk to some of these kids, I was told by some of them that I was wasting my time and that they should 'all just be locked up'.

It would have been so easy to give up on the gun crime kids. They were antisocial, didn't really want our help and were resigned to their bleak and anticipated short futures. Just getting the small amount of information out of them that you've just read took half a day of building trust. But they had talked to us and it was only right that we tried to do something for them. One strong theme that had emerged from the discussions was the importance of respect and loyalty, both to the gang and to their families. Their mothers, in particular, were obviously very important to them. So we invited their mothers to meet us at the same community centre a week or so later and we told them what their children had told us. They sobbed, they cried, they prayed. And, most importantly, they vowed to do something about it. They shared the problem ... and most emphatically.

I don't know how many of those kids managed to get out of their life-threatening lifestyles. It could be that they were just too firmly entrenched in gang culture. But I do know that mothers can achieve extraordinary things. The 'Not Another Drop' campaign was started by a group of mums in the London Borough of Brent in 2001 after 12 people were seriously injured and eight were killed by guns in the previous 18 months. 'Not Another Drop' eventually grew into a strong partnership between Brent Council, the police and the local community. It is satisfying to note that during 2007–2008 when the rest of London started to see a sharp increase in the number of gun- and knife-related fatalities, Brent reported none.

6

Many of the ideas we were to try out during my time in the Problem Solving Unit resulted from thinking about how people think and figuring out what we needed to do in order to disincentivise criminals or to make people feel safer. I saw so many operations and initiatives fail, or have little effect, because the police response was based upon faulty understanding; the nudges didn't work because nudges have to encourage behavioural changes that people feel comfortable making.

Richard Thaler and Cass Sunstein, authors of the hugely influential book *Nudge: Improving Decisions about Health, Wealth, and Happiness*, define a 'nudge' as: 'Any aspect of the choice architecture that alters people's behaviour in a predictable way without forbidding any options or significantly changing their economic incentives. To count as a mere nudge, the intervention must be easy and cheap to avoid.' Nudges surround us and we are prey to them all the time. For example, below you'll see two pictures of litter bins. Which one are kids more likely to use if given a choice? Which one is nudging them more?

The same 'Fun Theory' competition that produced the speed camera lottery, also once promoted a litter bin that made a noise like a whistling bomb being dropped from a height and then exploding whenever trash was placed in it. Children were observed picking up other people's rubbish just to hear the bin do its thing. And another initiative in Copenhagen showed that if you paint green footprints leading to a bin, it increases usage by 46 per cent. That's nudging: subtle influencing that doesn't override your right to choose other options but might inform your choices.

All too often, the police service insists on using sticks – metaphorical ones, I'm pleased to say – when a little psychology, humility, humour and nudging might result in a big bunch of tasty carrots.

10: THE SENSUOUS ADVENTURES OF KIKI AND BOUBA

Nothing we use or hear or touch can be expressed in words that equal what is given by the senses.
Hannah Arendt

Human Nature is not a problem that can be fixed by rules and regulations. All solutions to the existing problems must be based on how people behave, not on how we think they should behave.
Kirk Chisholm

1

After the Problem Solving Unit had been in existence for a few years, the team members were invited to become part of a larger, national problem solving group based at the Home Office. Every three months or so, we would meet at their smart new building in Marsham Street to swap ideas and good practice. The group was made up of police officers from around the UK, analysts, academics and representatives of bodies such as the Jill Dando Institute of Crime Science. The mix of participants brought fresh ideas and a wealth of experience to the table.

At one such meeting, we were discussing perception and how people's senses can be 'tricked'. The issue was that police staffing levels and budgets were going to be affected by some quite savage government cuts so we would all have to do more with less. How could police officers continue to prevent crime and catch the bad guys with reduced resources? And how could we reduce the fear of crime with fewer visible staff?[201]

A curious idea began to emerge from the discussion which, for want of a better description, I'll call 'placebo policing'. The idea went like this: people would feel reassured, or so they told us, if they saw more cops on the beat. But we couldn't afford to employ more cops, so, we

201 'Reassurance Policing' was the buzz-phrase of the time. For all sorts of reasons, the public's fear of crime was far greater than the actual level of crime. We were constantly being asked to find ways to close the 'reassurance gap'; a tricky task when every media outlet was giving the impression that the world was dangerous, scary and that crime was epidemic.

wondered, could we make it look like there were more without resorting to obvious ploys such as cardboard cutouts? What if we first identified the places where people felt most scared and vulnerable – let's call them Locations 1, 2, 3 and 4 – and then arranged for four officers (A to D) to make an appearance at each of those locations at, say, sometime between 9am and 9.30am.

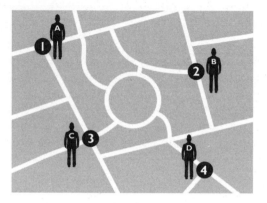

Then, an hour later at 10am to 10.30am, the officers rotate and all make an appearance at the next location.

And then, an hour after that you do the same thing again, and so on and so on throughout an eight-hour shift. Even if each officer is at one of those points for just a few minutes each time, the fact that it happens fairly regularly would give the impression that there were lots of cops about when, in fact, there are just four. The impression the criminals would get is that this is not a good place to commit crime. And people at those four locations would see a different cop at least once every hour. That's a much higher rate of sightings than you'd normally get at those locations unless you posted an officer there for a full eight-hour shift. If each officer made a point of talking to local people and purposefully being seen at each location, it would have a huge effect on public perceptions. Plus, for the rest of the time, those four officers could patrol other areas so there would be no loss of service.

Yes, it was a fanciful idea. I have no idea whether it would have worked but it would have cost nothing to try. Sadly, however, we couldn't find a borough commander who was willing to let us give it a go and the idea died. Maybe if we'd called the idea 'targeted reassurance patrols' instead of 'placebo policing' we'd have got further. There's that whole perception issue again.

Perception is all about how we interpret what we see, hear and feel around us. Our senses provide us with a number of different windows on the world. So it's not surprising that problem-solvers look to the senses to find solutions.

And not just human senses either.

2

When farmers plant their crops of maize, they are naturally concerned about pests. But it is not weevils or locusts that concern African farmers. You've already read about the problems that exist with rats and snakes. But think bigger than that. Much bigger.

In April 2008, the farmers of Bulawayo in Zimbabwe suffered massive crop losses at the feet – and trunks – of marauding elephants. The offending animals had escaped from Hwange National Park, an animal sanctuary, and then decimated the farms nearby. This was the final straw for many farmers already struggling with drought and the political and economic turmoil embroiling the country. About a third of Zimbabwe's 12 million strong population is receiving emergency food aid. 'Life has become unbearable because of these elephants which destroy our crops,' explained farmer Erica Hlongwane. 'On one hand we worry about the prospect of hunger because of crop failure, while on the other we count the losses stray elephants are causing daily. We also fear the elephants might demolish our pole-and-mud huts.'

Villagers attempted to scare the elephants away by using drums, pots and pans and anything else they could make a loud noise with. But the bull elephants saw this as a threat and would sometimes charge in response. To make matters worse, elephants are attracted to the smell of booze and would wreck villages while looking for brewing beer. Electric fences have been shown to be effective but disrepair and frequent power outages make them unreliable for elephant repelling. Among other deterrents developed by researchers are ropes soaked in chilli or tobacco oil, fireworks, air-pressure horns, and early warning systems such as trip wires and observation towers. However, elephants are very big and not easy to threaten. Also, they are clever animals and soon become acclimatised to threats.

In February the same year, the *Hindu Times* newspaper reported that elephants were causing much the same problems in India. The elephants' traditional migratory paths have been shrunk by the expansion of agricultural land and in just one month, elephants had strayed into cultivated fields and had destroyed sugarcane, banana, ragi, pulses and maize crops. In Uthanapalli, the elephants attacked farmers Babu, Muniraj and Basappa Singh, who were defending their crops. Basappa was killed outright. Muniraj and Babu Singh were admitted to the Hosur Government Hospital with serious injuries. Although true figures are hard to come by, at least 150–200 people a year are killed by elephants in India.

This problem exists wherever elephants and humans are in close proximity. In the Xishuangbanna area of Yunnan Province, China, the problem is so frequent that the authorities plant special 'dinner halls' – plantations of banana and sugarcane that keep the elephants occupied and stop them from destroying crops and raiding local villages. There are many such schemes in existence all over Africa and Asia where elephant numbers are dwindling and the animals are protected. However, farmers can and will kill the animals that are destroying their livelihoods. In Sri Lanka in 2009, the end of hostilities in the long-running civil war caused an opening of hostilities between humans and elephants. Not only are the animals wandering into redundant minefields but, with no more conflict in their way, they've returned to using elephant 'motorways' – the straightest path between two points, which is taking them through plantations and refugee villages. It's estimated that up to 150 wild elephants are shot or poisoned by farmers every year – and this is in a country where elephants are important to the economy, being used in place of expensive plant machinery. So what's the answer?

One possible solution has come from the most unlikely of sources: bees.

While working in Africa in 2008, Dr Iain Douglas-Hamilton and Professor Fritz Vollrath of Oxford University discovered that elephants hate bees. They even hate the sound of bees. Lead researcher on the team Lucy King found that the animals' aversion is probably due to the sensitivity of their trunks; solitary bee species are always looking for holes to live in and an elephant's nostrils are very attractive, as are the folds in its skin. A sting at the tip of a trunk can be hugely painful and could cause breathing difficulties. And elephants are totally reliant on their trunks for drinking and eating; without full use of them they will die. During field trials, King's team played either buzzing sounds recorded at beehives, or a control sound of white noise. 94 per cent of elephants moved away from the buzzing noise while only 27 per cent left the white noise. However, recorded noise was not the answer that farmers were looking for.

'Farmers don't have money to pay for a loudspeaker and a minidisc and on that level it's not practical,' she explained at the time. 'Secondly, elephants are smart and would work out that there are no painful bee stings; we don't know if that would happen after three playbacks or 30, but it is clearly going to happen. More research is needed to understand to what extent beehives could be used […] but using bees in this way would enable local farmers to reduce elephant crop raiding and tree destruction, while at the same time providing some income through the sale of honey. This would be a valuable and significant step towards sustainable human–elephant coexistence. It is vital that we find new approaches so that we avoid extreme solutions such as shooting problem animals.'

Photo: Lucy King

Research continued and eventually culminated in projects being set up in Kenya, Botswana, Mozambique, Tanzania, Uganda and Sri Lanka, using specially constructed, low-cost hives hung at intervals along the length of a fence. And the results are looking good. In Mozambique, for example, the beehive fences are working well against crop-raiding elephants and the first seven and a half kilos of Mozambican Elephant-Friendly Honey were produced in June 2013, giving a huge moral boost to the project and farmers. And in Uganda, Community Liaison Officer Innocent Kahwa reported that: 'We tried trenches and failed because elephants could cover them with soil. We used gun shooting to scare away the animals. It also failed. Now, we have resorted to bee fencing – and so far, so good.'

3

In Japan they say that the first bite is with the eyes. It's part of their whole philosophy of food that the more beautifully presented a meal is, the better it will taste. There is some evidence that this is true because sight is our primary sense. It's so dominant that it can subvert all of the others. Think back to a particularly badly-prepared presentation that you've had to sit through. If the speaker's slides were covered in text or complex diagrams, chances are you completely missed what was being said as you were concentrating on reading; your ears 'switch off' to allow you to take in the visual input. Good presenters know to use images rather than words to support what they're saying so that there's no distraction. And, if they have to put words up on the screen, they stop speaking and give people time to read before moving on.

Think too about Broken Windows Theory, which we discussed in the previous chapter. If you visit an area and see uncared-for buildings covered in graffiti, piles of litter, dark stairwells with broken lighting and overgrown areas of grass and planting, how does your brain interpret that visual input? How does what you see make you feel?

I once saw a lecturer melt chocolate and pour it into a mould shaped like a dog poo. Even though everyone in the room knew that it was chocolate, only a few would have a bite of the resulting object. The visual input created a sense of disgust that outweighed taste, smell, touch, and even common sense. This visual bias was used by designer Sherwood Forlee when he invented clear sandwich bags pre-printed with what looks like spots of mould. The effect of putting your sandwiches inside the bags is that no one steals them from communal fridges (I reckon he'd had his lunch swiped on more than one occasion).

Photo: Sherwood Forlee

Because we have a natural propensity to recognise patterns, we build a mental 'directory' of visual shortcuts to help us make sense of the world as we go through life. One obvious example of this is how we interpret colour. As we've discussed, nature uses some colours as warnings and we've learned to recognise them and even to incorporate them into our lives: the yellow and black of wasps is used on warning signs,[202] and the red that means hot or danger, and the green that means 'it's safe to proceed' are used for things like traffic signals. So how do we see pink?

Deep in the Arizona desert, in Maricopa County, there is a very unusual prison. For a start, the inmates live in tents rather than cells, despite the fact that temperatures regularly top 100°F. Smoking is banned and so is pornography. The only TV channels are the Weather Channel and Disney, and the prison radio broadcasts classical music, Frank Sinatra, patriotic music and bedtime stories. During the day the prisoners work in chain gangs, doing free work on county and city projects thus saving taxpayers' money. There are male and female chain gangs; there is no discrimination here and they work hard for their keep as they have to pay for their meals. It's the only exercise they get as there is no gym. On top of all this, the prisoners are forced to wear old-fashioned striped outfits and pink underwear.

Sheriff Joe Arpaio created this prison in 1993 and is unrepentant about the harsh regime he has created. 'Criminals should be punished for their crimes,' he says, 'not live in luxury until it's time for parole, only to go out

---

202 It's not just elephants that can be driven away by the threat of stinging insects. I once met an enterprising Cornishman whose method of discouraging young people from loitering outside his pasty shop in Penzance involved wasps. He could be seen several mornings a week slopping his shop windows with sugared water that quickly dried clear in the summer sunshine. 'Brings the wasps in,' he explained to me. 'They don't stop people coming in my shop because they like my pasties but no one wants to hang around outside for very long.' I'm reminded of something that Dylan Thomas once wrote. 'As I child I was given books that told me everything about the wasp, except "why?"'

and commit more crimes so they can come back in to live on taxpayers' money and enjoy things many taxpayers can't afford to have for themselves.' When questioned about the discomfort caused by the high temperatures, he says: 'It's between 120 to 130° in Iraq and our soldiers are living in tents too, and they have to walk all day in the sun, wearing full battle gear and get shot at, and they have not committed any crimes.' Arpaio, a former DEA (Drugs Enforcement Agency) officer, claims to have saved the taxpayer around $70 million. Reducing the quality of the food to a basic diet of Bologna (baloney) sandwiches saved $500,000 a year and they don't get 'treats' like coffee, which has no nutritional value (and saves $150,000 a year). The prisoners cost less to feed per day than a family dog.

The prison is not without controversy, as you can imagine. Human rights campaigners are constantly attacking Arpaio's methods and there have been a number of lawsuits filed on behalf of inmates. In April 1999, a jury awarded $1.5 million to an inmate denied medical treatment for a perforated ulcer. And in January of the same year, Maricopa County settled a $8.5 million wrongful death suit filed by the family of Scott Norberg who died, allegedly, of asphyxiation while struggling with prison guards in 1996. The vast majority of suits cite the 'inhumane treatment' of the inmates. Even Amnesty International has expressed concerns.

Despite all this, Arpaio is hugely popular with the voters and enjoys an 85 per cent approval rating in the county, which at 9,200 square miles, is larger than some US states and includes the city of Phoenix. Arpaio claims he's not after public approval; what he wants is for justice to be seen to be done and to stop people committing crimes once they leave his prison. On the face of it, his system works. A study by the Grant Sawyer Center for Justice Studies at the University of Nevada in 2008, claimed that Arizona has the nation's lowest rate of reoffending (24.5 per cent). By comparison, the highest rates were in California (53.4 per cent), Utah (64 per cent) and Alaska (66 per cent).[203] This news is scant comfort for the inhabitants of the tent city prison. 'It feels like we live in a furnace,' says inmate Ernesto Gonzales, a man with 10 years of his sentence still to serve. 'This is hell.'

Some aspects of Arpaio's prison system are being copied elsewhere. The Mason County Jail in Texas now makes all of the inmates dress in pink jumpsuits. 'I wanted to stop reoffenders,' says Sheriff Clint Low. 'They don't want to wear them. Working inmates get a choice to work outside or sit inside, and some choose to sit inside because they don't want people to see them.' So many of the male inmates have now refused to go outside that the county doesn't have the use of chain gangs any more. But even indoors, the prisoners are not spared; they sleep on pink sheets and wear pink slippers. Even the walls and the bars of the cells are painted pink. Sheriff Low claims that the colour has a calming effect.

The origins of this idea lie in the work of Alexander Schauss in the 1960s and 70s. Together with fellow researcher John Ott, he tested the idea that colours have a psychological effect on humans. They discovered that experiments involving a particular shade of pink – labelled P-618 (a pastel bubblegum pink) – produced some surprising results. After staring at an 18 x 24 inch card painted with P-618, people's heart rate, pulse and respiration slowed more than those of people who'd been looking at other colours. P-618 also seemed to work as an appetite suppressant but, most surprisingly, it appeared to sap people's strength; those who spent time looking at the colour found they could no longer lift the same weights that they had lifted before. Excited by the results, Schauss persuaded the US Navy to try the colour in one of its correctional facilities. The two governors agreed and Schauss renamed P-618 after them to say thank you: Baker-Miller Pink was born.[204]

---

203 However, I've not found any figures that measure the number of ex-Arpaio prisoners that commit crimes in other states after release.

204 If you're interested, the ratios are: R:255, G:145, B:175. It equates to around a pint of red paint being added to a gallon of white.

The facility later reported that there was a substantial drop in violent incidents, which seemed to confirm Schauss's theory. In no time at all, word spread throughout the world of law enforcement, and Baker-Miller Pink became *de rigueur* in jails, holding cells, and even psychiatric wards, all over the USA. It soon acquired the nickname of 'drunk tank pink'.

Photo: Reece Lodder

However, some psychologists have suggested that rather than calming some people, pink could actually make their behaviour worse. For prison inmates, being made to wear pink is primarily about embarrassment. The colour's associations with softness and femininity are in sharp contrast to the tough guy, macho reputation that hardened prisoners try to cultivate. No one likes to feel humiliated and being made to wear pink could actually foster resentment and make things worse. There are stories of prisoners scraping paint off the walls with their fingernails out of sheer hatred.

More study is needed, but whatever the truth turns out to be, several US college football teams believed in the stories enough to engage in a little psychological warfare. In the early 1980s, the visiting-teams' locker rooms at Iowa and Colorado State Universities were painted Baker-Miller Pink in a deliberate effort to demoralise and enfeeble the opposition.

However, such shenanigans were soon stopped when a rule was passed by the Western Athletic Conference that all locker rooms – home and away – had to be painted the same colour. Pink had effectively become a controlled substance.[205]

Curiously, the relationship between pink and femininity is a fairly modern phenomenon in Western culture. Up until the late nineteenth century most babies wore white and gender wasn't differentiated by colour or clothing style; the design of baby clothes was fairly unisex, being mostly patterned on dresses and smocks. By the 1850s, coloured baby clothes had become more popular, but there was still no gender-specific colour code. Fashion reports of that era describe both boys and girls dressed in white, pink, blue or violet. But as the twentieth century approached, things began to change. Boys' clothes became more obviously masculine and girls' more feminine. And colours began to be attached to gender, although not necessarily the colours we know today. *The Times* wrote in 1905 that pink was the colour for boys and blue was for girls, as did *Parents* magazine as late as 1939. It was argued that pink was a form of red – the colour of blood and passion and redolent of soldier's uniforms – while blue was calm and welcoming and strongly associated with images of the Virgin Mary. But, by the end of World War II, things had become fairly settled as pink for a girl and blue for a boy, and the association of colour with gender has become very culturally powerful in such a short time.[206] It's why pink is used as an anti-theft device: we tend to notice anything pink that's being carried by a man. Academics at Birmingham City University Business School have found that painting things pink, like

---

205 Red might one day find itself in the same boat. A 2004 study by scientists at Durham University found that 55 per cent of all sports they analysed were won by teams that wear red. And a 2009 study by sports psychologists at the University of Münster, Germany, found that teams who wear red are often given more points by judges than teams wearing other colours.

206 The fact that the Nazis used pink triangles to denote homosexuals seems to indicate that it was, by then, seen as a non-masculine colour.

plant equipment for example,[207] reduces theft because thieves, who are predominantly men, don't want to draw attention to themselves and because pink items are harder to sell on. Remember we mentioned pink bicycles in Chapter 7? And it's why bicycles, umbrellas, street furniture – literally anything that can be walked away with – is better off pink.[208]

But pink has one more card to play. Pink as a weapon of offence.

4

Back in the early 2000s, I began hearing stories about the use of green lighting to move people away from an area. The story went that in Amsterdam ... or Birmingham ... or London ... or New Orleans ... or *somewhere* that had problems with kerb-crawlers and street prostitution, the local council had turned the Red Light Zone into a Green Light Zone. By using green street lighting, sex workers were made to look grotesque and undesirable.[209] The idea seemed unlikely but I researched the story nonetheless and, unsurprisingly, it turned out to be an urban myth.

There's no doubt that green light does make people look like extras from a Hammer Horror film. Most nightclubs don't use it for that very reason. As John Dziel of DAE Concert Lighting puts it: 'Green light doesn't exist naturally so it's a good subconscious nod to something being wrong/sick/dead. Green makes anyone look bad. Use with caution ... or

---

207 'Plant' is a general term for industrial machinery and vehicles. It includes things like diggers, generators, cranes, steamrollers, cement mixers, bulldozers, pneumatic drills, etc. Approximately £1.5 million worth of plant is stolen *every week* in the UK. It's a huge problem.

208 It's also why, if you want to sell a predominantly male product – like a rifle – to women, you make it a bit smaller and change the colour or, as US marketers say, 'Pink it and shrink it'.

209 You might recall that it was a suggestion that came up during a problem solving 'think tank' discussion about prostitution that I mentioned in Chapter 6.

on actors that no one likes.' However, despite this promising start, the Green Light Zone story doesn't hold up for several important reasons. Firstly, it assumes that sex workers stand under street lights, which is a strong cultural image but, frankly, isn't terribly true, at least not in the UK. But even if it were, street lighting simply isn't powerful enough to illuminate someone in a hugely green way. It takes a serious amount of candle-power to light a person green on a West End stage. Most street lamps have only 200–250w bulbs and a green light of that power would be even dimmer. Plus, in a domestic street, the lamp posts are usually at least 18–20 feet high, which is around the height of the eaves of a two-storey house (so they don't shine directly into a window). Secondly, if it's summertime, the lights would be pretty ineffective as the days are much longer. Certainly, I couldn't find a single, documented instance where this idea had been tried and had worked.

However, just because green light probably doesn't work, it doesn't mean that other coloured lights won't. One residents' association in Mansfield, Nottinghamshire, believes firmly in the power of pink. In March 2009, the residents of Layton Burroughs, a residential housing estate, successfully applied for funding to light three underpasses with fluorescent pink lighting of the kind used by beauticians and skin specialists to examine blemishes and highlight acne. Their aim? To put teenagers off hanging around. Marianne Down, a member of the Layton Burroughs Residents' Association told the BBC: 'We used to have quite a problem with large groups of young people hanging around in the underpasses drinking, which felt quite intimidating, but the pink lights have really made a difference. The groups aren't there as much and it feels safer walking through there now, particularly at night.'

The idea, first developed by officers from Lancashire Constabulary, is now being used all over the UK. However, the issue of human rights has been raised. Peta Halls, development officer for the National Youth Agency, said: 'Anything that aims to embarrass people out of an area is not on. The pink lights are indiscriminate in that they will impact on all young people and older people who do not, perhaps, have perfect skin. Why waste limited resources on something which moves all young people out of an area? They will move on to somewhere else. They have a right to congregate, it's part of being a teenager and most young people are good, law-abiding people.' But that hasn't stopped it being used. As recently as 2010, Cardiff City Council was said to be considering it. Of course, the tabloids chose to cover the story with sensitive headlines such as *'Acne lights to shame hoodies off streets'* (*The Sun*) and *'Acne-Social Behaviour: Council considers pink lighting to stop teenage yobs congregating in ASBO blackspot.'* (*Daily Mail*).

Many people see blue light as calming and peaceful, redolent of summer skies and warm shallow seas. Certainly, the belief is shared by the East Japan Railway Company who, in 2009, spent £100,000 installing blue lights on the platforms of all 29 stations on Tokyo's busy Yamanote Line. Suicide by leaping in front of trains had been on the increase and the blue lights were installed in the hope that they would calm the eight million frantic, stressed and unhappy commuters who use the line every day. But did it work? One 2013 review by the University of North Texas found that the introduction of blue lights had resulted in an 84 per cent decrease in the number of suicides.[210]

But blue light is also used to make things go away. It's not uncommon to find blue or ultraviolet (UV) lighting in the restrooms of many night clubs and in public toilets to discourage illegal drug taking. The idea is that it makes it significantly harder to identify the position of a vein. And, in principle, it works; I've been in a number of such venues and have had a look for myself. However, it didn't take long for users to get around the problem by simply drawing the veins on their arms with a black marker before going inside. And there are plenty of hardened groin injectors who don't need

---

210 The researchers do point out that their analysis relies on data from a single railroad company and it 'does not examine the underlying suicide-mitigation mechanism of blue lights.'

light to find a vein. Some social commentators have made the point that dimmer blue lighting could lead to an increased risk of injections being botched – maybe multiple times – which isn't a desirable situation for anyone.

One unexpected drawback of using UV lights in public toilets has been an increase in graffiti. Certain types of pen and paint look spectacular under UV lighting, and artists and taggers have been quick to exploit that fact. And some public toilets have had to revert to normal lighting because the blue light was acting like a red light. 'Here in Rugby the blue lighting scheme has not achieved its aim,' explained David Johnson, head of the council's Engineering and Works Department. As he told the *Coventry Telegraph*: 'It's created an atmosphere conducive to sexual activity. Plus, the subdued lighting is off-putting to the public wishing to use the facilities.' Another development has been people writing contact names and mobile numbers on toilet walls using pens developed for security marking. During the day, the walls look plain. But come nightfall and the UV lights are turned on, the wall becomes a 'cottaging' or 'dogging' telephone directory.[211]

5

Smell is a very powerful sense, often overlooked. Along with taste, it's connected directly to the hippocampus, the part of our brain concerned with long-term memory and strong emotions. It's why a smell or a taste can be so evocative and why experimental chefs like Heston Blumenthal use aromas and other props to enhance your dining experience. Amazingly, 90–95 per cent of what you think is your sense of taste is actually a mingling of your senses of taste and smell. Try eating some foods while pinching your nose and then without pinching – the difference in flavour is quite astonishing.

211 Interestingly, if you see a blue light in Amsterdam's famous Red Light District in De Wallen, it won't be a police station. Blue lights are used to indicate that the lady in the window wasn't born a lady, or may not be wholly a lady yet.

Marketing people know the power of smell. Supermarkets and retail outlets know that wafting the aroma of freshly baked bread around the premises will get the shoppers reaching for their purses and wallets. Some cinemas pump the smell of popcorn into their foyers and the aroma of coffee is added to instant coffee packaging before sealing. In the USA, the army is experimenting with sealing delicious smells inside soldiers' field rations to make the food seem more palatable.

Smells can help us solve problems. As mentioned in Chapter 6, the smell of lemons can subconsciously make people wash their hands more often. And natural gas – such as we have in our kitchen stoves – is odourless and could be very dangerous if we weren't able to detect a leak. Therefore, methyl mercaptan (also known as methanethiol) – a gas found in animal faeces and rotting vegetation – is added so that we can smell it.[212]

In 2012, I met Japanese scientists Dr Makoto Imai and Dr Hideaki Goto whose research into smells led to the discovery that, even though we don't often register smells when we are asleep, a potent aerosol made from pungent Japanese wasabi horseradish – the active ingredient is allyl isothiocyanate – will irritate the mucus membranes to such a degree that you have no choice but to wake up. Their practical application of this was to develop a fire alarm for the deaf.

212 Incidentally, asparagus is rich in mercaptan, which is why urine can smell 'gassy' after we've been eating it.

In 2009, the border town of Vierlinden in Germany had a problem with sex workers gathering in large numbers near the B1 motorway between Seelow and Müncheberg and on the B87 near Beeskow. As many as 1,500 women – mainly from Ukraine, Bulgaria and Romania – worked in and around the border, targeting truckers on their way to and from nearby Poland. Mayor Dirk Illgenstein decided that the problem had to be eradicated by 'any means possible' because, as he put it: 'Our territory must be completely taboo for the red-light scene.' The main difficulty he faced, however, was that prostitution is legal.

He began by ticketing the sex workers for endangering traffic and started filming the punters on secret cameras and putting their car number plates on a 'website of shame'. Then he hit upon the idea of spreading around dollops of fake vomit. Quite how he came up with this idea is unknown but, it must be said, the stench and sight of vomit would probably dampen the ardour of even the horniest trucker. Fake vomit can be bought from specialist movie supply stores but it is (apparently) pretty tasteless and doesn't smell of much. Illgenstein decided to beef his up by adding butyric acid $(C_4H_8O_2)$ – basically rancid butter – to the mix. This same substance was used between 2005 and 2010 by the Sea Shepherd Conservation Society to 'butter bomb' the decks of Japanese whaling ships. Despite being harmless and non-corrosive, it stinks strongly of vomit, and it put the whalers off wanting to go out on deck and fire harpoons at things. Illgenstein hoped it would have the same effect on the sex workers. Not surprisingly, they were unimpressed by his plan.

'This is completely macabre and discriminatory, and reminds me of mediaeval witch hunts,' said Uta Ludwig, head of women's outreach clinic Belladonna, which works with many of the sex workers in question. 'Running the women off doesn't help. They'll just turn up somewhere else.'

I've not found a review of the action to date so, as to whether the idea worked, watch this space.

Just don't sniff this space.

6

When I was studying biology at school, I was told that there were five senses: sight, hearing, taste, touch and smell. However, if a sense can be said to be any form of input that allows us to figure out where we are and what's going on around us, then there are a lot more than five. We have a sense of direction and we have a sense of time (time cannot be perceived by any of the five traditional senses). We have pain sense (nociception), a balance sense (vestibular) and heat sense (thermoception). Then there's proprioception: our facility for knowing where we are in space. Shut your eyes and wave your arm around and, amazingly, you know where your hand is. If you keep your eyes shut and wiggle your fingers you feel as if you can almost see them. Plus there's *synaesthesia*, a condition that causes a curious blending of the senses that, in extreme cases, has some people tasting words or seeing numbers. However, we're all mildly synaesthetic; we've already talked about smell and taste overlapping significantly and the fact that we associate colours with feelings and temperature (blue is cold, red is hot, etc.). There's a degree of synaesthesia in our speech too and it's fairly easy to show you the effect.[213] Have a look at these two shapes. If I tell you that they are called 'kiki' and 'bouba', can you tell me which one is which?

213 I'm not terribly synaesthetic but I sometimes have to describe things in synaesthetic ways. For example, I have described camomile tea as 'tasting like the smell of cut grass' and root beer as 'tasting like the smell of embrocation'.

The chances are you'll imagine 'kiki' as the sharp, angular shape and 'bouba' as the softer, rounded shape. Most people do. You are, in effect, 'seeing' the sounds. And the effect is very deeply buried in our subconscious; this test works on people all over the world, no matter what language they speak. Recent research demonstrates that even children as young as two years old (too young to read) show this effect as well, and there is a theory that this facility for attaching certain sounds to certain characteristics, colours and shapes may be the origins of language.

Scientists believe there may be upwards of 20 different senses constantly feeding us input – so it's no surprise that problem-solvers have always understood the power of targeting one or more of them. We've looked at sight and the use of colours. We've explored smell with wasabi fire alarms, gas leaks and fake vomit. And we've seen how sound allows bees to herd elephants. But what about our senses of taste and touch? Obviously, people with visual impairments rely a great deal on clever use of tactile surfaces to keep them safe, such as the knobbly paving slabs that line the edges of train platforms, for example, or the ridged cones on the underside of the press button boxes at pelican crossings which rotate to tell the person when it's safe to cross.

Chewing gum is a good example of a problem relating

to taste and feel. For a start it's very sticky. It poses a huge problem for cleaners who have to employ steam guns to clean it up off the streets (or paint it black as they do on some tarmac pavements) or pick it off the underside of furniture. It's a problem for some bird species that eat it and can't digest it. It's a problem for monuments and important venues where the gum detracts from the beauty and/or atmosphere of the place. And it's a problem for the taxpayer; the government spends around £150m each year on cleaning up gum on the UK's streets. One set of figures I've seen suggests that cleaning up one piece of dropped gum costs 50 times more than the stick of gum itself.

So what can you do to stop people sticking chewing gum where it shouldn't be stuck? It's a question that we were asked several times in the Problem Solving Unit. At the time, there were people saying that it should be banned in public areas, like smoking is in many places. Gum bans do exist in some places but they are difficult to police. In Singapore, they've tried. The import and sale of gum is illegal but it's not illegal to chew gum and plenty of it goes on, especially among tourists. Punitive fines are imposed if anyone is caught spitting their gum onto the floor, but catching someone in the act is difficult. There is still gum on the pavements of Singapore despite the ban, albeit not nearly as much as in places like London where it's estimated that Oxford Street alone has, at any one time, around a quarter of a million gum pieces on its pavements.

One of the first questions we asked is – why do people drop their gum? We found a number of reasons, all of them related to the senses. The first was due to taste or, rather, the loss of it. Chewing gum and bubblegum very quickly lose their sweetness as the sugars are dissolved and swallowed. Then the flavour seems to go; I say 'seems' because it's actually truer to say that your brain gets 'bored' and stops responding to it. As the sweetness reduces, so does our perception of other flavours and aromas, such as mint. They're still there but the brain tunes them out. If you want to see this effect for yourself, chew some gum until it becomes tasteless, then remove it from your mouth and keep it somewhere safe and clean for 24 hours. Then pop it back in your mouth – it will once again have flavour: a weak flavour admittedly, but one you could no longer taste the day before. I was reminded of this fact in 2006 when visiting Ayrshire in Scotland. One particular small street was pointed out to me that was covered in gum. 'You should be here when it rains,' a police colleague told me. 'All the gum comes back to life. We call it Minty Street.'

I did wonder if it could be possible to make a gum that dissolves in your mouth at the same rate as the flavour fades. However, a quick email to the Wrigley company resulted in the simple and obvious response that 'it wouldn't be gum then'. The very chewability and firmness of chewing gum is what makes it attractive. However, they did tell me that their chemists are looking into ways to make the gum more biodegradable than it currently is.

So what do you do with your gum once you no longer want it? You could swallow it. It won't take 'seven years to dissolve in your stomach', as you might have once been told by a parent, and it's a biological impossibility for it to get 'wrapped around your heart' or other organs. While it's true that gum is made of fairly indigestible things like elastomers, waxes, resins and emulsifiers – the very things that stop it dissolving in your mouth or in the rain – the body will eventually push it out of the other end of the digestive system. You would have to swallow an awful lot of gum in a very short period of time to create any kind of medical problem. But if you don't fancy swallowing it, you need to get rid of it some other way. And here's the other tactile problem: gum is moist and sticky and often has bits of food embedded in it and it's not a lot of fun to touch. Had you saved the foil wrapper – as gum companies advise – you could have wrapped it in that but most people discard the wrapper when they pop the stick of gum in their mouths. But wrapped or unwrapped, you still have to hold it until you find a bin and people will generally only walk, on average, about 12 paces with a piece of litter in their hands before getting a deep and impatient urge to be rid of it.[214] Unfortunately the feeling of revulsion caused by holding a piece of chewed gum is often more powerful than a person's compulsion to do the right thing and the gum is dropped onto the pavement. Or there's no bin nearby. And, of course, there are some ignorant and lazy people who just don't give a damn; the sort of people who leave their litter about for someone else to clear up.

We can make disposal of gum easier by providing gum bins. My particular favourite design at the moment is the 'Gumdrop' which is actually made from recycled gum (the company makes a handy small one for your key-ring too if you're between bins). Founded in 2009 by Anna Bullus, the Gumdrop company recycles the gum collected into a range of polymers that can be used in the plastics and rubber industries.

214 There is a story that Walt Disney made a similar observation, which is why – apparently – the litter bins are all around 30 paces apart in Disney resorts; if a person can see one approaching they might hang on to litter until they get there.

Photo: Gumdrop Ltd

The Gumdrops are globular and bright pink – a colour much discussed in this chapter – and they attract attention. In a six-month trial project in Cardiff in 2013, 100 Gumdrops collected enough gum to make six new city benches, 60 pairs of Wellington boots, 1,003 rulers or 1,134 new Gumdrop bins. Interestingly, placement was important; gum bins outside pubs and food outlets got the most use, presumably because people remove their gum in order to eat and drink. The company's website states that Gumdrops reduce gum litter by up to 46 per cent in the first 12 weeks of use. And, of course, the gumdrops can also be recycled.

But, as effective as bins can be, they entice rather than actively encourage people to use them. Gum boards, however, go one step further by being fun to use. A gum board is just what it sounds like, a board on which to stick your gum and some have a simple message such as 'Thank you for sticking your gum here'. But the most successful gum boards draw people in by engaging their sense of devilry or naughtiness. You pick an unpopular but well-known person and put their photo on the board. That's often enough. But if you add a message such as 'Use your gum to show what you think of him/her' people will do exactly that. You do have to be careful; as we discovered while trying them out in west London, some celebs and their agents do not have a sense of humour. But gum boards work; in 2004, Preston council in Lancashire started to use boards with a peelable plastic film cover that could be cleaned every day and announced that the boards helped reduce gum litter in the town by nearly 80 per cent. In the first year of their use in Luton, Bedfordshire, the boards collected in excess of 75,000 pieces of used gum that would otherwise have probably ended up on the pavement.

Photo: Gum Election

And during the Obama/Romney US election campaign of 2012, creatives Stefan Haverkamp, Hedvig Astrom and James Cooper ran a project called 'Gum Election' where they asked people to use their gum to indicate 'Who sucks the most?'[215] The purpose of the project was, in their words, 'to encourage people to vote on Election Day as well as keeping the city

215 They had run the same project in the previous Obama/McCain election in 2008.

a little cleaner'. The posters were put up all over New York City, as well as cities in California and Canada (who couldn't vote, of course, but enjoyed joining in the fun). People were encouraged to post pictures of the gummed posters on photo sharing sites like Instagram and Tumblr and the results flooded in. And they pretty much mirrored the final election result. As Havercamp said at the time, 'Our campaign cost nothing but we had more responses than any official party ad. It just shows that, even in politics, you don't need money – just a great idea.'

This chapter and the previous one were all about nudges; how little hints and suggestions can shepherd people towards better behaviour or lesser likelihood of becoming a victim. Our senses are our windows on the world so, if you want to get a message across, the more 'windows' you can nudge open, the better.

11: THE R FACTOR

The measure of success is not whether you have a tough problem to deal with, but whether it's the same problem you had last year.

                     - John Foster Dulles

When a measure becomes a target, it ceases to be a good measure.

                     Goodhart's Law[216]

1

I'm not an obsessive person by nature. While I collect all sorts of weird and wonderful things, my tastes are eclectic and I don't have the fanaticism of the completist. I'm not at all competitive or compulsive and I'm quite sanguine about gaps in my various modest collections. But I did once get quite obsessive about a burglar. Let's call him Terry.

It was 1982 and I'd just passed my probation. I was a fully fledged cop. Terry was about the same age as me – 20 or 21 – and he was a fully fledged burglar. I knew this because he'd been caught a couple of times as a teenager and because lots of people told us that he was. Terry wasn't just prolific; he was prolific and cocky. He boasted to people about his ability to run circles around the police. And his boasts were pretty justified. Terry was clever. When he broke into a house he

---

216 Coined by and named after the economist and former advisor to the Bank of England Charles Goodhart.

only ever took small, portable, nondescript items that were hard to identify and easy to dispose of: things like cash, popular brands of electronics (Walkmans were very big back then) and unmarked, generic jewellery such as plain rings and gold necklaces.[217] Consequently, even if you caught him with property on his person, it was next to impossible to prove that it didn't belong to him. He wasn't greedy either; he stole just enough to pay his bills and to keep him in beer, petrol, and a few other small luxuries.

Terry took delight in the fact that all we ever had against him was hearsay evidence and anecdote, none of which was admissible in court. He'd wave and smile whenever we saw him and was always extra polite and helpful whenever he was stopped and searched. The result of this was that most of my colleagues hated him with a passion and several became quite fixated upon catching him. No one likes a mickey-taker.

I wasn't immune to Terry Fever either. Whenever I had a spare minute during a shift, I'd spend it tailing him in the hope that I'd be lucky enough to get something on him. Unfortunately, it tended to work the other way round; he'd spot me before I spotted him – I was a particularly rubbish undercover cop – and one day, just for kicks I suspect, he wrote a letter to my Chief Superintendent stating that I was harassing him and that, if I didn't stop, there would be an official complaint made.

I'm not proud of that period of my police career. People are innocent until proven otherwise and, until I saw him actually do something wrong, he had exactly the same rights as any other law-abiding citizen. Therefore, I guess it could be said that I was harassing him. My Chief Super knew how frustrated we all were but his hands were tied. The law is the law. I agreed to back off.

But here's the thing: during my most intense periods of Terry-watching, the burglary rate in the area dropped

---

217 Remember the mnemonics of CRAVED (Concealable, Removable, Available, Valuable, Enjoyable, Disposable) and VIVA (Visible, [has] Inertia, Valuable, Accessible) mentioned back in Chapter 4?

significantly. As soon as I stopped, the numbers rose again. At the time, I couldn't prove an absolute correlation between the fluctuations and my 'stalking' activities; after all, it's quite possible (if unlikely) that there were other factors involved that I knew nothing about. But there's little doubt in my mind that my colleagues and I were able to put him off his stride, which resulted in fewer burglaries. Our problem was that, without something tangible and countable to justify any further action against him, we were forced to leave him alone. I returned to reporting his crimes instead of preventing them, while the CID figured out how to catch him without receiving their own harassment complaints. Everyone felt frustrated and miserable except Terry.

You'll be pleased to know that there is a happy ending to this story; Terry was eventually caught red-handed while burgling a house that, unusually for that time, had a CCTV system installed.[218] And it wasn't long after this that I became convinced, more than ever, that normal policing methods were badly thought-through. What my colleagues and I should have been doing was frustrating him by making people's houses harder for him to burgle.

What stopped us from doing so was the fact that, at that time, any such police activity wasn't measured as 'performance'. While I was doing my best to stifle Terry's burgling habit, I wasn't arresting as many people as my colleagues were. The number of burglaries may have dropped significantly but, on paper, I appeared to be doing bugger all police work. Consequently, one of the other reasons that I was advised to leave Terry alone was that it was 'bad for my career'.

Looking back on events now, it's extraordinary to think that my performance wasn't judged on the things I did and

---

218 As I recall, the owner of the house was a store detective who had been given his store's old system when they'd upgraded. And, being a gadget lover, he'd set it up in his house. How Terry had missed it, I don't know. The cameras were not small and compact like they are now. Maybe his cockiness got the better of him. I'd like to think so.

the results I achieved. Whether I was deemed a good worker or a bad worker depended solely upon the method used to measure my performance.

So how do you measure the effectiveness of policing?

You might remember back in Chapter 1, when I talked about the origins of organised policing, that I quoted Sir Richard Mayne's 'Primary Objects' in which he stated that *'The protection of life and property, the preservation of public tranquillity, and the absence of crime, will alone prove whether those efforts have been successful and whether the objects for which the police were appointed have been attained.'* I don't see any mention there of arrest figures, do you? And Professor Herman Goldstein, the father of Problem Oriented Policing (POP), made the point that, traditionally, policing had focused on the 'means' of policing rather than its 'ends'. In other words, the measures used to gauge police success were wrongly targeted on inputs (what cops do) instead of ouputs (what cops achieve).

I do appreciate that measuring outputs is a lot trickier in policing than it is in, say, a manufacturing business. For them, it's quite easy. You can quantify success with simple, easy-to-obtain statistical data like company profits, orders and sales, expansion, buy-outs and take-overs, staff turnover, customer feedback, etc. And if the public doesn't like a product or the quality of service, they will vote with their feet and buy their products from your rivals. In contrast, something like policing is a lot harder to measure because it has no profits to count and no 'product' that you can measure in physical units. That's why, for many years, when asked to provide evidence of police efficiency, senior managers fell back to measuring inputs; what their troops did all day.

In the early days of my police career I was required to keep a record of all stops, stops and searches, arrests and process (reporting people for minor offences – mostly traffic) that I was involved in. I also had to keep a 'court card' that showed how many appearances I'd made and the outcome of each case. These constituted my 'figures' – my return of work, as it was properly called – and they were reviewed monthly by a senior officer throughout my two-year-long probationary period and then yearly thereafter. Quite how the benchmark for satisfactory performance was set is still a mystery to me; there didn't seem to be any official guidance coming out from New Scotland Yard, and every station I worked at seemed to have a different idea of what 'satisfactory' was. It even seemed to vary between senior officers working at the same station. Was there a point below which the number of arrests an officer made became unacceptable? How do you know when you've stopped and searched enough people? These were questions I often asked myself. And they were questions I asked my sergeants who invariably replied with something like, 'Look, do you want to keep your job or not?' It all seemed so arbitrary, especially because faking data is so easy. After all, you can claim to have driven 100 miles and produce the petrol gauge and odometer of your car as hard evidence, but if all you did was go around the same roundabout 1,000 times you haven't achieved anything except maybe nausea. I also suspect that the figures forced cops to make arrests and to do stops and searches that maybe they might not have done; there was definitely a culture of 'What gets measured gets done' at supervisor level. I certainly saw officers making up their stop numbers with names randomly chosen from telephone directories. After all, who would ever check? All I know for sure is that measuring activity isn't the same thing as measuring performance. If you want to measure success, you need to make sure that you're measuring the right criteria.

In addition to my figures, I was also judged on such things as 'uniform dress, bearing, personal appearance' and 'detective ability, crime investigation, interrogation'. It's notable that, back then, there were no headings for things like 'has engaged with the community', or 'has helped to reduce crime and the fear of crime'.

However, things did get better. Later on in my service, the annual performance review forms were redesigned and new categories appeared that included, for the first

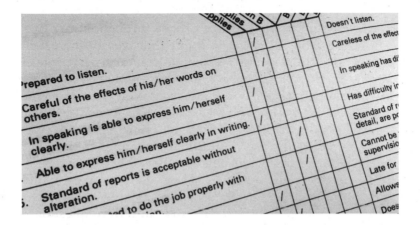

time, behavioural measures such as 'has an understanding attitude towards the public', 'has an awareness of local problems', and 'has a helpful attitude'. Once these sorts of things started to be measured, my annual reports suddenly seemed to get much better even though I hadn't changed the way I worked at all. All that had changed was what was being measured.

I'm sure you're familiar with the quote, often but erroneously attributed to Einstein (more Churchillian Drift there), which goes: *'If you judge a fish by its ability to climb a tree, it will live its whole life believing that it is stupid'*. On paper I must have looked like the stupidest and laziest fish in the forest.

2

In 2001, Hampshire Constabulary published its annual crime figures and announced a substantial drop in motor vehicle crime across the county. It is worthy of mention that sterling work in Portsmouth by a project called 'Operation Cobra' had reduced crime by 31 per cent. However, the biggest reduction had been in the New Forest area, normally a hotspot for theft from motor vehicles. Anyone noticing this might have been tempted to congratulate the local police for their particularly excellent work; the statistics were there in black and white. However, the actual reason for the drop was the outbreak of Foot and Mouth Disease. Visitors' cars were banned from the forest for some four months in what proved to be a successful effort to keep the disease from the wild ponies and other animals. And, to their credit, Hampshire Constabulary was quite open about the causes of the drop and never once claimed credit for something they hadn't done. But it does show that statistics alone do not tell the whole story.

And in 2007, a colleague of mine from Nottinghamshire told me that a similar thing happened in a town called Gedling. The local police chief was in very high spirits after hearing that there had been a sudden 80 per cent reduction in the number of thefts of, and from, cars in pub car parks. However, before he began singing the praises of his staff and policies, it was pointed out to him that, maybe, he should wait until some analysis confirmed the cause. And, thankfully, he was wise enough to take the advice, because it turned out that police action had not contributed to the reduction at all. It was entirely due to the introduction of the Health Act 2006, which, from July 1st, 2007, made it illegal to smoke inside pubs. The result was an exodus of smokers to outside the pub where they unconsciously became 'capable guardians' and made it almost impossible for the poor old car thief to operate.

These two stories – and there are many more like them – demonstrate the importance of evaluating results properly.

The word 'evaluation' comes from the same root as the word 'value' and that's what it's all about; measuring what value a project or initiative has added. When we looked at projects we'd been involved with in the Problem Solving Unit we went through two stages: an *Impact Assessment* followed by a *Process Review*.

The Impact Assessment meant asking ourselves two simple questions:

1. Is the situation better than it was before? (e.g. crime

figures have gone down, people feel safer, more public engagement); and

2. If the situation has improved, was it our response that made the difference?

The second question was just as important to answer as the first. It wasn't enough to show that the problem had diminished or vanished. We also needed to know what exactly – let's call it the *R Factor* – was responsible for the reduction. If we were the R Factor then it was cause for celebration and we'd know that maintaining what we were doing would lead to continued success. But if the R Factor was something beyond our control – like in the examples above – then the problem could always come back. Consequently, we'd need to plan for that eventuality.

In our Nottinghamshire car thefts example, the R Factor was a change in people's smoking habits. But, since 2007, e-cigs have become readily available and many pubs now allow them to be smoked on the premises. If the pubs in Gedling have now allowed this, the R Factor might have been removed. It would be interesting to see if letting people smoke e-cigs indoors has caused the number of car crimes to rise. And, if so, did the local police plan for it?

I'm not going to go into the mechanics of evaluation too deeply in this chapter as (a) it'll interrupt the narrative, (b) there are plenty of books that explain it better than I ever could, and (c) it can be a bit dull. You can find out all about aims, objectives, baselines, milestones, quantitative and qualitative measures and stuff like that elsewhere. I will, however, talk briefly about setting aims.

Your aims should always be ambitious – it's good to push the limits of what you believe you can achieve. But you do also have to be realistic. Throughout my career my colleagues and I were often set impossible targets by our senior officers who, in turn, were often set impossible targets by the government. They were so unrealistic at times that I can only assume that some Home Office minister plucked a number out of thin air or threw some dice. Simon Guilfoyle, the author of

Intelligent Policing, says: 'There has never been any obvious science behind why a target would be set at, for example, 30% instead of 32%, 27%, or 80%. Some targets appear to have been set purely because they are slightly higher than whatever was achieved during the previous period. This is purely based on the unenlightened assumption that the last period's performance must have been 'normal'.'

Obviously, we'd all love to eliminate problems completely so that they no longer blight people's lives. But, as we discussed in Chapter 3, elimination is an almost impossible state to achieve when you're working with complex, human issues. Admittedly, there are times when you have to been seen to aim for elimination. For example, imagine that the Home Office decided to set an 85% reduction target for domestic violence. Although any sane person would realise that it doesn't in any way imply that 15% of current totals is 'acceptable', the tabloids would have a field day with it. And if it were done for especially emotive crimes such as rape or child abduction, it would be quite rightly seen as insensitive and insulting. There are times when you have to carefully consider your words.

Our mantra within the Problem Solving Unit, as you might recall, was 'transforming one set of circumstances into another, preferred state'. We knew that we may not be able to get rid of a problem completely and forever, but we also knew that we could usually make a situation better, often much better. This was reflected in the way that we set our aims. One useful tool that we used to help decide the degree of effect we could have on a problem was the Impact Scale: [219]

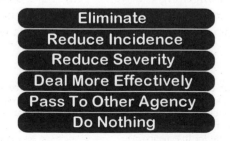

Eliminate
Reduce Incidence
Reduce Severity
Deal More Effectively
Pass To Other Agency
Do Nothing

219 Based on work by Professors John Eck and William Spelman.

If you say that you're going to eliminate a problem, no matter how good your interventions are, you're probably setting yourself up to fail. But you can still aim to stop a problem from happening so often. Reducing the number of incidents was the most common level of aim that my colleagues and I used.[220]

But even if you can't limit the number of times a problem occurs, you can still make a difference by minimising the effect it has on people's lives. A good example of this is the use of traffic calming measures around premises like schools. Children have always and will always run out in front of cars when leaving school. You may not always be able to stop them being knocked down but, by using speed humps and barriers, you can slow down both the children and the cars so that if they do meet, the impact results in minor injury rather than serious injury or death.

However, there are problems where neither elimination nor reduction are possible. I'm talking about sudden unexpected and rare events like train crashes or falling buildings or even terrorist attacks that are, by their nature, unpredictable. But even if you can't prevent them from happening, you can still develop detailed contingency plans to ensure the quickest and most effective response possible. You can plan to minimise the impact of the problem when and if it occurs.

If all else fails, you may have to ask yourself, 'Am I the best person to deal with this?' or, 'Could I pass this on to a more suitable person/agency?' or even, 'Is there someone I could work with?' A police officer is often the first port of call when something is adversely affecting someone's life. But that doesn't necessarily mean that the police service is the best agency to tackle their problem. This is when having

---

220 I say reduction by numbers because percentages are so deceptive. I recall that I once looked at some issues in one of the Royal Parks and was told that about 40% of all crimes reported to police in July were sexual offences. As alarming as that sounded, the reality, in raw figures, showed that there had been 13 crimes reported in total for that period. Five were categorised as sexual offences and they were all reports of indecent exposure.

a wide and varied range of partners comes in handy. If one or more of them seems to be better equipped to tackle the problem, you pass it to them for action and support them in their efforts.

Above all, aims should be realistic. Unrealistic aims won't be met and that can be both damaging to your credibility and demoralising for all of those involved. I saw a powerful example of that in February 2015 when most newspapers carried a headline which read something like 'A&E departments miss patient target'. The story was that NHS trusts had been set the task of ensuring that 95% of patients were seen and treated within four hours. Some A&E departments hadn't met the target and the words 'fail' and 'failure' were given prominence in every news report I read about them. But hidden further down in the text of the story was that fact that the 'failures' had, nevertheless, achieved levels of over 90% despite the number of emergency admissions being higher than ever.[221]

Getting more than 90% of people through a busy A&E unit within four hours is a pretty excellent level of service, if you ask me. How many organisations can boast over 90% efficiency as the norm? But that's no comfort for the staff who were labelled as failures. What kind of effect is it going to have on their morale? The saddest thing is that it could have all been so different. Firstly, setting the same single target for every hospital is ridiculous. They're all different. An average evening in A&E is very different in a deprived inner city area to one in a quite well-to-do county town. Perhaps what the NHS and the Health Ministry should be doing is assessing performance by outcomes - public satisfaction, reduction in deaths, and people's quality of life following treatment of serious injuries - rather than simply measuring how many people are pushed through the system. And how about rewarding those who did hit their targets

---

221 It's also notable that I didn't once see any national newspaper headline dedicated to the A&E departments that did hit their target.

and encouraging those that didn't by saying, 'Thank you for trying your hardest to get there.' Will they be more likely to try harder next time than those who've been branded as failures? I know I would.

What's particularly annoying about stories like that is that failure isn't always the bad thing that it's painted to be. In fact, the concept of 'embracing failure' has become something of a cliché within business circles in recent years because, if you think about it, failure increases our knowledge about what doesn't work. It reveals the weak links in a chain. It uncovers the sticking points. That's hugely useful because that knowledge may help to prevent other people from making the same mistakes in future. I once heard someone say: 'Uncertainty is the basis of all science. If we were sure of everything, we'd have finished by now.' I have no idea who first said it and I haven't been able to track it down as a quote, but it's a wise observation. If an experiment proves that something is not true, it's useful knowledge for future experimenters. It's what I would call a noble failure because it was the result of well-meaning effort. We should learn to embrace noble failure and turn it into something positive.

Sometimes I didn't achieve my aims. Sometimes things happened over which I had no control. At other times, my initiatives didn't work quite as I'd planned; there is always scope for things to go unexpectedly awry. But I maintain that any win – however small – is still a win. If things are better than they were, then people's lives have been improved and that's never a bad thing.

Just ask the people who were treated by all those 'failed' A&E units.

3

While an Impact Assessment is about what was achieved and how, the second part of evaluation – the *Process Review* – is all about looking back over the project and asking things like:

- What went well?
- What didn't go well?
- What were the highlights and why?
- What were the low points and why?
- What were the sticking points (if any)?
- Who performed well?
- Who didn't perform well?
- What mistakes were made (if any)?
- How well were mistakes rectified?
- How well were resources managed?
- What could have been done better and how?
- What have we learned that would be useful to pass on to others running similar projects?

The Process Review provides useful information to pass on to others involved in similar projects. It points out where we might have gone wrong and provides opportunity to rethink our interventions and to try using a different approach in future. When the Problem Solving Unit was asked to tackle complex issues of crime and public safety, it wasn't uncommon for our first attempt to fail. But we didn't give up. We reviewed what we'd done, regrouped, tweaked our responses and tried again. Sometimes they didn't work either. So we ran through the process once again. We did that as many times as necessary. Occasionally, very occasionally, we were asked to look at a problem for which there seemed to be no hope of a solution and which people described as impossible to solve. But we always gave it our best shot. Perseverance, realistic aims, and a willingness to accept noble failure and learn from it, resulted in some extraordinary success stories. And we became involved in projects where local police officers, local authority staff and the community exhibited exactly the same determination as we did to make things better.

4

Photo: Tom Bastin

Kingswood, in the London Borough of Southwark, is a large housing estate of around 700 households that sits in the middle of prosperous Dulwich village. Despite its size, the estate feels quite isolated, like an island afloat in a sea of leafy green suburbia. All around it there are very expensive properties and, nearby, you'll find the celebrated Dulwich Picture Gallery and several public schools including the prestigious Dulwich College. But Kingswood is very different to its surroundings. The estate is fairly self-contained and has its own shops, housing office, primary school and secondary school. But most of the estate takes the form of social housing and the residents live with high levels of deprivation and low employment. And Kingswood had some serious problems.

In July 2007, a 16-year-old boy with no connection to

gangs or crime was savagely attacked on the estate by a gang member from neighbouring Lambeth Borough. Thankfully he survived multiple stab wounds, but the attack raised the fear of crime on the estate considerably, especially among young people. Squabbles and fights between gangs had been escalating in recent months, usually when gangs from other areas came onto the estate to commit offences like robbery and drug dealing. Few of these crimes were ever officially reported because the young victims were afraid of retribution. Following the stabbing, the estate was designated a priority policing area due to residents' concerns about increasing crime, gang violence and antisocial behaviour. Then, in July 2008, a fifteen-year-old gang member from Kingswood was lured off the estate and murdered. For some young people, this was a wake-up call. For others, it hardened their resolve to join a gang for protection. Young people living on the estate were as much the victims as they were the offenders. Large groups of youths started to regularly gather in what they considered to be safe, defensible areas like stairwells and near shops, which made other residents feel threatened. A lack of youth facilities exacerbated the problem. Tensions on the estate heightened and residents began to withdraw from their community. Things were falling apart. Worryingly, anecdotal evidence and graffiti seemed to indicate that, for a few, the murder victim was seen as a 'fallen soldier' and there was talk of revenge in the air.

PC Mark Deacon of the local College Ward Safer Neighbourhoods Team (SNT) and Joan Leary from Southwark Council's Antisocial Behaviour Unit knew that something had to be done before things got out of hand. In addition to crime and emerging gang issues, there were also frequent fights when schools finished for the day. Most of these took place near the estate's shops or at nearby Sydenham Hill Station.

Photo: Tom Bastin

Like the aforementioned Welland Crescent and so many other areas with multiple issues, it was clear from the outset that no one single agency was going to turn Kingswood around. So Mark and Joan set out to get as many agencies who 'shared the problem' on board as they could and, in a short time, pulled together a strong problem solving forum involving their own teams, the British Transport Police, Southwark Borough Youth Services, Youth Offending Team and Housing Department, Kingsdale School, the Kingswood Tenants' and Residents' Association and local community wardens. Myself and a colleague from the Problem Solving Unit were also invited along to pitch in ideas and to advise where we could as we'd been involved in tackling similar problems on other estates.

The first task was research and analysis. Local people were consulted and crime reports were examined. Every source of data we could find was examined for patterns and intelligence; even things like council maintenance and cleaning records so that the main problem areas for littering, graffiti and damage could be identified.

Ultimately, all of this work led to the formation of three aims: Firstly, to reduce the number of young people becoming victims of violent crime; secondly to achieve a reduction in concerns about youth antisocial behaviour and fear of crime amongst residents; and thirdly, to increase residents' confidence in the ability of the police and Southwark Council to effectively tackle issues of concern. To meet these aims, we set objectives which included: identifying individuals involved in crime and antisocial behaviour; creating and supporting activities for young people to divert them from gangs and crime; increasing community cohesion; and reducing ASB by secondary school students on the estate.

What followed was a raft of measures put into action to meet the three aims. Regular public meetings were held on the estate. The SNT and community wardens increased the number of visible patrols and youth workers engaged with the estate's young people. Enhanced support was given to the victim of the 2007 stabbing (and a witness), which led to a successful prosecution and imprisonment of the offender, which increased trust in the police and the judicial system. A youth club was set up on the estate with a wide range of activities focusing on personal safety, drug awareness and strategies to help young people leave gangs. Chaotic families and parents that were identified as struggling to cope with their kids were visited and help was provided wherever possible. Young people were encouraged to sign Acceptable Behaviour Contracts (ABCs) and educational schemes were offered to children excluded from school. Residents were made aware that they were in real danger of losing their homes if they breached tenancy obligations by taking part in crime or by allowing illegal activity on their premises.

Meanwhile, the schools – which had been resistant to police officers visiting – got involved and teachers joined police staff and wardens patrolling key areas during school start and end times. In addition, CCTV was installed covering the school gates, which reduced disorderly behaviour to almost zero. Truancy on the estate was dealt with by way of truancy patrols and the numbers dropped to negligible levels. And the council's environmental staff had been busy too, organising regular 'clean sweeps' of the estate to remove graffiti, abandoned vehicles, litter and bulkier fly-tipped items, and deep cleaning communal areas. Gardens were tidied, repairs made to properties (no more broken windows) and surveys were carried out to ensure that problems were being addressed.

Enforcement went on too: fixed penalty notices were issued for minor crimes, a number of drugs warrants were successfully executed and arrests made. It was made very clear that Kingswood now had a zero tolerance policy for carrying weapons.

Another issue that needed tackling was community cohesion, something I was very keen to see happen. We wanted Kingswood to develop a 'tribe'. We wanted the community to own and care for their space and to look out for each other. Therefore, a series of events were organised to bring people together. They included a summer fête, music and talent contests, a children's fun day, cycle safety events, and a 'Kingswood Carnival'. They all proved to be very popular and did a great deal to help break down barriers between social groups. My personal favourite was a dog show. I'd already seen the power of dogs on another south London estate where setting up a dog show had helped to bring a fractured community together. Dogs create a bridge; it's awkward to approach a total stranger to say hello. It's a lot easier if they have a dog and you can ask to pet it and then open a conversation. There were lots of dogs on the Kingswood estate and the dog show brought the owners out of their homes. Battersea Dogs' Home, the RSPCA and the PDSA got involved, offering dietary advice and discounted neutering and spaying, and the Met Police dog team did a display. But the high point for me was seeing a Yorkshire-terrier-owning pensioner, probably in her late 70s or early 80s, having a go at a tall, muscular young black guy because his dog, an American Bulldog, was overweight. These were people who, on any other day, would probably have crossed the road to avoid each other. Dogs had brought them together. It was wonderful to see.

Throughout the entire operation, residents were kept informed and updated on all interventions by phone calls, emails, leaflet drops, public meetings, street briefings and home visits. And if any initiative didn't work as intended, it was discussed, assessed, and then either abandoned, retried or adapted for a second attempt. Everyone refused to give up on Kingswood.

It was an extraordinary effort by a partnership of dedicated problem solvers and an evaluation of their efforts proved to be enlightening. By comparing crime data for the same periods in 2007 and 2008, it became immediately apparent that there had been a 66 per cent reduction in common assaults and a 50 per cent reduction in violent crime against youths (under 18). There was a 40 per cent reduction in criminal damage. There was an increase in reports of drug crime ... but only because there had been a crackdown and several arrests, and because people now felt confident enough in the police to report incidents.

On the qualitative side of things, an independent and comprehensive 'citizen impact' survey was undertaken which revealed that 59 per cent of respondents had noticed an improvement in the behaviour of young people, 69 per cent said that they felt safe while alone on the estate, and 72 per cent thought the police and council had done a 'good' or 'very good' job with regard to these matters. Other measures of success included Southwark Antisocial Behaviour Unit reporting a 70 per cent reduction in calls to their 24-hour ASB Hotline.

The biggest challenge had been to win the trust of young people and so they were invited to take part in discussions about the estate. Ten young people subsequently volunteered to work with the police to represent their peers at meetings. A survey conducted as part of the evaluation revealed that 77 per cent of young people now felt either 'safe' or 'very safe', and 53 per cent stated that they now felt comfortable and confident enough to report being a victim of crime.[222] Incredibly, 50 per cent of young people stated that the amount of stop and search used on the estate was 'about right' and 17 per cent thought there should actually be more.

One final survey question was posed to all of the residents of Kingswood. It asked, simply, 'Do you believe that Kingswood is now a good place to live?' An overwhelming majority – 84 per cent – said 'yes'.

And that, perhaps, is the most important result of all.

5

Back in 2004, the Met – assisted by funding from Mayor Ken Livingstone's office – had embraced the POP approach by creating a two-pronged form of policing; the existing response teams would continue answering the 999 calls, chasing the bad guys and reporting the crimes, but brand new *Safer Neighbourhoods Teams* (SNTs) would take on the POP work of crime prevention, tackling community concerns and fear of crime issues. Supporting both policing 'strands' would be local Intelligence Units staffed by trained researchers and analysts. A trial of the model in London and at several other UK sites worked so well that it was adopted across the country and much of the training that we'd developed in the Problem Solving Unit was adapted by the Home Office to support new SNTs nationwide.[223] However, as the recession began to strangle the budgets, the old ways started to re-assert themselves. The SNTs were given more and more response duties and, once again, performance started to be measured by inputs rather than outputs.

---

222 This is higher than the national average which is believed to be between 30% and 44%.

223 It wasn't just our best practice; the Home Office drew on the experience of many police forces around the UK. Among the best at POP were Lancashire, Hampshire, Merseyside, South Yorkshire, Surrey, Avon and Somerset, West Midlands and Nottinghamshire but many others developed superb working practices too.

In 2006, North Wales Police instigated a system where officers were awarded points for the number of arrests and car seizures they made. And, in 2007, the police commander for the London Borough of Merton issued a memo stating that unless the number of arrests improved, he was 'fully prepared to use police regulations' to punish what he regarded as under-performance. These are just two examples; there were a great many more. To her credit, Home Secretary Theresa May was keen to stop this and, in 2010, announced that she wanted an end to police target-setting. 'I couldn't be any clearer about your mission', she told senior police officers. 'It is to cut crime. No more, and no less.' It was, no more and no less, precisely what Sir Richard Mayne had stated back in 1829, what Professor Herman Goldstein had advocated a century later, and what I had believed for three decades. If those old ideas about measuring police performance had been used for the Kingswood Estate project, chances are that the officers concerned might have come up short on their 'figures' as they were deeply involved in crime prevention.

In 2013, the Home Secretary was forced to reiterate her message and expressed concern that some senior police officers were bringing back targets as an easy option. 'Those targets certainly aren't coming from me, and they aren't being used to increase the effectiveness of policing', she said. 'Their main function seems to be to act as a security blanket for senior officers - a way to avoid taking responsibility for the decisions they have to make.' At the same time, the Met's reorganisation of its SNTs – which involved cutting staffing levels from five to two per team - was being blamed for the force scoring the third lowest visibility rate in the country. In July 2014, Commissioner Sir Bernard Hogan-Howe admitted that the balance between response policing and community policing had 'gone the wrong way' and that the policy was being reviewed. Catherine West, the MP for Hornsey and Wood Green, welcomed the news: 'Residents are consistently telling me that properly resourced Safer Neighbourhoods Teams are vital in making them feel safer and deterring crime and antisocial behaviour,' she told the *Broadway Ham and High* newspaper. I couldn't agree more.

Right at the start of this book I said that police and communities working together is the key to making our lives safer, happier and crime-free. The Kingswood project is the epitome of what I believe good policing should consist of; close links with the community, working effectively with other agencies, solving local problems and preventing new problems from occurring whether they be crimes or nuisances. Governments love to tell us that we're 'all in this together', but they don't always practise what they preach. Politicians and parties come and go but we don't need MPs and other notables to tell us how to live well. We just need to find ways to be the kind, caring, law-abiding, communal beings that we undoubtedly are. And if police officers can help to make that happen, the world will be a better place.

The value of a police officer should never be measured solely by the number of countable things they do – arrests, stops etc. The job is far too important and complex to be measured in simple numbers.

EPILOGUE: TO GET TO THE OTHER SIDE

It isn't that they can't see the solution. It's that they can't see the problem.

G K Chesterton

'Some of us will do our jobs well and some will not, but we will all be judged by only one thing – the result.'

Vince Lombardi

1

Thirty years is a long time to spend working for one employer but I never got bored. The Metropolitan Police Service is a huge organisation and there were lots of opportunities to get involved in a variety of areas of work. And it's hard to get bored in London. It is the most extraordinary city with an extraordinary population to match.

Over 13 million people live within the Met Police area and the population density is around 14,000 people per square mile. These numbers are bolstered daily by nearly a million commuters and, every year, by 14 million international visitors and 27 million overnight stay visitors. Every major religion and faith is represented and over 300 languages are spoken. And while London is not the most deprived area of the UK, it does have the largest gap between rich and poor, with areas of desperate poverty and deprivation and, sometimes just a few streets away, the highest concentration of billionaires in the world (72 at time of writing). It is a city of airports and rail networks, sporting and concert venues, national and international company headquarters, major banks, and hundreds of miles of roads. It houses the royal family, the seat of the UK government and almost every foreign embassy and consulate. Such a diverse city produces a constant stream of unique problems and every one of them needs a tailored solution.

For three decades I tried to find those tailored solutions and did what I could to make things better. I didn't always get it right and, occasionally, I got things wrong. But most of the time I made a difference. Then, when the Problem Solving Unit came along, my new colleagues and I were able to make a bigger difference together. It opened my eyes to a smarter, more effective and more inclusive form of policing.

I retired in 2010, 30 years to the day after I'd joined. On that final day, there was no golden handshake, no ceremony, nothing to officially mark my leaving.[224] That isn't how cops retire, at least not in the Met. I got a handshake from my Chief Superintendent, a framed copy of my 'Certificate of Completion of Service', and that was that. I checked my Met Police email address for the last time, set an automated reply saying that I'd retired, and handed in my warrant card at the HR office. Then I walked out of the front doors and the cord was cut. I was now no longer part of the Met 'tribe'; my access

---

224 There was, of course, a very pleasant drinks party with close colleagues.

to police buildings, computer systems and data was gone. But I didn't need any of that. Not any more. That part of my life was over. Or so I thought.

I have no idea why people find policing so fascinating. But they do; the enormous number of cop shows and crime fiction books is testament to that fact. People were always asking me questions about my career and they seemed particularly fascinated by the work of the Problem Solving Unit. So, now that I was retired and had some time on my hands, I began to wonder whether I should write a book about it. The idea had occurred to me as long ago as 2006 and I'd been gathering material and writing small pieces for possible inclusion ever since. So I sat at my computer and began to type.

This book is the result. I hope that I've given you a reasonable vision of how I believe that policing could be better. I also hope that I've managed to pass on some of what I've learned in an interesting and entertaining way.

Each chapter of this book had a general theme to it and I've tried to incorporate at least one lesson about effective problem solving in each chapter without it sounding like a business book. For example, Chapter 1 was all about the power of community, Chapter 2 looked at demand and Chapter 3 was about research ... and so on and so forth. What I've done, in fact, is share a process for solving problems with you. It can be whittled down into these five basic stages:

- **Demand** (Chapter 2 and some Chapter 1)
- **Research** (Chapter 3)
- **Analysis** (Chapter 4)
- **Response** (Chapters 5 - 10)
- **Evaluation** (Chapter 11)

This five-stage process is what I use for solving problems in every sphere of my life. I'm afraid that DRARE isn't a terribly memorable acronym but I've deliberately chosen to use unambiguous plain English terms – it doesn't need a catchy name in order to work.[225] If you don't believe me, try it on a problem that is currently affecting you. It can be any kind of problem; it's not just for crime. Think about what the demand is and who's making it. Do some research and then take the time to make sense of what you find out. Share the problem with people who think differently from you and you'll get some original ideas and insights. Consider partners; – who might be able to help you? Tackle the problem from different directions; look at the cause and the effect and the place and time that it happens. What could you change to prevent it? Then evaluate what you've done; did you make a difference? If so, how? Review what happened and learn from your success and your noble failures. Reward good work and celebrate the fact that you've made things better.

2

I recently met Jimmy Wales, the founder and public face of Wikipedia. Here is a man whose aim is to 'give every single person on the planet free access to the sum of all human knowledge' which, as aims go, is pretty damned good. Whether it's achievable is another matter, but I applaud his vision. We talked about the 'wiki' philosophy, the fact that absolutely anyone can alter, add or delete information on Wikipedia and I asked him whether this was a worry. Wasn't it possible that bad people could misuse that kind of free

---

225 There are lots of different models. In the USA, law enforcement agencies engaged in POP use a system called *SARA* (Scan, Analyse, Respond, Assess). No one seems to be entirely sure who created SARA but the good money is on Professor John Eck and Police Chief Darrel W Stevens. Some organisations in the USA use Professor Paul Ekblom's *Five Is* (Intelligence, Intervention, Implementation, Involvement, Impact). The Royal Canadian Mounted Police use *CAPRA* (Client, Acquire/Analyse intelligence, Partnerships, Response, Assessment), and, here in the UK, some use SARA and some use Sixth Sense's ID PARTNERS (Identify demand, Drivers, Problem, Aim, Research and Analysis, Think, Negotiate, Evaluate, Review, Sustainability). There are many more but they all pretty much follow the same sequence of activities.

access to do bad things? 'I don't think so,' he said. 'Wikipedia works on the radical assumption that mostly people are okay. If you read commentary in newspapers and on the internet, you weep for the future of the species as it seems there are so many horrible people out there. But if you really think about everyone around you, out of every 1,000 people you meet, 990 of them will be perfectly nice, maybe another nine will be extremely annoying but there's only maybe one in a thousand that is actually malicious or a troublemaker. And yet we go through life designing everything around the bad people, locking things down. We should be designing things around the majority of good people and then deal with the bad people when we need to.'

I couldn't agree more. But I wish the media did too.

The TV schedules are filled with 'misery porn' shows about people on benefits, dodgy builders, rip-off Britain, people with ghastly medical conditions, beaches that will kill you, holidays from hell and any number of *When XXX Attack!* style shows. There are hundreds of sensationalist crime shows with titles like *Fear Thy Neighbour*, *The Devil You Know*, *Wives with Knives* and even *Momsters – When Moms Go Bad*, that go to great pains to remind you that danger is (apparently) on your doorstep and all around you. You'd think that the TV news would balance things out with a dose of reality but, sadly, they rarely report happy stories and are increasingly sensationalist as they fight among themselves for viewers. Not content to state the facts, they pad out their programmes with supposedly expert opinions and *vox pops* asking people on the street with barely any knowledge of the issues: 'How do you feel?' or they ask you to text into the programme and share your opinion.[226]

Things are even worse in the printed news. A chap called Hugh Davies maintains a list of all of the stories he finds in just one newspaper – the *Daily Mail* – in which something

---

226 Comedians David Mitchell and Robert Webb spoofed this aspect of news broadcasting in a sketch on their radio, and later TV, show *That Mitchell and Webb Sound/Look*. The sketch is called, 'What do you reckon?' Do look it up.

is reported to give you cancer. The list includes air travel, baby bottles, being black, being a woman, being a man, bras, bubble bath, candlelit dinners, childlessness, constipation, crayons, Facebook, flip-flops, being left-handed, menstruation, milk, money, pastry, potatoes, poverty, pregnancy, retirement, shaving, soup, turning on the light at night to go to the loo, water, working and many, many more. He also publishes a list of the things that the newspaper reports could cure or prevent cancer. It's a much shorter list and it includes acid, apples, Brazil nuts, circumcision, dynamite, horseradish, housework, magnets, masturbation, migraines, strip-search scanners, toilet paper, yoghurt and zinc. He also keeps a third list of things that, confusingly, appear in both of the previous lists. Among the things that can apparently give you cancer and prevent you getting cancer are aspirin, beer, breastfeeding, bread, Chinese medicine, curry, dogs, eggs, fried food, measles, mobile phones, rice, sex, tea and vitamins.[227] What Davies finds particularly notable is not the range of things the paper reports but the frequency. There is pretty much a 'XXX will give you cancer' story every day. And that's just one of the thousands of newspapers, magazines, journals, websites, blogs and forums that assault us daily with bad-luck stories and tales of misery.

But, like Jimmy Wales, I remain an optimist. I believe that people are essentially good; if they weren't, there would be a lot more crime than there is. Most of us don't steal or rob or murder or assault our fellow humans. Every single day, we are presented with ethical dilemmas and the opportunities to do bad things that we might get away with, but most of us don't. Admittedly, laws and sanctions keep us in check, but so too does an inherent sense of what is right and what is wrong. Common sense comes into it too, and self-preservation. As historian and comedian Natalie

---

227 I've presented a very small selection from the lists. You can see them in full (with links to original newspaper articles) by searching Facebook for The Daily Mail List of Things That Give You Cancer. But only if you're happy to risk Facebook giving you cancer.

Haynes once so perfectly put it: 'An eye for an eye and a tooth for a tooth isn't sustainable as everyone ends up blind and toothless.'

Most of us want to live in a place where we feel safe and valued and part of a 'tribe'. And there's no reason why we can't.

There is a great deal more good in this world than bad.

3

In March 2015, just a few miles from where I grew up, a Cornish town mourned the loss of an extraordinary man. Thousands of people lined the streets of Falmouth as the funeral cortège passed through the town. Thousands more followed the hearse for an hour-long walk of tribute. A Royal Marine band led the parade and windows displayed banners saying things like 'Thank you, Andy' and 'Gone too soon'. But this was no celebrity or sporting hero that the town was mourning. It was a police officer.

Source: Western Morning News

PC Andy Hocking, described by his friends and family as 'iconic, approachable, respectful, proud, smiley, gentle, legend, hero, committed, friendly, Gooner (Arsenal fan) and professional, loving husband and dad' died unexpectedly of heart failure at the age of just 52. But he'd had such an impact on the town that the outpouring of grief made the national news. Falmouth Town Council described PC Hocking as 'the epitome of a true community police officer. An ever-present and ever-able patroller of our town centre', and one of his best friends, photographer Hugh Hastings, said: 'He was always a fantastic person. He represented Falmouth in such a superb way. He was wonderful at his job and always had a smile for everybody but he could do his job well at the same time.'

The tragic death of PC Andy Hocking brings this book back to where it started, to my childhood in Cornwall and the bet with my homicide detective father that I couldn't survive six months as a cop; the bet that gave me a 30-year career. Looking at the differences between policing in Cornwall and policing in London is what convinced me that city policing had lost its way. It prompted me to try to bring some of that Cornish spirit to the capital: getting neighbours to talk to each other; building functional caring communities; forming strong partnerships; tackling quality of life issues that policing had traditionally seen as 'nothing to do with us'; and solving problems at a local level. Three decades after I left home, and despite society changing significantly, community policing in Cornwall is as strong as ever because that's what the public wants. The thousands of tributes to Andy Hocking prove that fact in spades. People are people wherever they live, and I believe that people who live and work in big cities like London want their own Andy Hockings too.

I know that massive change takes time, something that short-sighted politicians working to four-year terms of office always seem to fail to acknowledge. But just because something is hard doesn't mean it's not worth trying. Politicians and police chiefs come and go, but communities remain. Real change comes from the people, from the masses, from the bottom up. Just think about all of the biggest changes that have come from protest, from demonstration, from appeal and challenge and petition. If people decide that they want to live in a better world they can help make that happen. I can help. You can help.

Get to know your neighbours – create or strengthen your tribe. Offer to pull each other's bins off the street on bin day. Organise a Zocalo or a Big Lunch. Look out for each other, especially the old and the vulnerable. Make your community a place where people want to live and where criminals don't feel confident enough to operate. Make positive little changes to your behaviours and to your home and to the things you own to make life difficult for the bad guys. Give kids somewhere to hang out and meaningful activities to get involved in. Talk to your local police officers and CSOs and get to know them. Be their eyes and ears and share information.

If we want to live in a nicer world, we all need to get involved in policing, together. Call me an idealist but I believe we can change the world if we move away from reactive change to proactive change.

We just need to cross that road.

ACKNOWLEDGEMENTS

Many people have helped to make this book a reality. But three people in particular deserve special mention.

I wrote the first draft of this book in 2010. And it was horrible. It read like some kind of instruction manual. But one night, after a recording of *The Museum of Curiosity*, I got talking to my friend and boss, the legendary TV producer John Lloyd, CBE.[228] The course of that conversation involved me telling him some of my favourite police stories.

'This is fantastic stuff, Steve,' he said, 'You have to get these down in a book.'

'I've tried doing that,' I said, 'but it reads like the most tedious business book in the world.'

'Can you send me what you've written so far? Or some of it anyway,' said John. 'Perhaps I can see what the problem is.' So I did. And after the recording the following week I asked him if he'd had time to look it over.

'Yes I did. I didn't like it,' he said with characteristic honesty. 'The problem is that you've left yourself out of the stories. They don't work unless you're telling them.'

And he was right.[229] I'd written everything in the third person, mostly in passive voice and, consequently, it was as dull as ditchwater. I had, as John pointed out, completely

---

228 This was a year after my meeting with Tim Minchin and before I was properly involved in the show. I didn't officially start work on *Museum* until Series 5 in 2012. However, I was, at this time, already part of the 'QI family' and was writing and illustrating for the *QI Annuals*.

229 John usually is. He has an unerring eye for spotting how to make things just right – just look at his track record: *The News Quiz, Not the Nine O'Clock News, Blackadder, Spitting Image, The Meaning of Liff, QI* ...

removed myself from the narrative. But writing a book about myself seemed a little ... well ... egotistical. And besides, I'm not a celebrity or a noteworthy sportsperson or a famous explorer. Who'd want to read about what I'd done?

And so I ummed and ahhed about the book for a further year or so, continuing to gather more content and trying different formats and voices, but never quite getting it right. I turned it into a talk as a way of putting myself back into the narrative and, to my surprise, it became something of a hit. Throughout 2013 and 2014, I performed *The Skeptical Bobby* at over 100 venues and events around the UK, including the Cornbury, Harrogate International, Village Green and Edinburgh festivals, the Hay Festival of Literature and the Arts, Latitude, QEDcon, Salon London, the Ig Nobel Prizes, Science Showoff, countless 'Skeptics in the Pub' meets and at universities and colleges. I got some fantastic reviews: the British Humanist Association called it 'brilliant, beautiful and inspiring'. And Professor Richard Dawkins described it as 'superb, intelligent and humane'. I even got to do a TED talk. The experience was hugely valuable and helped me to understand how best to tell my story.

I then had the good fortune to meet two people who completely turned the project around for me. The first was the journalist and comedy writer Jane Bussmann. I'd read her amazing book *The Worst Date Ever*[230] and realised that her style of writing – a mix of personal anecdote, humour and factual research – was just what I needed to emulate. And, after meeting her and talking to her about it, I quickly developed a much clearer idea of how to write the book.

The other person was Graham Linehan of *Father Ted*, *IT Crowd* and *Big Train* (and many more) fame. I'd met Graham before and we'd become pally. And when I took *The Skeptical Bobby* talk to his home town of Norwich, he invited me to

---

230 It tells the story about how Jane – a comedy writer – followed a UN peacekeeper (that she fancied) to Africa and, quite by accident, became the person who broke the story of Joseph Kony's brutal kidnapping of thousands of children. It's a brilliant book and I highly recommend it.

ACKNOWLEDGEMENTS

pop around to see him at home. We walked his dog in the woods, sat and drank tea in his kitchen and chatted about all kinds of things, including this book. One thing Graham is brilliant at doing, is getting you to hack everything back to basics so that you have a clear idea of the direction to take. I guess that's the director in him. And why a director is called a director. I came away with a much clearer vision of what the book should be like and, thanks to John and Jane, I also knew how to write it and what my 'voice' should sound like. I owe them all a great debt of gratitude.

I must also thank the following people without whom this book would have been much shorter and considerably less interesting:

Firstly, retired Acting Commissioner Tim Godwin OBE, Commander Mike Hoare, and Detective Chief Superintendent Martin Stevens for believing in us and for giving the Problem Solving Unit the opportunity to be what it was.

Secondly, my Problem Solving Unit colleagues, bosses and associates Matt Bell, Steve Bloomfield, John Chadwick, Paul Dunn OBE, Rob Elliot, Gary Fryer, Neil Henson, Neil Hutchinson, Marshall Kent, Paul King, Ian Morris, Andrew Nimmons, Ruari Robertson, Paul Scott, Jan Strachan and Nick Tittle.

And thirdly, my heartfelt thanks go to the following people who have provided me with 30-years' worth of material, advice, friendship and support (brackets show organisations they were working for, or contracted to, at the time I worked with/contacted them):

Douglas Adams, Ken Pearce (Uxbridge Local History and Archive Society)

Chaz Akoshile, Alex Birtwistle, Jo Fogg, Andrew Kent, Darren Kristiansen (UK Home Office)

Rick Allard, Jill Andrews, Venetia Barton, Billy Cotsis, Jaylan Veseli (Safer London Foundation)

Terry L. Anderson (PERC)

Paul Anstee, Simon Brooker, Sarah Burrows, Jonathan Clack, Sue Clisby, Dr Nina Cope, Alan Cousins, Mark Deacon, Annie Donelan, Jane Farmery, Matt Fox, Lance St Clair, Dr Andy

Bryars, Chris Hale, Stuart Hutchinson, Mark Jenkins, Steve Kelsey, Peter Kirkham, Tony Laffan, Dr Alistair McBeath, Ian Oldfield, Tim Otway, Aimee Passant, Martin Peirson, Dave Pridige, Colin Riley, Mark Warwick, Ian Webber, Chris Weston-Moore, Paul White, Chris Williams (Metropolitan Police Service)

Hedvig Astrom, James Cooper and Stefan Haverkamp (Gum Election)

Ian Barber (Central Scotland Police)

Alex Barnett (Press Office, UK Highways Agency)

Guy Beattie, Cindy Butts and Naomi Simpson (Metropolitan Police Authority)

Terry Bergin QC

Dr Sue Black OBE

Neil Boast (Suffolk Constabulary)

Dom Boothroyd (National Lobster Hatchery)

Dr David Bramwell

Dr Karen Bullock (University of Surrey)

Anna Bullus (Gumdrop Ltd)

Warwick Cairns

Si Colgan

Sarah Corbett (Craftivist Collective)

Dr John Curran, Gary Walker, Huw Williams (Left/Field London)

Hugh Davies

Stephen J. Dubner (Freakonomics)

John Dziel (DAE Lighting)

Marc Abrahams (Annals of Improbable Research and Ig Nobel Prizes)

Professor Gary Cordner (Kutztown University, Pennsylvania)

Steve Burton (Transport for London)

Paul Davies, Rachel Lilley, Kate Robinson, Justine Wieteska (South Yorkshire Police)

Eddie Derriman (Cornwall Fisheries)

Emanuele Faja

Dr Adam Feather (Barts and the London Teaching Hospitals)

Dr Robin Fletcher (University of Middlesex)

Kate Fox (Social Issues Research Centre, Oxford)

Professor David Forrest (University of Salford Business School)

David Gavin (NHS)

Ross Gibert (QED Property Ltd)

Malcolm Gladwell

Professor Mark Griffiths (Nottingham Trent University)

Simon Guilfoyle, Debbie Hodson (West Midlands Police)

Whit Haydn (NYPD)

Chrissie Hernandez

Glenn Hester (Glynn County Police Department, Brunswick, Georgia)

Steve Hills

Professor Mike Hoare (Cranfield University)

Dr Makoto Imai and Dr Hideaki Goto (Shiga University of Medical Science)

Andy Kerr

Dr Lucy King (University of Oxford)

Professor Joseph Lampel (City University)

Professor Gloria Laycock (Jill Dando Institute of Crime Science)

Joan Leary (Southwark Council)

Thea Litschka-Koen (Anti-Venom Swazi Charity)

Robert Llewellyn

Robert Loch (YesAnd Club)

Dr Dan Lockton (Royal College of Art)

Professor Mike Maguire (University of Wales)

Mo McFarland

Ross MacFarlane (Wellcome Library and Collection)

Keith McGrory, Steve Postlethwaite (Hampshire Constabulary)

Barbara Mikkelson (Snopes)

Tim Minchin

Tim Moore

Cate More

Mel Morgan (Interserve)

Linda Morris (RoSPA)

James Murphy (US Airways)

Dr David Nutt
Dr Ciarán O'Keeffe, Dr Matthew Smith (Buckinghamshire New University)
Richard Osman
Mark Page
Carl Parker, Flore Pirard (Wandsworth Borough Council)
Shelley Reed, Andy Winter (Brighton Housing Trust)
Oliver Payne (The Hunting Dynasty)
Tim Reynolds (National Museum of Computing & Ceravision)
Sir Gerry Robinson
Sir Ken Robinson
Sid Rodrigues (Ethical Society and Skeptics in the Pub)
Jon Ronson
Jimmy Fields, Harold Medlock, Bobby Morton, Darrel Stephens (Charlotte Mecklenburg Police Department, North Carolina)
Dan Schreiber, Richard Turner (*The Museum of Curiosity*)
Rob Schütze
Helen Slinger (Government Office for London)
Sir Tim Smit (Eden Project)
John Soanes (National Police Improvement Agency)
Janice Staines
Rory Sutherland (Ogilvy Partners UK)
Keith Taylor (Merseyside Police)
Professor Nick Tilley (Nottingham Trent University)
Tyler Vigen (Spurious Correlations)
Jimmy Wales (Wikipedia)
Mike Ward (City of Alexandria Police, Kentucky)
Andrew Webb
Geoff Williams (National Centre for Applied Learning Technologies)
Charlie Wilson (OgilvyOne)
Janice Winder (Ayr Community Safety Partnership)
Professor Richard Wiseman (University of Hertfordshire)

... and to all of the brilliant police officers, police staff and problem solvers I've met or worked with this past 35 years.

Huge thanks to my followers on Twitter who have never let me down whenever I needed laughter, advice, information, inspiration or support. They also provided some of the photos in this book and are credited where appropriate. All uncredited illustrations and photographs are by me.

Finally, massive thanks are due to Emily Bryce-Perkins, Mat Clayton, Phil Connor, Isobel Frankish, Caitlin Harvey, Jimmy Leach, Georgia Odd, Emily Shipp and everyone else at Unbound for pushing me to write this book and for making the process so enjoyable.

I love to hear about innovative problem solving from all walks of life. If you have a story, do share it with me. I can be contacted by email at stevyncolgan@me.com or on Twitter where I'm @stevyncolgan.

I also keep a blog about interesting problem solving in my Unbound shed here:

http://unbound.co.uk/books/why-did-the-policeman-cross-the-road/shed

And a bibliography and full list of sources used in this book can be accessed at: https://colganology.wordpress.com/why-did-the-policeman-cross-the-road-references-and-sources/

Finally, turn the page to see a list of the people who were generous enough to become patrons of this book and who pledged their money and support to make it a reality. Thank you, each and every one of you.

SUPPORTERS

Pamela Abbott
Lily Adams
Rosie Adams
Moose Allain
Dave Appleby
Martin Archer
Helen Armfield
Bob Ashwood
Michael Atkins
Tim Atkinson
Laurie Avadis
James Aylett
Caz Bailey
Tara Ballantine
Sally Banks
Tony Bannister
Fionnuala Barrett
Bruce Barrow
Mark Barry
Chris Bartlett
Matthew Bate
Richard Bates
Adam Baylis-West
Barbara North Beck
Adrian Belcher
Simon Bennett
Catherine Benson
Terry Bergin
Geoff Berriman
Adam Betts
Kathy Bibby
Dr Sue Black

Emma Black
Rob Blake
Robert Bluck
Steven Bond
Stephen Bonner
William Bonwitt
Ruth Bourne
Luke Bowyer
Tony Brandrick
Donal Brannigan
Richard W H Bray
Toby Bray
Kirsten Braybrook
Brian Breczinski
Tony Brent
Dave Briggs
Ben Brignell
Holly Brockwell
Jo Brodie
David Bromley
Anne Brophy
Alex Brown
Margaret JC Brown
Alan Bucher
Paul Burkey
Peter Burling
Joseph Burne
Alison Burns
Susan E Burton
Marcus Butcher
Alan Buxey
John Byron

Ian Calcutt
Ben Cameron
Duncan Cameron
Andrew Campling
Andy & Joy Candler
Phillipa Candy
Xander Cansell
David Catherall
Stephen Cawood
Claire Chambers
Kenny Chapman
Paul Charlton
Emma Clifford
Garrett Coakley
Eddie Cochrane
Simon Cole
Dawn M Colgan
Liam Colgan
Pat Colledge
David Collins
Louis Constandinos
Tim Cook
David Cooke
Neil Cooper
Paul Cooper
Ben Cope
Sarah Corbett
Isabelle Couchman
Adam Coventry
John Crawford
Karen Crawford
Andrew Croker

Heather Culpin
Ruth (@rutitoottoots)
   Curtis
Ade Dann
Peter Davey
Suzanne Davidson
Martyn Davies
Matt Davis
Christopher Dawson
Neil Denham
JF Derry
John Dexter
Rhona Dick
Mar Dixon
Andy Doddington
Jenny Doughty
Connor Doyle
Liz Drabble
Ian Dryland
Helen Ducker
Christopher Dudman
Jody Duke
Rachael Dunlop
Alan Dunn
Ben Dupré
Caius Durling
Daniel Durling
Claire Eades
Daryl Edwards
Lorna Edwards
Heiko Egeler
Michael Ellerby
Joanna Ellis
Chris Emerson
Andrew Evans
Simon Evans
Tahnee Evans
Oliver Facey
Kash Farooq
Gary & Ali Fellows

Heather-Louise Fewins
Alistair Fitchett
Joanna Fitzgerald-
   Gibson
Lindsey Fitzharris
Piers Fletcher
John-Paul Flintoff
Bevin Flynn
Bas Fordy
Melissa Forrest
Iain Forsyth
James Fowkes
Chris French
Julia Frost
Phil Gallagher
Hilary Gallo
Martin Gardner
Alison Garner
Richard Garner
Tom Gauld
Amro Gebreel
Mark Georgiou
Julie Gibbon
Alex Gilbert
David Gilray
Helen Glassborow
Tim Godden
Teresa Goede
Allen Goodreds
Dave Gorman
Ben Govier
Heather Govier
Christopher Grabowski
Maeve Grant
Katie Green
Matt Griffith
Clair Griffiths
Mike Griffiths
Paul Groom
Tina Groves

Geoff Haederle
Miranda Hale
Richard and
   Ruth Hammond
Chris Hapka
Nicola Hargreaves
Paul Hargrove
Pat Harkin
Steve Harris
A.F. Harrold
Faye Hartley
Steve Hartley
Matt Harvey
Joanna Haseltine
Andrew Hearse
Di Heelas
Tannice Hemming
David Hicks
Julie Hicks
Chris Higgins
E O Higgins
Daniel Higham
Matthew Hill
Steve Hills
Andrew Hodge
Lisa Holdsworth
Rich Honess
Connie Honigs
Emily Hopkins
Stephen Hoppe
Andrew Horne
Andy Horton
Clive Howard
Tom Howard
John Howe
Charlie Humphries
Toby Irvine
Huma Islam
David James
Paul James

Beth Jenkins	Peter Maloy	Joe Morrison
Marjorie Johns	Hedy Manders	Daryl Moughanni
Adam Johnson	Dave Mansfield	Liane Mount
Roger Owen Jones	Julia Mariani	Chris Mountain
Simon Jones	Mandy Marshall	Lucy Mountfort
Steve Jones	Phil Marshall	Sami Mughal
Keith Kahn-Harris	Dawn Mason	Karen-Babette Müller
John Kearon	Patricia Matheson	Regan Naughton
Patric Keller	Katrin Mäurich	Carlo Navato
Andrew Kelly	Pamela McCarthy	Simon Needham
Chloe Kembery	Iain McCulloch	Richard Neville
Andrew Keogh	Iain McCulloch	David Newsome
Dan Kieran	Greg McDougall	Dave Nicholls
Janneke Kimstra	Andrew McEvoy	Chris Nicholson
J Kniffler	Mo McFarland	Marie Jose Nieuwkoop
Michael Lane	Laura McGowan	Andy Nimmons
Valerie Langfield	Alan McHenry	Sabra Noordeen
Niki Lappin	Mike McHugh	Vaun Earl Norman
Caroline Lawrence	Karen McKenna	Nottingham Skeptics
Ewan Lawrie	Gavin McKeown	in the Pub
W Tom Lawrie	Samantha Mckeown	Lauren O'Connell
Jane Learner	Aven McMaster	Eugene O'Gorman
Craig Lewis	Rob Medford	John O'Hagan
Monika Lewis	Laura Menard	Steve O'Hear
Suzy Lishman	Andrew Meredith	Dr. Ciarán O'Keeffe
John Lloyd	Will Merrifield	Jan O'Malley
Dan Lockton	Andrew Merritt	Mark O'Neill
Sarah Loftus	Caroline Metcalf	Greg O'Toole
Angela Lord	Alison Metcalfe	Georgia Odd
Ian Lorimer	Nigel Metheringham	Lisa Oldham
Payne Loss	Libby Miller	Monica Ormonde
Ulrich Lübke	William Milliken	Tony Orr
Karl Ludvigsen	Ron and Corinne Mills	Vicky Osborne
David Luke	Margo Milne	A. Ottey
Mike Lythgoe	John Minshall	Ed Owen
Calum Macaulay	John Mitchinson	Sarah Pannell
Geoff MacDonald	Ken Monaghan	Yianni Papas
Ross MacFarlane	Cate Moore	Mike Parry
Alisdair Maclean	Michael Moran	Rebecca Pascoe
Cait MacPhee	Julie Ann Morris	Jenette Passmore

Andrew Peacock
Lesley Pearson
Andy Pegg
Edward Penning
David Perry
Chris (furrie) Phillips
Morgan Phillips
Andy &
    Elaine Pickering
Greg Pickersgill
Helen Pickford
Justin Pinner
Justin Pollard
Dan Pope
Finnegan Pope-Carter
Matthew Porter
Niall Porter
Jackie Potter
Janet Pretty
Francis Pryor
Jennie Pyatt
Simon Quin
Mikael Qvarfordh
Elliot R
Sam Randall
Rebecca Read
Colette Reap
Simon Reap
Jenny Reaves
Jim Redpath
Vic Reis
Jennette Rennie
Elizabeth Ann Rice
Kathryn Richards
Sioned-Mair Richards
Christopher Richardson
Jean Roberts
Imogen Robertson
John Roden
Angella Rodgers

Sid Rodrigues
Lucy Rogers
    (@DrLucyRogers)
Wojciech Rogozinski
Robyn Roscoe
Deb Ruddy
Craig Rushforth
Dave Russell
Adrian Ryder
Any Salyer
Riccardo Sartori
Neil Sayer
Chris Scarfe
Sebastian Schleussner
Dan Schreiber
Hugo Scott-Slade
Richard Selwyn
Ibrahim Sha'ath
Tony Shannon
Arsha Sharma
Lynette Sherburne
Keith Sherratt
Jon Shute
Charles Skeavington
London Skeptics
Al Smith
Janet Smith
Leighanne Smith
Mathew Smith
Peter R Smith
Sarah-Jane Smith
Simon James Smith
Tanya Smith
Colin Smythe
Claire Snodgrass
Lili Soh
Jenny Sparks
Chris Spath
Liam Spinage
Teresa Squires

Janice Staines
Damian Steer
Richard Stephens
David Stokes
Kay Stratton
Michael Strawson
Mark Sundaram
Giles Sutcliffe
Rory Sutherland
Rory Sutherland
Peer Sylvester
Lee Symes
Tall Man with
    Glasses
    (@stuartwitts)
Chris Taylor
Georgina Taylor
Karen Taylor
Matthew Taylor
Sonia Tennant
Sonia Tennant
George Theo
Richard Thomas
Caz Thomson
Mark Thurley
Carl Tipple
Jonathan Tisdall
Espen Torseth
Liz Tothill &
    Mike Hayward
Liz Townsend
Twisty
Dawn Upson
Georganne Uxbridge
David Valls-Russell
Mark Vent
Ian Vince
Emma Visick
Jose Vizcaino
Jenny Wade

Erica Wagner
Steve Walker
Helen Ward
Stewart Ware
Adam Warn
John Wates
John Wells
Andrew West
Paul Whelan
Levin Wheller
Ben Whitehouse
Senga Whiteman
Heather Wilde
Kitty Wilkinson
Cordelia Williams
Geoff Williams
Huw Williams
Julian Williams
Sean Williams
Derek Wilson
Elizabeth Wilson
Christopher Wilton
Laurie Winkless
Tobias Winterhalter
Gem Witchalls
Daniel Wood
Stacey Woods
Liz Wooldridge
Paul Woolgar
Colin and
     Rachel Wright
Lindsay Wright
Neil Wright
Steve Wright
Nicholas Yates
Linda Youdelis
Alice Young